Lecture Notes in Computer Science   8460

Commenced Publication in 1973
Founding and Former Series Editors:
Gerhard Goos, Juris Hartmanis, and Jan van Leeuwen

T0224063

Kostas Magoutis   Peter Pietzuch (Eds.)

Distributed Applications and Interoperable Systems

14th IFIP WG 6.1 International Conference, DAIS 2014
Held as Part of the 9th International Federated Conference
on Distributed Computing Techniques, DisCoTec 2014
Berlin, Germany, June 3-5, 2014
Proceedings

Springer

Volume Editors

Kostas Magoutis
University of Ioannina and FORTH-ICS
Dept. of Computer Science and Engineering
45110 Ioannina, Greece
E-mail: magoutis@cs.uoi.gr

Peter Pietzuch
Imperial College London
Dept. of Computing
Queen's Gate 180, London, SW7 2AZ, UK
E-mail: prp@doc.ic.ac.uk

ISSN 0302-9743   e-ISSN 1611-3349
ISBN 978-3-662-43351-5   e-ISBN 978-3-662-43352-2
DOI 10.1007/978-3-662-43352-2
Springer Heidelberg New York Dordrecht London

Library of Congress Control Number: 2014938621

LNCS Sublibrary: SL 5 – Computer Communication Networks and Telecommunications

Typesetting: Camera-ready by author, data conversion by Scientific Publishing Services, Chennai, India

Printed on acid-free paper

Springer is part of Springer Science+Business Media (www.springer.com)

Foreword

In 2014, the 9th International Federated Conference on Distributed Computing Techniques (DisCoTec) took place in Berlin, Germany, during June 3–5. It was hosted and organized by the Technische Universität Berlin. The DisCoTec series, one of the major events sponsored by the International Federation for Information Processing (IFIP), included three conferences:

- COORDINATION 2014, the 16th IFIP WG 6.1 International Conference on Coordination Models and Languages
- DAIS 2014, the 14th IFIP WG 6.1 International Conference on Distributed Applications and Interoperable Systems
- FORTE 2014, the 34th IFIP WG 6.1 International Conference on Formal Techniques for Distributed Objects, Components and Systems

Together, these conferences cover the complete spectrum of distributed computing subjects ranging from theoretical foundations over formal specification techniques to systems research issues.

Each day of the federated event began with a plenary speaker nominated by one of the conferences. The three invited speakers were:

- Frank Leymann (University of Stuttgart, Germany)
- Maarten van Steen (VU University Amsterdam, The Netherlands)
- Joachim Parrow (Uppsala University, Sweden)

There were also three satellite events, taking place during June 6–7:

1. The 5th International Workshop on *Interactions Between Computer Science and Biology* (CS2BIO) with keynote lectures by Marco Pettini (Université de la Mediterranée, France) and Vincent Danos (University of Edinburgh, UK) and a tutorial by Jeffrey Johnson (Open University, UK)
2. The 7th Workshop on *Interaction and Concurrency Experience* (ICE) with keynote lectures by Kim Larsen (Aalborg University, Denmark) and Pavol Cerny (University of Colorado Boulder, USA)
3. The First International Workshop on *Meta Models for Process Languages* (MeMo) with keynote lectures by Joachim Parrow (Uppsala University, Sweden) and Marino Miculan (Università degli Studi di Udine, Italy)

This program was an interesting and stimulating event for the participants. Sincere thanks go the chairs and members of the Program Committees of the involved conferences and workshops for their highly appreciated effort. Moreover, organizing DisCoTec 2014 was only possible thanks to the dedicated work of the Organizing Committee from TU Berlin, including Margit Russ, Kirstin Peters (also publicity and workshop chair), and Christoph Wagner. Finally, many thanks go to IFIP WG 6.1 for providing the umbrella for this event, to EATCS and TU Berlin for their support and sponsorship, and to EasyChair for providing the refereeing infrastructure.

June 2014   Uwe Nestmann

Preface

This volume contains the proceedings of DAIS 2014, the 14th IFIP International Conference on Distributed Applications and Interoperable Systems, sponsored by IFIP (International Federation for Information Processing) and organized by the IFIP Working Group 6.1.

DAIS was held during June 3–5, 2014, in Berlin, Germany, as part of the DisCoTec (Distributed Computing Techniques) federated conference, together with the International Conference on Formal Techniques for Distributed Systems (FMOODS and FORTE) and the International Conference on Coordination Models and Languages (COORDINATION). DAIS received 53 submissions, with each submission reviewed by at least three Program Committee members. The committee decided to accept 12 full papers and four short papers, giving an acceptance rate of 23% for full research papers. The conference program presented state-of-the-art research results and case studies in the area of distributed applications and interoperable systems. The main themes of this year's conference were cloud computing, replicated storage, and large-scale systems.

In the area of cloud computing, there are papers on service-level agreement differentiation and trust-aware operation of providers in cloud markets, and adaptive and scalable high availability for infrastructure clouds. A significant number of the papers cover distributed storage, including a strongly consistent relational model for metadata in HDFS, and distributed exact deduplication for primary storage; there is a special focus on eventually consistent stores with papers on scalable causality tracking for eventually consistent stores, and operation-based conflict-free replicated datatypes (CRDTs). Papers on large-scale systems include autonomous multi-dimensional slicing, bandwidth-minimized distribution of measurements in global sensor networks, and coordinated scheduling for inter-grid architectures. We also have papers on behavioral caching for Web content, implementing Web protocols based on formal modeling and automated code generation, energy efficiency, and distributed algorithms.

Finally, we would like to take this opportunity to thank the many people whose work made this conference possible. We wish to express our deepest gratitude to the authors of submitted papers, to all Program Committee members for their active participation in the paper review process, and to all external reviewers for their help in evaluating submissions. We would like to thank the publication chair, Eva Kalyvianaki, for her excellent work in producing the conference proceedings. Further thanks go to the Steering Committee of DAIS, and in particular the chair, Rui Oliveira, who provided useful advice and help. We would also like to thank Maarten van Steen, our invited keynote speaker. Finally we are thankful to the Technical University of Berlin for hosting the event in Berlin, to the past DAIS chairs Jim Dowling, Francois Taiani, and Karl Goschka for their advice and documentation, and to Uwe Nestmann for acting as a general chair of the joint event.

March 2014

Kostas Magoutis
Peter Pietzuch

Organization

Steering Committee

Jim Dowling	KTH Royal Institute of Technology, Sweden
Frank Eliassen	University of Oslo, Norway
Pascal Felber	Université de Neuchâtel
Karl Goeschka	Vienna University of Technology, Austria
Seif Haridi	KTH, Sweden
Rüdiger Kapitza	Technical University of Braunschweig, Germany
Rui Oliveira	Universidade do Minho, Portugal
Romain Rouvoy	University of Lille 1, France
Francois Taiani	Université de Rennes 1, France

Program Committee Chairs

Kostas Magoutis	Foundation for Research and Technology, Greece
Peter Pietzuch	Imperial College London, UK

Publication Chair

Evangelia Kalyvianaki	City University London, UK

Program Committee

Stergios Anastasiadis	University of Ioannina, Greece
Cosmin Arad	Google, USA
Danilo Ardagna	Politecnico di Milano, Italy
Carlos Baquero	Universidade di Minho, Italy
Gordon Blair	Lancaster University, UK
Wolfgang De Meuter	Vrije Universiteit Brussel, Belgium
Jim Dowling	KTH Royal Institute of Technology, Sewden
Frank Eliassen	University of Oslo, Norway
David Eyers	University of Otago, New Zealand
Paulo Ferreira	INESC ID/Technical University of Lisbon, Portugal
Kurt Geihs	Universität Kassel, Germany
Karl M. Goeschka	Vienna University of Technology, Austria
Franz J. Hauck	University of Ulm, Germany

Peter Herrmann	NTNU Trondheim, Norway
K.R. Jayaram	IBM Research, USA
Evangelia Kalyvianaki	City University London, UK
Boris Koldehofe	University of Stuttgart, Germany
Dejan Kostic	Institute IMDEA Networks, Spain
Reinhold Kroeger	Wiesbaden University of Applied Sciences, Germany
Kostas Magoutis	Foundation for Research and Technology, Greece
Benjamin Mandler	IBM Research, Israel
Rene Meier	Trinity College Dublin, Ireland
Hein Meling	University of Stavanger, Norway
Pietro Michiardi	Institut Eurecom, France
Alberto Montresor	University of Trento, Italy
Kiran Muniswamy-Reddy	Amazon, USA
Dirk Muthig	Lufthansa Systems, Germany
George Papadopoulos	University of Cyprus, Cyprus
Nikos Parlavantzas	INSA Rennes, France
Jose Pereira	INESC TEC and University of Minho, Portugal
Peter Pietzuch	Imperial College London, UK
Etienne Rivière	University of Neuchatel, Switzerland
Giovanni Russello	University of Auckland, Australia
Lionel Seinturier	University of Lille, IUF-LIFL and Inria ADAM, France
Liuba Shrira	Brandeis University, USA
Francois Taiani	Université de Rennes 1, France
Luís Veiga	Instituto Superior Técnico-UTL/INESC-ID Lisboa, Portugal
Spyros Voulgaris	VU University Amsterdam, The Netherlands

Additional Reviewers

Achilleos, Achilleas	Guerrieri, Alessio
Almeida, Paulo Sérgio	Haque, Tareq Rezaul
Azab, Abdulrahman	Jesi, Gian Paolo
Baraki, Harun	Kambona, Kennedy
Cardozo, Nicolas	Krikava, Filip
Ciavotta, Michele	Lea, Tormod Erevik
Dibak, Christoph	Lopes, Nuno
Esteves, Sérgio	Matos, Miguel
Evensen, Pål	Mayer, Ruben
Florio, Luca	Mettouris, Christos
Fonte, Victor	Meyer, Fabian
Gibilisco, Giovanni Paolo	Miglierina, Marco

Noureddine, Adel
Ottenwälder, Beate
Pandey, Navneet Kumar
Philips, Laure
Provensi, Lucas
Renaux, Thierry
Salem, Maher
Shoker, Ali

Simão, José
Sobe, Anita
Taherkordi, Amir
Textor, Andreas
Thoss, Marcus
Tirado, Juan Manuel
Witsch, Andreas

DAIS 2014 Keynote

A Perspective on the Future of Computer Sciences
(Through a Technical Example)

Prof. Maarten Van Steen

VU University, FEW/Informatica
De Boelelaan 1081a, 1081 HV Amsterdam
The Netherlands

`m.r.van.steen@vu.nl`

Abstract: Computer sciences have always moved, and continue to move, swiftly. On the one hand, we have seen many subjects come and go. On the other, many of these subjects are becoming the core of new sciences, most recently those emerging from big-data discussions. Where does this place the computer scientist? As a natural reaction, people tend to build a fence around what they believe is "real" computer science, and what is considered to be an application of computer science.

In this talk, I argue that drawing such a line is not only pointless, it is even dangerous. Computer sciences are more than ever in the core of new sciences, and that is where the computer scientists should be as well. Building a fence will place the computer scientist out of the core, potentially leading to isolation.

I illustrate this point by means of a project on crowd management. It is a technical talk, one by a die-hard systems researcher who can only make the project a success by understanding how his science can contribute to the bigger picture and what that means for collaborating with scientists from other disciplines.

From federated conferences to federated sciences?

Speaker: Maarten Van Steen is a professor of large-scale distributed systems at VU University Amsterdam and currently the chair of its Department of Computer Science. For several years, a large part of his research is concentrated on understanding very large networked systems of small, wireless devices such as massive sensor networks. Next to such extreme distributed systems, his interests also reach out to complex-network science and understanding the behavior that emerges from very large networked systems. He is (co-)author of three text books, including *Distributed Systems, Principles and Paradigms* (with Andrew Tanenbaum) and *Graph Theory and Complex Networks, An Introduction*.

Table of Contents

A Risk-Based Model
for Service Level Agreement Differentiation
in Cloud Market Providers

Mario Macías and Jordi Guitart

Barcelona Supercomputing Center (BSC) and
Universitat Politecnica de Catalunya - Barcelona Tech (UPC)
Jordi Girona 29, 08034 Barcelona, Spain
{mario.macias,jordi.guitart}@bsc.es

Abstract. Cloud providers may not always fulfil the Service Level Agreements with the clients because of outages in the data centre or inaccurate resource provisioning. Minimizing the Probability of Failure of the tasks that are allocated within a Cloud Infrastructure can be economically infeasible because overprovisioning resources increases the cost and is economically inefficient. This paper intends to increase the fulfilment rate of Service Level Agreements at the infrastructure provider side while maximizing the economic efficiency, by considering risk in the decision process. We introduce a risk model based on graph analysis for risk propagation, and we model it economically to provide three levels of risk to the clients: moderate risk, low risk, and very low risk. The client may decide the risk of the service and proportionally pay: the lower the risk the higher the price.

1 Introduction

Cloud Computing arisen as a successful commercial solution to sell computing resources as a utility: clients dynamically size the resources according to their workloads, and pay only for what they use. Cloud resources are usually sold as Virtual Machines (VMs) that can run isolated in the same hardware as other VMs and scale at runtime. In current commercial Clouds, infrastructure providers price the resources and clients may decide to buy them or not. There is no negotiation. Our research, however, is framed in research Cloud Market implementations such as the SORMA [10] Market Middleware. In Cloud Markets, both resource users and providers are autonomous agents that negotiate the terms of the Quality of Service (QoS) and the price that the client will pay to the provider. When the negotiation is finished, the terms of the contract are established in a Service Level Agreement (SLA) that keeps contractual information about the terms of the QoS as well as the pricing information (price and penalty to pay in case of violation of the SLA).

Cloud providers may not always fulfil the SLAs they agree with the clients because of outages in the data centre or errors in the hardware. Not fulfilling

K. Magoutis and P. Pietzuch (Eds.): DAIS 2014, LNCS 8460, pp. 1–15, 2014.

the agreed SLAs would lead to economic penalties [8] and a loss of reputation that can cause clients with high reliability requirements to not allocate their tasks in the provider [7]. Minimising the Probability of Failure (PoF) of the tasks that are allocated within a Cloud Infrastructure can be economically infeasible. Overprovisioning resources increases the cost and is economically and ecologically inefficient because the overbooked resources are underused most of the time.

This paper has a main goal: to increase the fulfilment rate of SLAs at the infrastructure provider side by providing risk-aware policies that maximize the economic efficiency. We introduce a risk model based on graph analysis for risk propagation, and we model it economically to provide three levels of risk to the clients: moderate risk, low risk, and very low risk. The client may decide the risk of the service and proportionally pay: the lower the risk the higher the price.

To achieve the stated goal, this paper introduces the following contributions:

1. Model of the PoF of a multi-tier service that is hosted in a Cloud data centre by means of the analysis of the links between virtual resources.
2. A new revenue model that will help providing different levels of risk at different prices, while adapting prices to the present value of the resources (that is, the rate the resources decrease their value over time).

This paper is structured as follows. After the related work section, Section 3 introduces the baseline negotiation and revenue model that is used as framework for this paper; Section 4 shows the risk model and Section 5 shows the revenue model; Section 6 describes the experiments and evaluates their results; at the end, Section 7 show the conclusions and the future work lines.

2   Related Work

This paper extends our previous work [7,8], which demonstrated that differentiating SLAs according to their QoS level could lead to economic benefits in an open market with many competitors, because there is a variety in the objectives of clients. Some clients may require high QoS guarantees and other clients may prioritize lower prices. This paper extends the previous research by modelling the risk of complex cloud appliances and defining a revenue model that would allow to provide accurate prices as a function of the offered QoS level.

Bayesian networks[4] define a graph model for describing the probability of an event from the probabilities of the events that would cause it, in terms like *"if event A happen, event B will happen"*. That is inaccurate for Cloud appliances, because a failure in a node would not always involve a failure in the linked node. In addition, it is difficult to express some complex relations like redundancy. Our graph model extends the Bayesian Network model with the addition of weighted links and introduces two special types of node for representing union and intersection operations. These additions ease the expression of some complex Cloud appliances and the risk propagation through their nodes.

Djemame et al. [2] described an architecture to assess risk in computing Grids that allow providers to estimate the risk of agreeing a given SLA and use management techniques to maximize its fulfilment. They use risk assessment for task scheduling. Our work intends to be an upgrade of some of their risk models to adapt them to the architecture of Clouds and using such risk assessment also for improving business objectives.

Yeo and Buyya [16] provide two methods for risk analysis: separate, which only evaluates the risk over a facet, and integrated, which evaluates the risk over multiple facets. In the integrated method, they assume all the facets are independent from each other. In our model, the facets are the multiple risks of all the independent resources in a multi-tier application, but we do not consider them as independent. The risk is propagated according how such resources are linked, and the effects of such uncertainty have different impact depending on the location of the risk within the resources graph.

Sawade et al. [12] consider that risk models may lose their validity over time for some reason (the environment changes, the inputs change, learning errors, ...). Our model can minimize these drawbacks, because it is dynamically built according to the SLA templates from the clients.

The pricing models from Becker et al. [1] consider the concept of Business Value: how much a client is willing to pay for any extra unity of QoS. We also consider this concept in our model. However, our intention is not to solve the issue of calculating it but consider it as an important part of a revenue model for providing multiple pricing and risk levels. They also calculate the penalty of the execution of multiple services, while distributing the risk between the different services. Our approach considers only a single project and calculates the risk of penalties by evaluating the internal topology of such service.

Simao et al. [14] propose a pricing model that allows clients and providers to negotiate the price and penalties, but also how much service degradation the client is willing to accept and how much it will pay proportionally to such degradation. As in this paper, they define three levels of QoS and propose a depreciation strategy to control the degradation of the SLAs for each profile when the resources are overloaded. Our model does not explicitly select the SLAs to degrade, but allocates them by risk levels according to the envisioned probability of failure. Both models are complementary and may coexist simultaneously.

Wee [15] profiles in detail the Amazon Spot Instances. He concludes that such model does not motivate enough users to move their workload to the off-peak hours. Our model provides an extra incentive to move because, in addition to the lower prices derived from the low market demand, users can benefit also of lower risks derived from the low workload.

Li and Gillam [6] apply risk assessment to the financial aspect of the grid. They provide node granularity risk assessment to calculate prices and penalties for the SLAs. Our approach combines assessments from several nodes and links them to consider a Cloud appliance topology.

3   SLA Negotiation Model

This paper focuses two stages of the Infrastructure as a Service (IaaS) provisioning: the negotiation of SLAs between the clients and an Infrastructure Provider (IP), and the provisioning of resources to fulfil the terms of the agreement. We consider the OCCI Standard [9] to describe the infrastructure: the client can get three types of cloud resources (compute nodes, networks, and storage nodes) and define how they are linked by means of network interfaces and storage links.

When a client wants to host a service, it calculates how many Cloud resources it needs and sends an offer to the IP to start a negotiation. Each IP owns a set of N physical hosts. Each physical machine can host several VMs. The SLA of a set of VMs is described as $SLA = \{\vec{S}, \vec{L}, \Delta t, RL, Rev(vt)\}$. $\vec{S} = (s_1, \ldots, s_k)$ are the Service Level Objectives (SLOs) that describe the amount of resources to be purchased by the client, and $\vec{L}$ describes how the resources are linked according to its OCCI description. Each s_* term represents the amount of CPUs, Memory, Disk, network bandwidth, and so on. RL is the risk level (medium, low, very low) that the client selects for its service, having an impact in the price. Δt is the time period during which the VM will be allocated. If the IP provider has not enough free resources to allocate the SLA, it can reject it.

Current commercial Clouds do not compel to specify Δt and sell resources at fixed price/hour. In contrast, research Cloud Market middlewares [10] require to specify Δt when a client and a provider negotiate a price. Market mechanisms would motivate clients to distribute their workloads across time, if possible.

$Rev(vt)$, which was originally proposed in [7], is a revenue function that describes the revenue of a provider after the operation of a SLA. The violation time vt is the total time during which the agreed QoS has not been provided. Let MP be the Maximum Penalty (seen as negative revenue), MR the Maximum Revenue, MPT the Maximum Penalty Threshold, and MRT the Maximum Revenue Threshold, Equation 1 describes the revenue function.

$$Rev(vt) = \frac{MP - MR}{MPT - MRT}(vt - MRT) + MR \tag{1}$$

Equation 1 allows a grace period where the provider can violate the SLA without being penalized. If $vt \leq MRT$, the provider will get all the negotiated revenue (MR); if $vt \geq MPT$, the provider will pay the maximum penalty (MP); for $MRT > vt > MPT$ the money to earn or the penalty to pay will be proportionally in between MR and MP as a function of vt (see Figure 1) . The Maximum Penalty MP is defined to avoid infinite penalties. Client and provider can negotiate the values of MRT, MR, MPT, MP for establishing different QoS ranges that would report different revenues and penalties. The client can assume that vt will be normally near zero and will have to pay MR most times.

When the client wants to acquire resources from the IP, it starts the next negotiation: it sends to the IP an SLA template with values for $(\vec{S}, \vec{L}, \Delta t, RL)$. According to its envisioned status for Δt, if the IP has enough resources, it returns a complete SLA that specifies the values for MRT, MR, MPT and MP

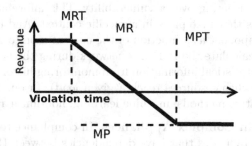

Fig. 1. Revenue of a SLA as a function of the violation time (Equation 1)

as a function of the number of resources, the market status, and the risk level requested by the client. A lower risk level would entail higher prices (MR), but higher penalties (lower MP and less tolerance to SLA violations (lower MRT and MPT)). If the client agrees the terms proposed by the IP, it confirms the SLA or, otherwise, rejects it and looks for another provider in the market.

4 Risk Management

This paper considers risk as the effect of uncertainty on objectives [3]. Risk depends on two facets: the probability of an unwanted event and how it deviates the desired outcomes. Given a time frame, an unwanted event may occur. This may impact or not in the desired outcomes. For example, if a single disk fails within a storage system with redundancy, an unwanted event occurred but its impact is low (cost of replacement, but no data has been loss). In our work, the impact of risk will be economically determined by the penalties that are specified in the SLA. Calculating the risk is calculating the PoF of a complex system, and calculating how the failure can impact the fulfilment of the SLA.

Measuring Risk in Individual Components. For each component based on OCCI types, we identify as failure each incident that causes this component to not work correctly. Although real computing resources may have multiple degrees of malfunction, our model adopts a binary definition of malfunction for single resources: working/failure. Our model does not care about the grade of performance for each individual component, but whether the propagation and aggregation of all the errors/misbehaviours of the individual resources will lead the system to fulfil the SLA or not.

The quantitative risk assessment for each component is based on the process proposed by Guitart et al. [3], which divides the risk assessment into the following stages: (1) Identify what weaknesses could prevent a component from functioning properly. In this paper we identify two: overload of resources and age of resources. (2) Identify which situations can exploit system vulnerabilities. Information from vulnerabilities and threats can be gathered from experts, historical databases and files. (3) The monitoring information is retrieved at different levels. We basically consider information from physical and virtual hosts. (4) Identify the likelihood of a threat acting over a vulnerability. This information is retrieved from historical facts that take place in a specific context. And (5) calculate the PoF of a single component as a function of the current monitoring status, given a time frame (e.g. calculate the PoF of a network during the next 24 hours). In this paper, we use statistical information from monitoring history (e.g. check the historic of failures when resources reach a given load). In our future work, we will explore alternative methods: machine learning, non-linear regressions, etc.

Measuring Risk in Complex Appliances. In compliance to OCCI, our risk model is composed by nodes that have dependencies between them. A node n_x is failing when it is not providing the agreed QoS (e.g. a disk is not able to read or write data, a compute resource is not providing all the promised computation power, a network fails...). The PoF of n_x is notated as $P(n_x)$ and it can be measured according to the steps as previously described.

Let n_x and n_y be two nodes that are linked to work together as a composite system. We consider that n_x has a risk link of weight ω_{xy} to n_y when the failure of n_y prevents n_x to work correctly (for example, n_x is an application server that uses n_y as a database). The weight $\omega_{xy} \in [0, 1]$ is the probability that a failure in n_y is propagated to n_x. In consequence, n_x can fail because an internal failure on n_x or a failure in n_y that is propagated to n_x with probability ω_{xy}. Equation 2 defines $P'(n_x)$ as the propagated probability of failure of n_x.

$$P'(n_x) = P(n_x) + \omega_{xy}P(n_y) - \omega_{xy}P(n_x)P(n_y) \tag{2}$$

Equation 2 is based on the formula for union of probabilities, which assumes that $P(n_x)$ and $P(n_y)$ are independent (unlike $P'(n_x)$ that depends on both $P(n_x)$ and $P(n_y)$). The graphical notation for such risk relation is the next:

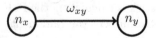

The aforementioned notation is used as a primitive for calculating the risk of complex systems. For example, let ws be a web server that handles requests from clients and contacts the application server as. We measured that the 30% of the times that as is invoked it accesses a database (db). If the database fails, the error will be propagated to as and, in consequence, to ws. In this example we assume $P(ws) = 0.05$, $P(as) = 0.01$, and $P(db) = 0.03$.

If the arrow between nodes does not show any number, we assume a weight value $= 1$ between risk nodes. From the client side, if the node ws fails, the complete web application is failing. The PoF of the complete super system is $P'(ws)$, which is calculated as shown in equation 3. Resolving it, the probability that the complete system fails (that is, the client cannot access ws) is ~ 0.068. It is always true that $P'(n_x) \geq P(n_x)$.

$$
\begin{cases}
P'(ws) = P(ws) + P'(as) - P(ws)P'(as) \\
P'(as) = P(as) + 0.3P(db) - 0.3P(as)P(db)
\end{cases}
\tag{3}
$$

In the previous example, the probability of failure of node as that will be propagated to ws is actually the probability of failure of the subsystem formed by as and db. By this reason, Equation 3 calculates $P'(ws)$ as a function of $P'(as)$ instead of $P(as)$. Our model allows simplifying complex systems by grouping many of their nodes and treats them as a single node.

In our model, a node can also have risk dependencies to many other nodes. We introduce two types of meta nodes to represent unions and intersections between risk probabilities. The next system is interpreted as follows: the system headed by n_x will fail when there is a failure in n_x OR there is a failure in n_y (with probability w_{xy}) OR there is a failure in n_z (with probability w_{xz}).

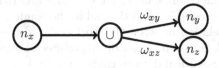

The node labelled as '∪' (union operator) is a meta node to which $P(\cup) = 0$. It is used to allow grouping the subsystem formed by n_y and n_z and treating it as a single node when calculating the risk propagation to n_x (calculated in $P'(\cup)$). In consequence, calculating $P'(n_x)$ is solving the next equations:

$$
\begin{cases}
P'(n_x) = P(n_x) + P'(\cup) - P(n_x)P'(\cup) \\
P'(\cup) = w_{xy}P(n_y) + w_{xz}P(n_z) - w_{xy}P(n_y)w_{xz}P(n_z)
\end{cases}
\tag{4}
$$

As example, imagine n_x is a VM that executes a disk-intensive task against a RAID-0 disk system which distributes the data chunks within two disks (n_y and n_z) for improving performance. If only one disk fails in a RAID-0 system, the complete system will fail, since there is no redundancy for recovering the data.

Our model also introduces the intersection operator '∩' to model redundancy in fault tolerant systems:

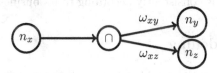

The probability of failure of the subsystem headed by the node '∩' is the intersection of probabilities of failure for nodes n_y and n_z, assuming that they are independent: $P'(\cap) = w_{xy}w_{xz}P(n_y)P(n_z)$. For example, imagine a RAID-1 disk system that mirrors two disks.

The combination of the union and intersection operators may also be used to model systems to which the redundancy is partial. For example, a master node M sends tasks to slave nodes A, B, and C. If one of the slave nodes fails, the other two nodes can handle the work; if two slave nodes fail, the complete system will fail.

Although we focus on the hardware failures at infrastructure level, our model allows also expressing software components as nodes within the graph, or simply considering the software failure within the PoF in the hardware node.

Risk-Aware Cloud Operation. Risk must be considered during the allocation and operation of cloud appliances. For example, a client that needs high availability would negotiate SLAs with a high penalty for the provider in case of SLA violation. In such scenario, the Cloud provider has to minimise the PoF of the application according to two complementary strategies:

- For each node n_x, minimizing $P(n_x)$, which is caused by risk in the node (not propagated). This paper considers two factors that influence in $P(n_x)$: hardware lifetime and workload [13]. The failure rate of hardware resources is high both at the beginning and the end of the components lifetime. There is also direct correlation between the workload and the failure rate, being higher during peak hours and lower during off-peak hours. We use statistical analysis based on historical data to calculate $P(n_x)$.
- Consider decreasing $P'(n_x)$ for each node n_x. Analysing risk graphs and providing redundancy in the critical points of the graph would noticeably reduce the risks of the system with reasonable economical performance.

Analysing the risk propagation graphs is itself a large research field that would require to deep within the research of machine learning and pattern recognition algorithms, and how to apply them to this problem. The aim of this paper is to keep the focus in the risk and revenue model. We simplify the graph analysis by experimenting only with one template of application. The graph analysis has been done off line and the risk minimization policies always apply the same action with the graph: to add redundancy to the nodes whose failures would entail a failure to the rest of the application.

Both strategies for minimizing risk would entail an increment in the cost of operation. Next section describes a model for the management of the revenue during both SLA negotiation and operation that would allow providers providing differentiated risk levels consistently according to its business objectives.

5   Revenue Modelling

This paper uses Equation 5 to establish the price of a set of Cloud resources, given a time frame. MR is the price for a service (Maximum Revenue, as previously defined in Equation 1).

$$MR = RP + DO + BV \tag{5}$$

In Equation 5, RP is the Reservation Price: the minimum price the provider can sell a resource without losing money. DO and BV are subjective terms that may depend on several conditions. DO is the demand/offer overprice: a client may be willing to pay more when there is more demand than offer. DO will tend to 0 when the demand is much lower than the offer. BV is the Business Value: the amount of money a client is willing to pay for an extra unit of QoS.

Our model calculates RP as the cost of amortization of all the resources that the client will use during a given period: the more amortized is a resource the lower is RP. Equation 6 shows how to calculate the amortization cost of a single Cloud resource that is allocated within a physical resource. The RP for a cloud appliance is the addition of the amortization costs for all its resources.

$$Cost_{Am} = (TCO - Amort)\frac{\Delta t}{(LT_{total} - LT_{now})H}\rho \tag{6}$$

TCO is the Total Cost of Ownership, the cost of the initial investment plus the common expenses in electricity and maintenance during the whole lifetime of a resource. $Amort$ is the sum of all the income associated to the provisioning of virtual resources for the given physical resource. Δt is the time that the client is willing to use the resource. LT_{total} is the Life Time that is planned for a group of resources: the time since it is provisioned until it is disengaged from the data centre. LT_{now} is the Life Time since a resource is provisioned until now. Finally $\rho = [0,1]$ is a density function that indicates the proportion of a group of resources to which the cost is being calculated. For example, if a VM requires 4 CPUs from a node with 16 CPUs, $\rho = 0.25$. Finally, H is the percentage of usage of the resources as envisioned by the provider to this time. If $H = 1$, the provider would consider that all the resources that are assigned to a VM are at full occupation during this time. If the resources are underutilized, the value H would proportionally increase the reservation price that is needed for actually amortizing completely a resource at the end of its lifetime.

To avoid inequalities in the amortization of individual resources with the same age, we group all resources from the same type and age into an accounting group. Then the values TCO, $Amort$, ρ and LT apply to the total of resources instead of individual ones. Equation 6 differs from the traditional way to calculate the amortization cost, TCO/LT_{total}, because this formula assumes full load and does not consider how the value of a resource decreases over time.

To calculate DO overprice, our previous work [7] demonstrated that the DO must be low when the offer/demand ratio is high enough to allow users to choose from a big enough set of providers, and high only in peak hours, when most resources are busy.

Calculating BV is difficult because it may rely on several hidden variables that depend on the client, the market status, the reputation of the provider, etc. Instead of trying to synthesize them in a mathematical formula, Machine Learning techniques can allow providers estimating this value. However, those techniques are out of the scope of this paper. We apply a fixed overprice for the SLAs in our experiments, according to their level of QoS and Risk.

We account DO and BV within the total of amortized cost, which are over-prices that accelerate the amortization of the resource and cause $Cost_{Am}$ value to decrease over time. That will allow the provider using different prices depending on the age of the resources that are being sold.

6   Evaluation

In our experiments, we used a Cloud Market simulator (available online [11]) that adopts the simulation architecture and methodology from our previous works [7,8]. We simulate 36 months of a IaaS provider that initially owns 50 hosts with 16 CPUs each one. The number of deployed services initially oscillates between 5 and 60 services/hour, according to a web workload that varies as a function of the hour of the day and the day of the week. To simulate the consolidation of the business of the provider, the average number of requests is linearly increased until it doubles its initial number at the end of the simulation. Because of the increase of the number of requests, the Cloud provider doubles its number of resources at month 18. From the point of view of Equation 6, there is initially an accounting group of resources and at the end of the simulation there are two accounting groups: the initial bunch of resources, and the new resources that were introduced at month 18.

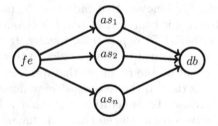

Fig. 2. Basic architecture of a web application

The clients can deploy several types of applications. In our experiments, the clients deploy web services according to the structure in Figure 2: a web front-end (fe) balances the job across a set of n application servers $(as_1, \dots, as_n)$ that use a database node (db) as persistence layer. The number of application servers varies from 2 to 4. The number of CPUs of each node follows a folded normal distribution [5] with both minimum value and variance equal to 1. The same distribution is used to determine the duration of the deployments, with minimum value and variance of 1 hour.

The allocation process of the SLA is the same as described in Section 3. The IP considers three different SLA allocation strategies, which offer three levels of risk for the SLA, from medium to lowest risk:

– **Cost Minimization** (CMin). The provider prioritizes the allocation of VMs in the hosts given two equally-weighted criteria: high consolidation, to save energy costs in hosts that are already running tasks and keep switched off those hosts that are idle [3]; and amortization, to allow lower prices according to the model in Equations 5 and 6. Because of high consolidation and resources age, SLAs allocated according this policy have the higher risk.

- **Node Risk Minimization** (NRMin). The provider prioritizes the allocation of VMs in the hosts according to two equally-weighted criteria: low consolidation, to lower the risks derived from overload in resources that would entail to not provide the agreed QoS; and resource age, trying to avoid the resources that are new and those resources that are near the end of their lifetime [13]. Figure 3 shows the used distribution of failures as a function of the age of the resource.
- **Graph Risk Minimization** (GRMin). The provider applies Node Risk minimization but, in addition, it analyses the OCCI links to try to detect single point of failures. Given the model in Section 4, the provider would detect that a failure in the database node would entail a failure in the whole application, so it decides to replicate it.

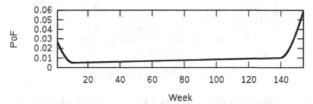

Fig. 3. Probability of Failure of resources over time

Table 1. Revenue function values for each group of SLAs

	CMin	NMin	GRMin
MP	-MR	-1.5MR	-2MR
MRT	$0.15\Delta t$	$0.1\Delta t$	$0.05\Delta t$
MPT	$0.75\Delta t$	$0.5\Delta t$	$0.3\Delta t$

The client selects the type of risk minimization strategy as a function of the risk needs of its application. When the IP calculates the price, it applies a fixed overprice of 50% to the NRMin SLAs and 100% to the GRMin SLAs. In addition to the overprice, that determines the MR value of Equation 1, the risk level also determines MP, MPT and MRT. Lower values for MP, MPT and MRT imply that there is less tolerance to failures for low-risk SLAs (see Table 1), because vt will reach MRT sooner (see Figure 1). These fixed values, as well as the other constants that the simulation relies on, are not intended to reflect real market data but to evaluate the model in terms of relative results and tendencies.

Evaluating Risk Minimization Policies. The graphics of this section show weekly average values to make them more clear and understandable, because hourly or daily averages are highly influenced by the workload oscillations. The weekly granularity for the values is also accurate enough because the simulation

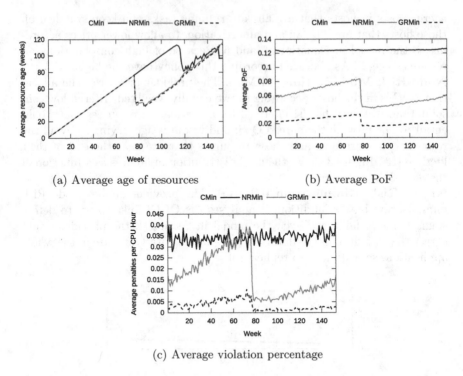

(a) Average age of resources   (b) Average PoF

(c) Average violation percentage

Fig. 4. Evaluation of risk metrics for different SLA policies

is long-term enough (36 months) to show clearly the tendencies of the metrics used to evaluate the effectiveness of the policies.

Figure 4a shows the behaviour of the policies with respect to the age of the selected resources. In the first half of the experiment all the resources are the same age. When a new bunch of resources is introduced at month 18 (week 77), the CMin policy still selects the older resources, which have the highest amortization rates. NRMin and GRMin progressively move their workloads to the new resources, after a short period in which new resources have higher risks than older resources (as shown in Figure 3). As explained before, the number of requests linearly increases over time. Around week 115 resources are highly loaded because of the high number of requests, and the provider has less possibility to choose resources for the different risk levels. This will influence the risk of the SLAs, as shown in Figures 4b and 4c.

Figure 4b shows the weekly average PoF of the SLAs, differentiated by the three different allocation policies (CMin, NRMin and GRMin). While CMin is near to constant over time, NRMin keeps much lower risk than CMin while is noticeably influenced by the load of the resources. The PoF for NRMin SLAs increases linearly over time as the number of application executions also increases because the possibility to choose is reduced. When the number of resources is doubled, the PoF of NRMin is reduced again, while the PoF of CMin is kept constant, because the policy still chooses the older resources. GRMin SLAs are also sensible to the load of resources because the allocation policy is the same as NRMin, but the elimination of the single point of failure causes the system keeping much lower risk rates.

The PoF has a direct impact in the economic penalties as consequence of the violations of the SLAs. Figure 4c shows the strict correlation of the economic penalties with the probability of failure. The economic impact of failures is higher in SLAs allocated with low-risk policies (NRMin and GRMin), because both the prices and the penalties are higher for these SLAs (see Table 1). Figure 4c, as well as the rest of figures with economic information in our evaluation, does not show absolute economic values, but values divided by CPU hours to facilitate the comparison of data from appliances with different size and different time.

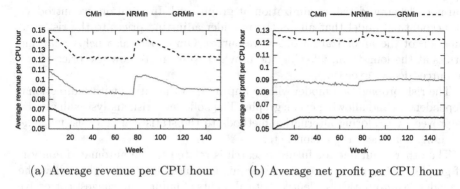

(a) Average revenue per CPU hour   (b) Average net profit per CPU hour

Fig. 5

Evaluating the Modelling of the Revenue. Figure 5a shows the average price per CPU hour for the different types of SLAs. During the initial part of the experiment, the price decreases because the resources are being amortized which, applying the pricing model of Equation 5, reduces RP. Figure 5b shows that during this period the profit (the revenue minus the reservation price minus the penalties) for CMin policy can be improved because the market allows higher profit margin: RP decreases but DO and BV may increase in a lower proportion to decrease prices while increasing the profit margin. On the other side, profit for risk minimization policies keeps near constant during this period (despite the price reduction) because the business value (BV) of low-risk SLAs is higher (the users are willing to pay more for this extra QoS). In consequence, the provider has more room to increase its margin profit with risk minimization policies.

Figure 5a shows that, when the resources are doubled at the half of the experiment, prices increase for risk minimization policies because they tend to allocate tasks in newer resources with a lower amortization rate than older resources. CMin policy keeps constant prices because this policy still allocates the services in the older resources.

Although the penalty rate increases for minimization policies in the first half of the experiment (from week 1 to week 77), as shown in Figure 4c, the impact of penalties in the net profit is proportionally low because of the different scaling of Figures 5b and 4c. For this reason, the profit of NRMin and GRMin policies slightly decreases over time. However, when new resources are added, the incurred price increment and the reduction of SLA penalties have some positive impact in the net profit. The influence of penalties in CMin SLAs remains quite stable during the whole simulation.

7 Conclusions and Future Work

This paper introduces a model to differentiate SLAs as a function of multiple risk levels and adapt the provisioning of resources to multiple client profiles in a Cloud Market. We introduce three policies for each differentiated risk profile that we present in the paper: cost minimization, risk minimization at individual node level, and risk minimization at graph level. In addition, we introduce an accounting model that allows the provider adjusting prices to the risk as a function of the amortization of the resources. Our model also helps adapting prices at the long-term, allowing the provider to estimate how the price of the resources decays over time.

The risk propagation model will be improved in the future with bidirectional dependencies and allowing cyclic graphs. The node-level risk analysis will also be improved by exploring alternative methods to the statistical analysis: machine learning, non-linear regressions, etc.

The other main line for future research is related to the automated analysis of graphs. New pattern recognition techniques must be introduced to allow the provider to automatically identify critical points of failure and suggest corrective actions that would minimize the risk only in the required points of the graph to avoid soaring the costs due to the excess of redundancy.

Regarding revenue modelling, we will work on techniques to discover the Business Value of resources. In other words, it is important that the provider estimates accurately how clients are willing to pay the additional QoS to maximize the profit of the provider without losing clients.

Acknowledgement. This work is supported by the Ministry of Science and Technology of Spain and the European Union (FEDER funds) under contract TIN2012-34557 and by the Generalitat de Catalunya under contract 2009-SGR-980.

References

1. Becker, M., Borrisov, N., Deora, V., Rana, O.F., Neumann, D.: Using k-pricing for penalty calculation in grid market. In: 41st Hawaii International International Conference on Systems Science (HICSS-41 2008), pp. 97–106. IEEE Computer Society, Waikoloa (2008)
2. Djemame, K., Padgett, J., Gourlay, I., Armstrong, D.: Brokering of risk-aware service level agreements in grids. Concurr. Comput.: Pract. Exper. 23(13), 1558–1582 (2011), http://dx.doi.org/10.1002/cpe.1721

3. Guitart, J., Macias, M., Djemame, K., Kirkham, T., Jiang, M., Armstrong, D.: Risk-driven proactive fault-tolerant operation of iaas providers. In: 5th IEEE International Conference on Cloud Computing Technology and Science (CloudCom 2013), Bristol, UK (December 2013)
4. Jensen, F.V.: An introduction to Bayesian networks, vol. 210. UCL press (1996)
5. Leone, F., Nelson, L., Nottingham, R.: The folded normal distribution. Technometrics 3(4), 543–550 (1961)
6. Li, B., Gillam, L.: Risk informed computer economics. In: Proceedings of the 2009 9th IEEE/ACM International Symposium on Cluster Computing and the Grid, CCGRID 2009, pp. 526–531. IEEE Computer Society, Washington, DC (2009), http://dx.doi.org/10.1109/CCGRID.2009.18
7. Macías, M., Guitart, J.: Client classification policies for SLA negotiation and allocation in shared cloud datacenters. In: Vanmechelen, K., Altmann, J., Rana, O.F. (eds.) GECON 2011. LNCS, vol. 7150, pp. 90–104. Springer, Heidelberg (2012)
8. Macias, M., Guitart, J.: Client classification policies for SLA enforcement in shared cloud datacenters. In: 12th IEEE/ACM International Symposium on Cluster, Cloud and Grid Computing, Ottawa, Canada, pp. 156–163 (May 2012)
9. Metsch, T., Edmonds, A.: Open Cloud Computing Interface - Infrastructure. Tech. Rep. GFD-P-R.184, Open Grid Forum (2011)
10. Neumann, D., Stoesser, J., Anandasivam, A., Borissov, N.: SORMA - building an open grid market for grid resource allocation. In: Veit, D.J., Altmann, J. (eds.) GECON 2007. LNCS, vol. 4685, pp. 194–200. Springer, Heidelberg (2007)
11. Risk-aware cloud market simulator, https://github.com/mariomac/riskCloud
12. Sawade, C., Landwehr, N., Bickel, S., Scheffer, T.: Active risk estimation. In: Proceedings of the 27th International Conference on Machine Learning (ICML 2010), pp. 951–958. Omnipress, Haifa (June 2010)
13. Schroeder, B., Gibson, G.A.: A large-scale study of failures in high-performance computing systems. In: Proceedings of the International Conference on Dependable Systems and Networks, DSN 2006, pp. 249–258. IEEE Computer Society, Washington, DC (2006), http://dx.doi.org/10.1109/DSN.2006.5
14. Simao, J., Veiga, L.: Flexible slas in the cloud with a partial utility-driven scheduling architecture. In: 2013 IEEE 5th International Conference on Cloud Computing Technology and Science (CloudCom), vol. 1, pp. 274–281 (December 2013)
15. Wee, S.: Debunking real-time pricing in cloud computing. In: 11th IEEE/ACM International Symposium on Cluster, Cloud and Grid Computing 2011, pp. 585–590 (May 2011)
16. Yeo, C.S., Buyya, R.: Integrated Risk Analysis for a Commercial Computing Service in Utility Computing. Journal of Grid Computing 7(1), 1–24 (2009)

Adaptive and Scalable High Availability
for Infrastructure Clouds

Stefan Brenner, Benjamin Garbers, and Rüdiger Kapitza

TU Braunschweig, Germany
{brenner,rrkapitz}@ibr.cs.tu-bs.de,
b.garbers@tu-braunschweig.de

Abstract. These days Infrastructure-as-a-Service (IaaS) clouds attract
more and more customers for their flexibility and scalability. Even critical
data and applications are considered for cloud deployments. However,
this demands for resilient cloud infrastructures.

Hence, this paper approaches adaptive and scalable high availability
for IaaS clouds. First, we provide a detailed failure analysis of OpenStack
showing the impact of failing services to the cloud infrastructure. Second,
we analyse existing approaches for making OpenStack highly available,
and pinpoint several weaknesses of current best practice. Finally, we
propose and evaluate improvements to automate failover mechanisms.

Keywords: Reliable Cloud Computing.

1 Introduction

Cloud computing is a big paradigm shift affecting almost all kinds of IT-provided
services. Both, for private and public cloud settings, people increasingly consider
shifting their applications to clouds. This naturally includes even critical applications, and thus, critical data [2,10]. As a result, reliability and availability of
cloud services become more and more important. Besides cost efficiency and
scalability, these properties are significant reasons for offloading applications to
clouds for many cloud customers.

Recent events show, however, even professional clouds still struggle with outages and failures [15,11]. Hence, support for high availability (HA) of Infrastructure-as-a-Service (IaaS) clouds has to be built from scratch, deeply integrated
in the cloud software stack.

In order to handle the aforementioned needs for reliability and availability in
infrastructure clouds, we present adaptive and scalable HA for the OpenStack[1]
infrastructure services. We consider typical failures like host, network, disk, and
process crashes.

Focus is set on HA of infrastructure services, so the actual virtual machines
(VMs) running on compute nodes are not covered. If this is necessary, there
has been research that combines live migration with failover techniques for

---

[1] https://www.openstack.org

K. Magoutis and P. Pietzuch (Eds.): DAIS 2014, LNCS 8460, pp. 16–30, 2014.

single VMs [8] and VM replication [1], or as a cloud-integrated service for highly available services [19].

In this work, first, we analyse the generic IaaS cloud anatomy, specialise on OpenStack later on, and show the impact and consequences of failing services and components. Second, we outline existing approaches and best practices for HA and identify their weaknesses and open problems. Third, we propose several approaches for the improvement of these mechanisms, tackling the discovered problems. Our approaches are based on replication of services and load balancing. Besides HA, they also improve the scalability of stateless infrastructure services when the load increases. Similarities between several infrastructure clouds, in combination with our generic approaches, allow universal application of our proposed principles.

There are existing approaches using passive replicas [5]. In that case, passive service endpoints are made active on failures of an active replica. In contrast to that, there are approaches using active replicas only, balancing the request load across all of them. This allows failure masking, because requests are only forwarded to correct replicas. At most one request being in flight while a failure occurs can be lost in this setup. Hence, we base our approach on this mechanism as well. Our contribution improves on existing ones by automatic failover procedures that do not require manual intervention and modifications that allow to handle more fine-grained failures. Furthermore, conflicts that may happen on failures when existing approaches are used, are solved and prevented with our improvements.

In our failure analysis, we identified that OpenStack's networking component *Quantum*[2], that manages and maintains virtual networks interconnecting VMs, runs into conflicts when only some processes of Quantum fail while other components keep running. To solve this problem, we provide a monitoring-and-cleanup solution that prevents the arising conflicts and implements automatic failover that does not require any manual intervention by an administrator.

This paper starts with an architecture overview of OpenStack in Section 2, with special focus on the Quantum architecture, because it is most relevant for the contribution of this work. Then, we provide a detailed failure analysis of OpenStack in Section 3. Next, we show current best practices making OpenStack highly available and their shortcomings in Section 4, followed by Section 5 that describes the improvements of our approach. In Section 6 we measure the performance of our approach compared to existing approaches and show the recovery times on component's failure. Finally, we conclude our work in Section 7.

2   Anatomy of an OpenStack-Based IaaS-Cloud

In the following section, we describe the anatomy of an IaaS cloud using Open-Stack as an example. OpenStack is only one open source implementation of an IaaS cloud system, and other implementations like Eucalyptus [14] and Open-Nebula [12] are quite similar in terms of architectural aspects [16]. Hence, our

---

[2] Will be renamed *Neutron* in the future.

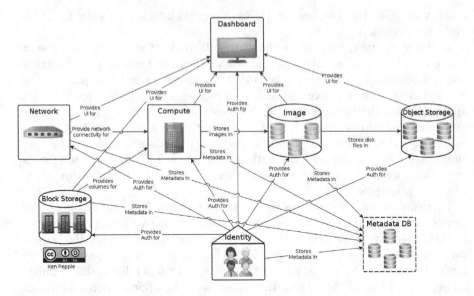

Fig. 1. OpenStack Architecture Overview based on [3]

generic approaches solving the HA questions, can be applied to them with small adaptions as well (see Section 5).

OpenStack-based IaaS clouds usually consist of several loosely coupled services, i.e. OpenStack components, that cover various cloud infrastructure building blocks like identity management, storage, networking, as well as the actual virtualisation fabric and the user interface. Figure 1 illustrates how the OpenStack services are interconnected and interacting with each other. All components interact with each other via a database and a messaging bus system. The database is mostly used for storage of relevant meta information about VMs and networks and can be implemented by a relational database system. As part of the default configuration MySQL is utilised here. The responsibilities of the message bus, cover the exchange of state information about compute nodes and scheduling tasks for example. Usually, the message bus is implemented using RabbitMQ[3], an AMPQ-compliant messaging system.

While OpenStack components interact with each other using a central database and the message bus, in order to provide functionality to the users, REST APIs are provided by the individual components. These APIs are widely compatible to the well-known Amazon Web Services[4].

Two important components of OpenStack are *Nova*, that provides the actual cloud computing fabric controller, and *Swift*, which provides object storage. These two components have been part of OpenStack from the very beginning of the development. Apart from *Cinder*, that provides block storage to VMs, further components are *Keystone* for identity and user management, *Glance* for

---

[3] https://www.rabbitmq.com

[4] https://aws.amazon.com/

virtual machine image management, and Quantum that maintains the (often-times completely virtual) network infrastructure interconnecting the VMs and real networks.

Most OpenStack components are divided up into several individual services working tightly together. Nova for example consists of the Nova scheduler service, the Nova compute service and several others. Similar to this, many components including Nova contain an API service. Clearly we have to consider all services of a component when making the OpenStack infrastructure highly available. Many of these services are stateless, which simplifies replication and makes them suitable for load balancing.

One of the most sophisticated OpenStack components is Quantum. It contains several services which are partly not stateless, and thus, sophisticated to make highly available because of consistency problems. The Quantum server is the main subcomponent and provides the management interface. It also controls the other subcomponents of Quantum, namely the DHCP-Agent, the L3-Agent and the Plugin-Agent. The agents in turn interact with system mechanisms for providing DHCP services to VMs, maintaining layer three networking capabilities, and managing firewalling.

Quantum supports several deployment modes. The simplest one is called *flat network*, bridging the VMs directly to an external network. Next, there is the mode *provider router with private networks* that isolates the VMs of one tenant in individual networks routed by an OpenStack networking router. The most flexible mode is called *per-tenant routers with private networks*. In this mode, each tenant can create virtual networks and routers and interconnect them. Virtual networks are isolated using Linux network namespaces, such that tenant's private networks could even have overlapping IP namespaces. In this work, we focus on the OpenvSwitch[5]-based variant of this deployment mode, that uses a OpenvSwitch Plugin-Agent running on the network node, that manages the virtual networking.

3 Vulnerability Analysis

The focus of this work lies on the analysis of the general cloud infrastructure services and its possible failure scenarios. HA for actual tenant VMs is out of scope for this work and has to be considered separately, for example by use of VM replication [8]. Special attention is payed to database failures and failures of virtual network components involved in stateful Quantum. Other stateless services can be grouped together and approached the same.

We further divide this section up into failures of building blocks the Open-Stack services rely on, such as the relational database and the messaging system. Apart from that, we consider failures of the actual OpenStack services itself, for example the identity management service *Keystone*.

In this work we consider crash-stop failures, complete host failures or individual process failures. If complete hosts fail, OpenStack loses its connections to

---

[5] http://openvswitch.org/

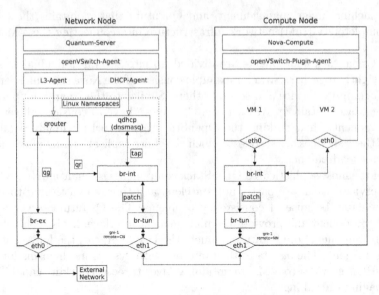

Fig. 2. Quantum with OpenvSwitch

all services running on that host, and has to offload these tasks to other hosts. More fine-grained are individual process failures, because only the specific failed process has to be handled by the failover procedure.

In our analysis we distinguish three different failure severity categories: *low*, *medium* and *high*. Failures, that render the whole infrastructure unusable are considered highly severe. Low severity of failures means the failure does not affect big parts of the infrastructure but mainly influences some VMs on a single physical machine. In between there are medium severe failures with major impact on the cloud infrastructure and a reduction of cloud functionality. Table 1 gives a quick overview over our analysis that is detailed in the remainder of this section.

3.1   Failures of OpenStack Building Blocks

Database Failures: The relational database is one of the core parts of an OpenStack cloud, as it stores the configuration and metadata. Most services directly rely on a relational storage backend in order to function properly. A failure of the database is considered highly severe, as it will cascade to the other OpenStack services.

Messaging System: The messaging system in OpenStack is another vital core component. It is used for internal communication of services directly or indirectly responsible for configuring and running VMs. Remote procedure calls (RPCs) are used for direct communication between OpenStack components, whereas tasks like scheduling requests are distributed within one component following a push-pull pattern. Periodic resource usage reports and events are also collected using the messaging system. Messaging system failures break inter-component communication which prevents the cloud from serving requests like VM creation, and thus, is considered higly severe.

3.2 Failures of OpenStack Services

Keystone: Keystone provides authentication and authorisation services for the remaining OpenStack components. If this service fails, requests can no longer be verified and are rejected by the services. The actual behaviour depends on the used authentication method of either unique IDs or a public key infrastructure. In the latter case, request validation is theoretically still possible without Keystone, but is prone to identity theft, as the revoked certificates are no longer updated. As a result Keystone failures are classified as highly severe.

Nova: Nova consists of several services. The API service handles internal and external requests and a failure will break all communication with Nova. The scheduler distributes VM requests among all compute hosts. Without it, new requests will remain in a pending state. So, scheduler failures will not render the whole cloud useless, but at the same time are not limited to a single host, so they are considered medium severe. The conductor service mediates all database accesses by compute hosts, mainly updating their current resource usage. A failure may lead to the scheduler making decisions based on outdated metadata. A failed compute service is of low importance, as just the VMs running on this host are no longer manageable but continue to run. Scheduling requests will ignore the affected host and no new machines are placed on it. The failure of the underlying hypervisor of a host (e.g. KVM) leads to the loss of all ephemeral data of the VMs. Resultant from our assumptions about the classification, we consider it being of low severity. The remaining services, Cert, Consoleauth and noVNC, are not always required or only provide additional functionality, which is not critical for general infrastructure operation.

Glance: Glance consists of an API service and a registry for storing metadata about VM images. A failure of either one will render the component useless, as incoming requests can not be served without the image's metadata (owner, visibility etc.). Because this is not limited to a single host, it is classified as medium severe.

Cinder: The Cinder block storage service of OpenStack is mostly out of scope in this work, because it can be implemented using renowned highly available block storage systems as backend providers. In this paper, we only need to consider the OpenStack-related parts of this service. The API service and the scheduler equals other component's API services and schedulers when considering HA. The severity of the volume and backup services is considered medium, since failures do not affect the cloud as a whole but also do not only affect single VMs on one host but all VMs using block storage.

Swift: Since Swift's architecture has been designed for HA and fault tolerance. Thus, the severity of failing storage nodes only depends on the Swifth config-uration parameters like the deployed cluster size and replication count. In this paper we only need to consider OpenStack-related parts. One of them, the Swift proxy service, can be handled like all stateless services.

Quantum: The Quantum component, that provides the network functionality, is divided into several parts: The Quantum server is responsible for management and includes the public API and scheduling facilities, that behave like the Nova API and scheduler. The DHCP-Agent handles automatic configuration of new VMs and manages the underlying Dnsmasq processes. A failure will break the network and routing configuration of VMs. The core parts of Quantum are the L3-Agent and the Plugin-Agents. Both are an abstraction for the actually used vendor-specific software switch, for example OpenvSwitch. In the evaluated setup, the L3-Agent handles the routing and bridging configurations for all deployed virtual networks. Traffic from tenant VMs is routed through a host running this service and then bridged to an external network. The Plugin-Agents are the respective counterparts, running on the compute nodes. They manage the connection of VMs to their networks and the tunnelling of traffic to the nodes running the L3-Agent. While Plugin-Agent failures only affect single hosts, L3-Agent failures may affect multiple virtual networks across many hosts. The networks continue to operate with the last known configuration until the L3-Agent is restored, but may experience inconsistencies due to the missing configuration updates. A failure of the L3-Agent is therefore medium severe, whereas the Plugin-Agents are of lower importance.

Horizon: Horizon is a web-based frontend for OpenStack and uses the API services of all other components in order to provide its services. A failure will not affect the regular operation of the infrastructure and therefore is classified low severe.

4   Best Practice for Providing Highly Available IaaS

Since the reliability of IaaS clouds is important, there have already been efforts dealing with HA. In the following, we summarise the current best practices.

The current most widely used approach for providing highly available OpenStack clouds is the Pacemaker cluster stack [4]. It consists of a collection of software tools to provide replication and failover capabilities for generic services. Corosync is used as messaging and membership management layer in order to connect all participating nodes of a cluster [9]. The communication between all nodes follows the virtual synchrony pattern and is realised using the Totem single-ring ordering and membership protocol [6]. Corosync can use multiple physical connections in a cluster to be resilient against link failures or routing errors, replicating all messages either in an active or passive fashion.

The Pacemaker cluster manager is responsible for monitoring and managing the cluster. All services are configured using *resource agents*, small scripts, which map the service specific status variables and init calls to standard Pacemaker calls. The internal policy engine can then query the services for their state and enforce failovers in the event of a failure. The affected resources will then be

Table 1. The table shows the criticality classification of the individual components, their usage of the database, the message queue, and whether they are stateful

Component	low	med	high	database	message-queue	stateful
Database			×	×		×
RabbitMQ			×		×	×
Keystone			×	×		
API Services		×				
noVNC	×					
Horizon	×			×		×
Hypervisor	×					×
Nova-Scheduler		×			×	
Nova-Cert	×				×	
Nova-Consoleauth	×				×	
Nova-Conductor		×		×	×	
Nova-Compute	×			×	×	×
Glance-Registry		×			×	
Cinder-Volume		×				
Cinder-Scheduler		×			×	
Cinder-Backup		×				
Swift-Proxy		×				
Swift-Storage	×					×
Quantum-Server		×		×	×	×
DHCP-Agent		×		×	×	
Metadata-Agent		×		×	×	
L3-Agent		×		×	×	×
Plugin-Agent	×			×	×	×

relocated to another host in the cluster. To guarantee a consistent cluster state, Pacemaker replicates configuration changes among all participating hosts. Failed hosts can be excluded by using fencing mechanisms to prevent a possible faulty behaviour. Fencing of hosts can be achieved following the shoot the other node in the head (STONITH) approach, where a failed host is separated from the remaining cluster through measures like remote shutdown or even stopping the power supply via manageable power distribution units.

The services of OpenStack are replicated following the primary-backup approach as described by Buhiraja et al. [7] and listen on a virtual IP-address also managed by Pacemaker. Some of the infrastructure services, like MySQL or the RabbitMQ messaging system, additionally require highly available block storage. For these applications, DRBD is used. DRBD stands for *distributed replicated block-device* and replicates write requests for a volume to another standby host in either synchronous or asynchronous fashion.

Pacemaker-based HA solutions can be more complex to implement and maintain compared to a lightweight load-balanced setup, that we use. Following the primary-backup approach, standby resources are only used in the event of a failure and reduce the overall efficiency of the cluster. The features of service and resource replication can often be directly achieved using the scheduling mechanisms in newer versions of OpenStack. The advantages of Pacemaker include its ability to be used for almost any generic service and its integrated support for most cluster related operations, such as monitoring, policy enforcement, and fencing.

Another cluster management software is the *Red Hat Cluster Suite* [17], a set of tools for monitoring and managing distributed resources in a group of hosts. The features and drawbacks are similar to the Pacemaker stack, as it is able to provide HA for generic services.

5   Scalable High Availability for IaaS

This section shows how our approach improves on the existing ones, tackling their shortcomings. At the same time we make use of simple and reliable mechanisms and allow to handle failures more fine-grained. Compared to existing approaches, we do not require any manual intervention on failures.

Our basic intention is to transparently mask service interruptions from OpenStack users, such that the services are always available to them, in order to encourage user's trust in cloud services. We can achieve scalability and availability at the same time involving replication and load balancing techniques. While many components are stateless and easy to replicate, we also have to consider stateful services like the central database and the message bus. Most sophisticated, however, is the Quantum component, consisting of many services and components.

We define an architecture with several roles of nodes. There are nodes belonging to the *persistence cluster* hosting the central database, the message bus and the HA tools Keepalived and HAProxy [4]. Then we have *cluster controller* nodes that host all the important infrastructure services like Keystone, Glance, Nova, Quantum and Horizon for example. Naturally, we additionally have *compute nodes* that run the actual VMs.

We tolerate single host failures and continue provisioning of all required cloud services even when failures occur. With our approach even multiple failing hosts at the same time can be tolerated, as long as they are part of different roles. Additionally, if they are of the same role, the remaining correct replicas only have to be able to handle the increased load to mask the failure.

In our approach we make use of virtual IPs, which allows us to implement automatic failover to other active service endpoint replicas. Virtual IPs allow, based on gratuitous ARP, to use one IP address as a service endpoint independently from the actual machine hosting the service. Hence, we can replicate the service on several machines and dynamically redirect traffic if one of them fails. Since we know which replicas are up and online, we can even apply load-balancing across the individual replicas in order to distribute the workload evenly. This works well especially for stateless services, for example the API services. Even though it is easily adaptable to any TCP-based services we focus on OpenStack-specific details here. The actual implementation of the above paradigms is done using Keepalived and HAProxy [4].

For stateless services, we can use active replicas and load balancing of requests instead of passive standby replicas. By this a better resource usage and easier failover can be achieved because requests and load are spread across all replicas. On failure we do not need to migrate service state or warm up a standby replica, but the load of the failed replica is directly distributed and adds evenly to the load of all other replicas.

Basically, we always try to minimise the failover times. That is, the time of service unavailability that is noticeable by the clients. Hence, we try to achieve automatic failover that does not require any manual intervention.

Making OpenStack services highly available using Keepalived and HAProxy is a very generic approach. It can be easily adapted to all kinds of services even beyond OpenStack. Basically, applying the approach only requires the service, which has to be highly available, to be stateless. Then it can be deployed on several hosts and requests are balanced evenly across all correct replicas. Stateful services always require a little more effort. However, sometimes there can be worked around the statefulness of a service, as it is described in this work for the DHCP-agents in Section 5.3. State is offloaded by the service to the database, so the DHCP-agent itself is actually stateless, but the database maintains its state. For the database in turn, there has to be a special approach for HA, which in our case is achieved using the Galera framework as described in Section 5.2.

5.1 High Availability for Stateless Services

For stateless services the basic idea involves HAProxy running on several hosts knowing all actual service endpoints. Clients can access any HAProxy instance they want and will be redirected transparently to the actual service. Here, HAProxy tries to involve stickyness of clients to services in order to support caching mechanisms. Since the HAProxy itself might fail as well, Keepalived is used, which applies gratuitous ARP in order to capture incoming packages from clients to a specific virtual IP [13]. This allows to transparently mask failing hosts (HAProxy instances) and to automatically redirect all traffic to another HAProxy instance. From the client perspective, this results in a virtual IP that is *always available*. Clearly, this approach requires the actual service (endpoints) to be replicated as well. This architecture is illustrated in Figure 3 with the dashed line showing one possible request-path. HAProxy is chosen over competitors like Nginx or Pen due to its resource efficiency and stability [18].

5.2 High Availability for Stateful Services

Apart from stateless services, we also have to consider stateful services and building blocks of OpenStack like the MySQL database and the Quantum networking services. The database can be made highly available using MySQL Galera [4],

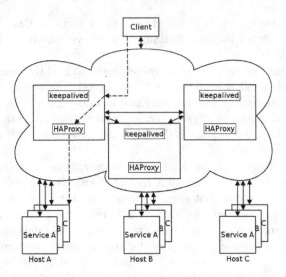

Fig. 3. Load-balancing Cluster with Keepalived and HAProxy

while the Quantum networking services require further considerations covered in Section 5.3.

Another fact that could bring further conflicts is inherently caused by the asynchronous network itself. It's not possible to decide whether services are responding slow or failed. Hence, hosts could misleadingly be considered faulty and later show up correctly again. However, in the HAProxy and Keepalived approach for stateless services this is no problem, because faulty hosts will be excluded from the load balancer until they respond back positively to the health checks. As a result, on failures, future requests by clients will be answered correctly (by another replica). However, the request sent to the service in the very moment of its failure will be lost and could be masked by the client library's timeout mechanisms using request repetition.

5.3   High Availability for Quantum Networking

When analysing Quantum, we discovered special consistency problems when agents fail but the underlying mechanism continues to work properly. This affects the L3-Agent, because OpenvSwitch is still working without the agent, but OpenStack assumes it has failed and reschedules the according networks. For this problem, we show our approach of cleaning up the old virtual infrastructure that has been managed by the failed L3-Agent, such that the newly commissioned replacement will not conflict with any legacy virtual networks. In addition, here we describe our monitoring approach, that is necessary to notice agent failures and trigger the cleanup accordingly.

Cleanup Legacy Virtual Networks. A trivial approach for the infrastructure cleanup would be a simple script, checking the affected components in short intervals triggering the needed action when a failure is detected. This has the advantage of low intervals between the checks, but recovery is problematic when the script itself terminates unexpectedly. The cleanup could also be implemented using a reoccurring tasks framework like Cronjob, that is considered well-tested and reliable. As with a simple script, the failure handling is not satisfying and Cronjob's minimum interval of one minute is too high in order to provide efficient failover. The current implementation uses Init systems (upstart or systemd) to manage the lifecycle of the cleanup utility. Like cron, the Init systems are well tested components and assumed to be reliable. They handle the activation and deactivation of the job, as well as failure handling in the event of an unexpected termination. The interval between checks can be chosen as low as in the simple scripted approach.

Rescheduling of Virtual Networks to Another L3-Agent. Network nodes have been limited to Master/Slave operation in the past [4]. Starting with Open-Stack Grizzly, virtual resources can be scheduled. This allows to operate multiple network nodes as a basic requirement for making the services highly available. However, virtual routers still require manual intervention to be relocated on another network node. We use OpenStack's integrated scheduling mechanism in order to automatically move routers to other hosts. The health of all L3-Agents is periodically monitored and router rescheduling is triggered, when a faulty agent has been detected. Then, the corresponding routers are migrated to other hosts. In our approach this is based on the active scheduling policy, while others involve custom schedulers[6].

The health checks are performed by the periodic task framework of Open-Stack, executed in configurable intervals[7]. By reducing the periodic interval, lower failover times can be achieved, but at the cost of additional resource usage. The lower bound is limited by Python's cooperative threading model, where long running tasks block all others inside the same process and might even delay the execution of the next periodic interval. New tasks are only started, after the previous one finished or yielded its execution to the next task.

In addition to highly available routers, this solution also enforces a consistent network configuration when only the L3-Agent fails but the underlying software switch (e.g. OpenvSwitch) continues to run but is no longer manageable by OpenStack. Our policy will remove all virtual routers and their configuration from the affected host, even without a connection to the Quantum server.

The reliability of this solution only depends on the reliability of the used Init system and its capabilities to handle failures. In our evaluation environment, failure handling was successfully tested with Upstart and systemd. The monitoring job will be loaded at boot time and restarted automatically in the event of an unexpected termination.

---

[6] http://lists.openstack.org/pipermail/openstack/2013-December/004226. html, last accessed Feb 3th, 2014.

[7] Defaults to 40s.

If a slow host is considered faulty and comes back online later, with our approach no conflicts arise. This is caused by our cleanup procedure, that prevents the same network to be maintained by more than one agent at the same time. The cleanup script itself will be maintained by the Init system and automatically restarted on failure, so the cleanup is still executed reliably.

Compared to the existing state, with our solution manual intervention is not necessary. In addition, our approach is very fine-grained, because we not only consider complete host failures but even handle failures of the individual processes.

High Availability for the DHCP-Service. Providing highly available DHCP services is not a problem in OpenStack Grizzly as multiple DHCP-Agents can be configured to serve a network. Since all agents synchronise their managed instances and configurations indirectly through the relational database, the underlying Dnsmasq configuration needs not to be changed.

6 Evaluation

In order to evaluate our approach and proof its functionality, we deployed it in a lab environment. Automatic failover allows the system to tolerate and mask any complete host and individual service failure in our testbed.

This evaluation focusses on failover times and special attention is paid to Quantum L3-Agent failures while other stateless services are grouped together and Keystone is evaluated as one arbitrary representative. The approach for this evaluation is to simulate failures by cutting network connections (complete host fail) and killing single processes. Then, we measure the time until clients experience the failed service available again served by another host.

For the Keystone evaluation we issued the `user-list` request repeatedly to the Keystone service. We expect all other stateless services to behave the same, different from Keystone only by a constant factor representing the difference in computing effort. Failures will be detected by the healthchecker from Keepalived which maintains an active replica list. Faulty replicas get removed from this list, and correct ones can be added back again later on. On failover we do not have any bootstrapping times, because the services are already up and running. Usually clients get sticked to one replica, to allow optimal use of caching mechanisms. Figure 4a shows that on failures the response time increases. Caused by the failure, requests time out and are retried by the client library. After the faulty replica is removed from the list, requests get responed by another replica.

The evaluation of L3-Agent failures is done in our testbed environment hosting 54 VMs based on CirrOS basically running idle. We evaluate failures by sending ICMP echo requests (pings) to a VM every 100ms while killing the L3-Agent process. Connectivity is measured by ICMP echo responses (pongs) from one arbitrarily chosen VM. Our cleanup mechanism is triggered on failure which disables all virtual infrastructure components maintained by the failed agent. Another agent notices the failure and cleans up the metadata and reschedules the failed router. The agent that has been selected by the scheduling algorithm

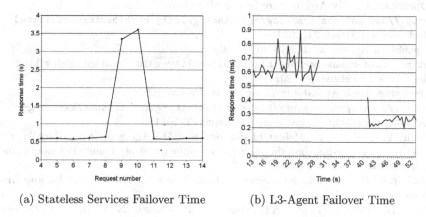

(a) Stateless Services Failover Time   (b) L3-Agent Failover Time

Fig. 4. Failover Times for Stateless and Stateful Services

receives a notification via the message bus and recreates the virtual infrastructure. Figure 4b shows a gap of pongs where the agent failed and a recovery of VM connectivity about 11 seconds later. This time period consists of the above parts of our automatic recovery procedure. The measurement shows that the automatic failover procedure is working without manual intervention and VMs are back online after a short period.

7   Conclusion

Since adoption of cloud computing is steadily increasing, the need for reliability is getting more relevant and important for both, providers and customers of IaaS clouds. In this work, we start with a general architecture discussion of IaaS clouds, then take OpenStack as an example and pinpoint shortcomings in existing approaches for HA. We provide a detailed failure analysis and classification describing effects of failing hosts and services to the cloud. In a next step, we solve the identified weaknesses of existing HA approaches. With our approach we want to minimise the time of unavailability of cloud infrastructure services as experienced by the cloud users and provide automatic failover procedures that do not require manual intervention by an cloud administrator.

References

1. vSphere - Replication, https://www.vmware.com/de/products/vsphere/features-replication (last accessed March 25, 2014)
2. Critical workloads, private deployments and market opportunities abound in the cloud (2013), http://insights.ubuntu.com/resources/article/critical-workloads-private-deployments-and-market-opportunities-abound-in-the-cloud/ (accessed March 23, 2014)

3. OpenStack Grizzly Architecture (revisited) (2013),
   `http://www.solinea.com/blog/openstack-grizzly-architecture-revisited`
   (last accessed March 24, 2014)
4. OpenStack High Availability Guide (2014),
   `http://docs.openstack.org/high-availability-guide/content/index.html`
   (last accessed February 3, 2014)
5. OpenStack High Availability Using Active/Passive (2014),
   `http://docs.openstack.org/high-availability-guide/content/ha-using-`
   `active-passive.html` (last accessed March 23, 2014)
6. Amir, Y., Moser, L.E., Melliar Melliar-Smith, P.M., Agarwal, D.A., Ciarfella, P.:
   The Totem single-ring ordering and membership protocol. Transactions on Computer Systems, 311–342 (1995)
7. Budhiraja, N., Marzullo, K., Schneider, F.B., Toueg, S.: The Primary-Backup Approach, pp. 199–216 (1993)
8. Cully, B., Lefebvre, G., Meyer, D., Feeley, M., Hutchinson, N., Warfield, A.: Remus:
   High Availability via Asynchronous Virtual Machine Replication. In: Proc. of the
   5th USENIX Symposium on Networked Systems Design and Implementation, pp.
   161–174 (2008)
9. Dake, S.C., Caulfield, C., Beekhof, A.: The Corosync Cluster Engine. In: Linux
   Symposium, pp. 85–100 (2008)
10. Greer, M.: Survivability and Information Assurance in the Cloud. In: Proc. of the
    4th Workshop on Recent Advances in Intrusion-Tolerant Systems (2010)
11. Krigsman, M.: Pain and Pleasure in the Cloud (2011), `http://www.zdnet.com/`
    `blog/projectfailures/intuit-pain-and-pleasure-in-the-cloud/14880` (last
    accessed February 5, 2014)
12. Moreno-Vozmediano, R., Montero, R.S., Llorente, I.M.: IaaS Cloud Architec-
    ture: From Virtualized Datacenters to Federated Cloud Infrastructures. Computer,
    65–72 (2012)
13. Nadas, S.: Virtual Router Redundancy Protocol (VRRP) Version 3 for IPv4 and
    IPv6. RFC 5798 (2010), `https://tools.ietf.org/html/rfc5798`
14. Nurmi, D., Wolski, R., Grzegorczyk, C., Obertelli, G., Soman, S., Youseff, L.,
    Zagorodnov, D.: The eucalyptus open-source cloud-computing system. In: Sym-
    posium on Cluster, Cloud, and Grid Computing, pp. 124–131 (2009)
15. Pepitone, J.: Amazon EC2 outage downs Reddit, Quora (2011),
    `http://money.cnn.com/2011/04/21/technology/amazon_server_outage/` (last
    accessed February 5, 2014)
16. Sempolinski, P., Thain, D.: A Comparison and Critique of Eucalyptus, OpenNebula
    and Nimbus. In: Cloud Computing Technology and Science, pp. 417–426 (2010)
17. Shiraz, K.: Red Hat Enterprise Linux Cluster Suite (2007),
    `http://www.linuxjournal.com/article/9759` (last accessed March 25, 2014)
18. Tarreau, W.: New benchmark of HAProxy at 10 Gbps using Myricom's 10GbE
    NICs (Myri-10G PCI-Express) (April 2009), `http://haproxy.1wt.eu/10g.html`
19. Thanakornworakij, T., Sharma, R., Scroggs, B., Leangsuksun, C.B., Greenwood,
    Z.D., Riteau, P., Morin, C.: High Availability on Cloud with HA-OSCAR. In: Proc.
    of the 2011 International Conference on Parallel Processing, vol. 2, pp. 292–301
    (2012)

Trust-Aware Operation
of Providers in Cloud Markets

Mario Macías and Jordi Guitart

Barcelona Supercomputing Center (BSC) and
Universitat Politecnica de Catalunya - Barcelona Tech (UPC)
Jordi Girona 29, 08034 Barcelona, Spain
{mario.macias,jordi.guitart}@bsc.es

Abstract. Online Reputation Systems allow markets to exclude providers providers that are untrustworthy or unreliable. System failures and outages may decrease the reputation of honest providers, which would lose potential clients. For that reason, providers require trust-aware management policies aimed at retaining their reputation when unexpected failures occur. This paper proposes policies to operate cloud resources to minimise the impact of system failures in the reputation. On the one side, we discriminate clients under conflicting situations to favour those that would impact more positively the reputation of the provider. On the other side, we analyse the impact of management actions in the reputation and the revenue of the provider to select those with less impact when an actuation is required. The validity of these policies is demonstrated through experiments for various use cases.

1 Introduction

Cloud Computing allows clients to acquire resources (usually Virtual Machines, VMs) and size them dynamically according to their spot requirements and pay only for what they use. Our research is framed in Open Cloud Markets [4] where both clients and providers are autonomous agents that negotiate the terms of the Quality of Service (QoS) and the pricing. After the negotiation, the terms of the contract are stored in a Service Level Agreement (SLA).

Cloud providers may not always fulfil the SLAs they agree with the clients. Online reputation systems [3] allow their users to submit and retrieve information about the fulfilment rate of the SLAs for each provider. Reputation systems enforce the confidence between parties and boost the number of commercial transactions, but they are vulnerable to reputation attacks: a group of dishonest clients may report false values about the QoS that a cloud provider is actually offering [1]. In consequence, reputation systems must also establish trust relationships between peers to avoid dishonest reports.

Reputation allows markets to exclude dishonest providers. However, spot failures or system outages may decrease the reputation of honest providers, having a double economic impact: the provider must pay penalties as agreed in the SLAs and it will lose potential clients due to the loss of reputation. For this reason,

K. Magoutis and P. Pietzuch (Eds.): DAIS 2014, LNCS 8460, pp. 31–37, 2014.

providers operating in a Cloud market require trust-aware management policies aimed at retaining their reputation when unexpected failures occur.

We propose policies to discriminate users in function of their reputation under some situations that force provider to violate SLAs, such as errors in resources allocation, or an outage that makes unavailable part of the resources in a data center, dealing with the issue raised by Xiong et al. [6] and Kerr et al. [1], which considered the necessity of a community-context factor to incentivise peers for reporting true feedbacks.

The main contributions of this paper are: (1) introduction of policies to minimize the impact of system failures in the reputation. We discriminate clients according to their reputation to favour those with high reputation under some conflicting situations, because the reports of those clients will impact more positively the reputation of the provider; (2) evaluation of the impact of the management actions in the reputation and the revenue of the provider to select those with less impact when an actuation is required.

The rest of this paper is organised as follows: Section 2 summarizes the reputation model and describes the policies, which are evaluated in Section 3. Then, we present the conclusions and some future research.

2   Trust-Aware SLA Management

We consider a group of providers that are competing in a market to sell their resources to the potential clients. The clients are also communicated between them by means of a Peer-to-Peer network. When a client wants to buy a resource, it sends an offer to the providers to start a negotiation and agree a SLA, which is described as $\{\overrightarrow{S}, \Delta t, Rev(vt)\}$. $\overrightarrow{S}$ are the Service Level Objectives (SLOs) that describe the QoS to be purchased by the client. Δt is the time period when the task will be allocated. $Rev(vt)$ is a revenue function that describes how much money the provider earns or loses after finishing a task. The Violation Time (vt) is the amount of time in which the provider has not provided the agreed QoS to the client. Let MR the Maximum Revenue, MP be the Maximum Penalty (a negative revenue), MPT the Maximum Penalty Threshold, and MRT the Maximum Revenue Threshold, we describe our revenue function as follows:

$$Rev(vt) = \frac{MP - MR}{MPT - MRT}(vt - MRT) + MR$$

If $vt < MRT$ the SLA is not violated (0 violations); if $vt > MPT$, the SLA is completely violated (1 violations). $MPT > vt > MRT$ is a partial violation. Please refer to Section 3 for more details about $Rev(vt)$ and its concrete values.

Both clients and providers are entities that have a degree of trust between them as individuals. Trust relations are provided by the reputation model described in our previous work [3], which demonstrated its validity to identify trustworthy providers and expel dishonest peers to protect the system against reputation attacks. In this model, a trust relation is expressed as $\overrightarrow{T}(A, B) = \omega_1 \overrightarrow{D}(A, B) + \omega_2 \overrightarrow{R}(B)$; $\overrightarrow{D}(A, B)$ is the direct trust from A to B, which is built based on previous experiences between A and B; $\vec{R}(B)$ is the reputation trust, which is calculated by asking to other clients about their past experiences with B; ω_1 and ω_2 are used to weight each term, and may vary in each particular client. Trust values vary from 0 (no trust) to 1 (maximum trust). Trust relations are continuously updated assuming that most peers are honest and, when asked, they report their true trust toward the provider. Related work considers many incentives to peers to report honestly [7]. Our contribution is complimentary to them, since we deal with the minimization of the impact of the dishonest reports.

To select a provider, a client sends SLA templates to all the providers that match its requirements. If the providers have enough resources to handle the request, they return a price. The client then scores all the providers and chooses the provider with the highest score, which may vary depending on the client preferences. In this work, we score providers as $\dfrac{-\vec{T}(c_x, cp_y)}{Price}$: the client would accept sending tasks to providers to which the trust is lower if the price they establish is low enough. That would motivate providers to keep its maximum trust level and, if not possible, to lower prices. The higher QoS is provided to a client, the higher trust values he will report to the reputation system; unless the client is behaving dishonestly and reporting false values.

We propose to maximise the reputation as a key objective that will help providers to increase their revenue due to the enforcement of the trust relationship with their clients. This paper considers selective SLA violation and/or cancellation for minimizing the impact of resource failures and overloading: to prioritise trustworthy users under certain situations in which a set of SLAs that are already allocated must be violated temporarily or directly cancelled.

When the monitoring system of a provider detects that there are not enough resources to fulfil the workload for all the VMs in a given node, the next process is triggered: the VMs are ordered according to a *given criterion* and the provider pauses the VMs on the top positions during t time. When the node can provide the QoS for the VMs that are still running, the provider stops pausing VMs. In reputation maximisation policies, the criterion to order VMs is the trustworthiness to the client that owns it. To calculate the trustworthiness to a client, the provider can join the reputation system as a normal peer, and poll several clients about several providers. If a given client is usually reporting values that are far away from the average, it will be considered unreliable.

The SLA violation algorithm is generic enough to achieve other BLOs, such as revenue maximisation [2]. Next section will evaluate the effectiveness of the trust maximisation policy by comparing it with the same policy for other BLOs.

We must emphasize that our policy cancels SLAs only when the provider is not able to fulfil them all. This should be infrequent, only when the violation is unavoidable, because the economic penalty is paid whatever the client trustworthiness is. The idea is at least to minimize the impact in the reputation of the provider. A bad usage of this policy could make the clients lose the confidence in the provider, thus losing profit.

3   Evaluation

To evaluate the effectiveness of our models, we have created a simulated environment [5] that is available online to facilitate replicating the experiments. The simulator reproduces the model and market negotiation steps that are described in Section 2 and the related work [3]. The trustworthiness of the clients follows a folded normal distribution with mean=0.5 and standard deviation=0.2. That means that most clients have trust values near 1 and a few clients are reporting dishonestly. The values for $Rev(vt)$ are the next: $MRT = 0.05$ (that means that if the agreed QoS is not provided during the 5% of the time or less, the SLA is not considered as violated); $MPT = 0.3$ (when the agreed QoS is not provided during the 30% of time or more, the SLA is completely violated); MR is dynamically established according to $\overrightarrow{S}$ and the market status [2]; $MP = -1.5MR$ (if the provider completely violates a SLA, it must pay back the 150% of the price that the client paid initially). The providers normally provide the 100% of the agreed QoS during off-peak hours and around 97% during peak hours. The workload follows a web pattern that varies in function of the hour of the day and the day of the week. The simulations rely on constant values that do not intend to reflect real market data, but to evaluate the model in terms of relative values and tendencies.

To evaluate the reputation-aware resources operation, we have simulated 5 days of a market operation with three types of providers, according to their policy for discriminating SLAs during resources overload: (1) a provider that randomly discards SLAs, used as a baseline to evaluate the system behaviour without any policy; (2) a provider that discards the SLAs that report less revenue [2]; and (3) a provider that discards the SLAs from the clients to which there is low trust. We introduced a global outage of the data centre at day 3 of the simulation. During the outage, the providers only have the 20% of their usual resources. The outage has been programmed to happen during a peak of workload. That means that about 80% of the allocated SLAs are to be violated during the outage.

Figure 1a shows reputation for day 2 (normal day) and day 3 (outage). Reputation is near the maximum value for all the providers at off-peak hours. During the peaks, the graph shows the effect of the increase of SLA violations in the reputation. The reputation maximisation policy keeps reputation near 1 during both peaks and off-peaks. The random policy shows that reputation decreases when no policies are applied. Although the revenue maximisation policy does not consider reputation, it indirectly keeps it between random and reputation maximisation policies: the provider tries to first pause the VMs whose SLA violation time is over MRT. In consequence, it violates less SLAs and, indirectly, the reputation of the provider is higher than the reputation of the provider that does not apply any policy.

Figure 1b shows the evolution of the spot revenue for the three providers during the outage, demonstrating that maintaining high reputation during the outage has a real impact in the revenue of the provider. However, we measured that during normal operation the revenue of the provider that maximises the reputation is slightly lower.

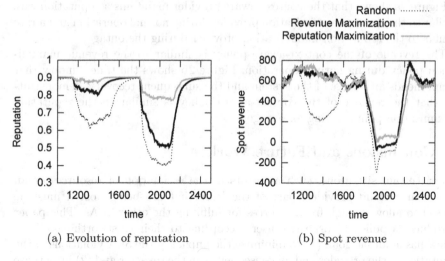

(a) Evolution of reputation   (b) Spot revenue

Fig. 1. Measurements after and before an outage

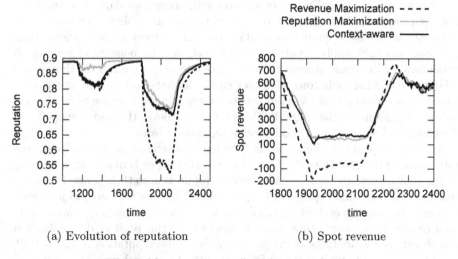

(a) Evolution of reputation   (b) Spot revenue

Fig. 2. Measurements for context-aware policy

Considering the previous observations, we have introduced a new provider that is aware of the environment (normal operation or outage) and dynamically switches the revenue/reputation maximisation policy in function of what is expected to report the highest economic profit. When the provider is operating normally it uses the revenue maximization policy; if the monitoring information shows that there is an outage in part of the resources, the provider switches to the reputation maximization policy and returns back to revenue maximization policy when the systems are again in normal operation.

Figure 2a shows that the context-aware provider maintains a reputation rate similar to the revenue-maximisation provider during normal operation and a rate similar to the reputation-maximisation provider during the outage.

The revenue of the context-aware policy is similar to the revenue maximisation policy during normal operation. Figure 2b shows the time window that comprehends an outage of the system and the subsequent recovery, demonstrating that the revenue of the context-aware policy is similar to the reputation maximisation policy during an outage.

4   Conclusions and Future Work

Under certain situations, such as errors in the estimation of resources or an outage in a cloud provider, part of the VMs that are being hosted must be paused to allow enough free resources for fulfilling the other SLAs. This paper introduces a policy to prioritize users according to their trustworthiness. This policy has a double goal: (1) to minimize the impact of the SLA violations in the reputation of the provider and, in consequence, in the revenue; and (2) incentivise users to report true validations of the providers.

After analysing the policy in comparison with others, we show that providers that behave honestly and apply revenue maximisation policies, in most cases indirectly keep a good enough reputation rate and achieve higher revenue than the providers that apply reputation maximisation. The benefits of reputation maximisation in terms of revenue are noticeable under conditions that imply a high rate of SLA violations. Considering the aforementioned, we introduce a new type of provider that switches between reputation or revenue maximisation policies depending on the context. This provider achieves the best revenue in all the cases, and always keeps good-enough reputation rates.

A key issue of reputation systems is to incentivise their users to report true validations of the providers [3]. The policies of this paper help solving it because clients that report true validations have high reputation to their peers. Providers that have interest on keeping high reputation will prioritize the QoS for trustworthy clients under certain situations such as peaks of demand or an outage. As a consequence, clients that want to benefit from this positive discrimination will report true validations of the providers. Since the reputation model is P2P, any provider could join a network for polling the trustworthiness of a client.

This paper validates the model by means of a simulated environment because there are no real market traces of this type of market model. In addition, we would need to fully use a large data centre during many days to generate data that is statistically representative enough. Using a simulated environment allows to solve such issues. Although the results do not reflect real information in *quantitative* terms, the objective of this paper is to evaluate the policies in *qualitative* terms: we measured that the application of a given policy can improve the trust or the revenue of a provider in a significant proportion.

This paper does not consider the ethical issues of using such policies by dishonest providers for always cheating the clients with low reputation: not only dishonest clients, but also clients that recently joined the reputation network.

In future work we will improve the context-aware provider by adding statistical analysis to dynamically learn how the actions of the provider during negotiation and operation can influence the future reputation. We also plan to improve the policy for selecting the SLAs that are going to be violated. The objective is to achieve a policy that is able to ponder both reputation and revenue maximisation objectives. In addition to the improvement in the model, future work will include new policies to complement the selective violation/cancellation of SLAs. For example, to apply price discounts to the clients to which there is high trust or to use migration capabilities to redistribute VMs for decreasing the violation rate of those SLAs from trusted clients.

Acknowledgment. This work is supported by the Ministry of Science and Technology of Spain and the European Union (FEDER funds) under contract TIN2012-34557 and by the Generalitat de Catalunya under contract 2009-SGR-980.

References

1. Kerr, R., Cohen, R.: Smart cheaters do prosper: defeating trust and reputation systems. In: 8th International Conference on Autonomous Agents and Multiagent Systems, AAMAS 2009, vol. 2, pp. 993–1000. International Foundation for Autonomous Agents and Multiagent Systems, Richland (2009)
2. Macias, M., Fito, O., Guitart, J.: Rule-based SLA management for revenue maximisation in cloud computing markets. In: 2010 Intl. Conf. of Network and Service Management (CNSM 2010), Niagara Falls, Canada, pp. 354–357 (October 2010)
3. Macías, M., Guitart, J.: Cheat-proof trust model for cloud computing markets. In: Vanmechelen, K., Altmann, J., Rana, O.F. (eds.) GECON 2012. LNCS, vol. 7714, pp. 154–168. Springer, Heidelberg (2012)
4. Neumann, D., Stoesser, J., Anandasivam, A., Borissov, N.: SORMA – building an open grid market for grid resource allocation. In: Veit, D.J., Altmann, J. (eds.) GECON 2007. LNCS, vol. 4685, pp. 194–200. Springer, Heidelberg (2007)
5. Reputation-aware cloud market simulator, https://github.com/mariomac/reputation
6. Xiong, L., Liu, L.: Peertrust: Supporting reputation-based trust for peer-to-peer electronic communities. IEEE Transactions on Knowledge and Data Engineering 16(7), 843–857 (2004)
7. Zhang, J.: Promoting Honesty in Electronic Marketplaces: Combining Trust Modeling and Incentive Mechanism Design. Ph.D. thesis, School of Computer Science, University of Waterloo, Waterloo, Ontario, Canada (May 2009)

Scaling HDFS with a Strongly Consistent Relational Model for Metadata

Kamal Hakimzadeh, Hooman Peiro Sajjad, and Jim Dowling

KTH - Royal Institute of Technology
Swedish Institute of Computer Science (SICS), Stockholm, Sweden
{mahh,shps,jdowling}@kth.se

Abstract. The *Hadoop Distributed File System* (HDFS) scales to store tens of petabytes of data despite the fact that the entire file system's metadata must fit on the heap of a single Java virtual machine. The size of HDFS' metadata is limited to under 100 GB in production, as garbage collection events in bigger clusters result in heartbeats timing out to the metadata server (*NameNode*).

In this paper, we address the problem of how to migrate the HDFS' metadata to a relational model, so that we can support larger amounts of storage on a shared-nothing, in-memory, distributed database. Our main contribution is that we show how to provide at least as strong consistency semantics as HDFS while adding support for a multiple-writer, multiple-reader concurrency model. We guarantee freedom from deadlocks by logically organizing inodes (and their constituent blocks and replicas) into a hierarchy and having all metadata operations agree on a global order for acquiring both explicit locks and implicit locks on subtrees in the hierarchy. We use transactions with pessimistic concurrency control to ensure the safety and progress of metadata operations. Finally, we show how to improve performance of our solution by introducing a snapshotting mechanism at NameNodes that minimizes the number of roundtrips to the database.

1 Introduction

Distributed file systems, such as the *Hadoop Distributed File System (HDFS)*, have enabled the open-source Big Data revolution, by providing a highly available (HA) storage service that enables petabytes of data to be stored on commodity hardware, at relatively low cost [2]. HDFS' architecture is based on earlier work on the Google Distributed File System (GFS) [4] that decoupled metadata, stored on a single node, from block data, stored across potentially thousands of nodes. In HDFS, metadata is kept in-memory on a single NameNode server, and a system-level lock is used to implement a multiple-reader, single writer concurrency model. That is, HDFS ensures the consistency of metadata by only allowing a single client at a time to mutate its metadata. The metadata must fit on the heap of a single *Java virtual machine* (JVM) [10] running on the NameNode.

K. Magoutis and P. Pietzuch (Eds.): DAIS 2014, LNCS 8460, pp. 38–51, 2014.
© IFIP International Federation for Information Processing 2014

The current implementation of HDFS does, however, support highly available metadata through an eventually consistent replication protocol, based on the Active/Standby replication pattern, but limited to having a single standby node. All read and write requests are handled by the Active node, as reads at the Standby node could return stale data. The replication protocol is based on the Active node making quorum-based updates to a recovery log, called the *edit log*, persistently stored on a set of journal nodes. The Standby node periodically pulls updates to the edit log and applies it to its in-memory copy of the metadata. The quorum-based replication protocol requires at least three journal nodes for high availability. Failover from the Active to the Standby can, however, take several tens of seconds, as the Standby first has to apply the set of outstanding edit log entries and all nodes need to reach agreement on who the current Active node is. They solve the latter problem by using a Zookeeper coordination service that also needs to run on at least three nodes to provide a high availability [7].

The challenge we address in this paper is how to migrate HDFS' metadata from highly optimized data structures stored in memory to a distributed relational database. Using a relational database to store file system metadata is not a novel idea. WinFs [13], a core part of the failed Windows Longhorn, was supposed to use Microsoft SQL Server to store its file system metadata, but the idea was abandoned due to poor performance. However, with the advent of *New SQL* systems [17], we believe this is an idea whose time has now come. Recent performance improvements for distributed in-memory databases make it now feasible. Version 7.2 of MySQL Cluster, an open-source new SQL database by Oracle, supports up to 17.6 million transactional 100-byte reads/second on 8 nodes using commodity hardware over an infiniband interconnect [17]. In addition to this, recent work on using relational databases to store file system metadata has shown that relational databases can outperform traditional inode data structures when querying metadata [5].

Our implementation of HDFS replaces the Active-Standby and eventually consistent replication scheme for metadata with a transactional shared memory abstraction. Our prototype is implemented using MySQL Cluster [14]. In our model, the size of HDFS' metadata is no longer limited to the amount of memory that can be managed on the JVM of a single node [10], as metadata can now be partitioned across up to 48 nodes. By applying fine-grained pessimistic locking, our solution allows multiple compatible write operations [8] to progress simultaneously. Even though our prototype is built using MySQL Cluster, our solution can be generalized to support any transactional data store that either supports transactions with at least read-committed isolation level and row-level locking. Our concurrency model also requires implicit locking, and is motivated by Jim Gray's early work on hierarchical locking [8]. We model all HDFS metadata objects as a directed acyclic graph of resources and then with a row-level locking mechanism we define the compatibility of metadata operations so as to isolate transactions for the fewest possible resources allowing a maximum number of concurrent operations on metadata. We show how serializable transactions are required to ensure the strong consistency of HDFS' metadata, by showing how anomalies that can arise in transaction isolation levels lower than serializable [1] can produce inconsistencies in HDFS metadata operations. As our solution produces a high level of load on the database, we also introduce a snapshot layer (per-transaction cache) to reduce the number of roundtrips to the database.

2   HDFS Background and Concurrency Semantics

Distributed file systems have typically attempted to provide filesystem semantics that are as close as possible to the POSIX strong model of consistency [19]. However, for some operations, HDFS provides a consistency level weaker than POSIX. For example, because of the requirement to be able to process large files that are still being written, clients can read files that are opened for writing. In addition, files can be appended to, but existing blocks cannot be modified. At the file block level, HDFS can be considered to have sequential consistency semantics for read and write operations [19], since after a client has successfully written a block, it may not be immediately visible to other clients. However, when a file has been closed successfully, it becomes immediately visible to other clients, that is, HDFS supports linearizability [6] at the file read and write level.

Metadata in HDFS. Similar to POSIX file systems, HDFS represents both directories and files as inodes (*INode*) in metadata. Directory inodes contain a list of file inodes, and files inodes are made up a number of blocks, stored in a *BlockInfo* object. A block, in its turn, is replicated on a number of different data nodes in the system (default 3). Each replica is a *Replica* object in metadata. As blocks in HDFS are large, typically 64-512 MB in size, and stored on remote DataNodes, metadata is used to keep track of the state of blocks. A block being written is a *PendingBlock*, while a block can be under-replicated if a DataNode fails (*UnderReplicatedBlock*) or over-replicated (*ExcessReplica*) if that DataNode recovers after the block has been re-replicated. Blocks can also be in an *InvalidatedBlock* state. Similarly, replicas (of blocks) can be in *ReplicaUnderConstruction* and *CorruptedReplica* states. Finally, a *Lease* is a mutual grant for a number of files being mutated by a single client while *LeasePath* is an exclusive lock regarding a single file and a single client.

Tying together the NameNode and DataNodes. Filesystem operations in HDFS, such as file open/close/read/write/append, are blocking operations that are implemented internally as a sequence of *metadata operations* and *block operations* orchestrated by the client. First, the client queries or mutates metadata at the NameNode, then blocks are queried or mutated at DataNodes, and this process may repeat until the filesystem operation returns control to the client. The consistency of filesystem operations is maintained across metadata and block operations using *leases* stored in the NameNode. If there is a failure at the client and the client doesn't recover, any leases held by the client will eventually expire and their resources will be freed. If there is a failure in the NameNode or a DataNode during a filesystem operation, the client may be able to retry the operation to make progress or if it cannot make progress it will try to release the leases and return an error (the NameNode needs to be contactable to release leases).

HDFS' Single-Writer Concurrency Model for Metadata Operations.
The NameNode is the bottleneck preventing increased write scalability for HDFS applications [16], and this bottleneck is the result of its multiple-reader, single-writer concurrency model [20]. Firstly, metadata is not partitioned across nodes. Secondly, within the NameNode, a global read/write lock (*FSNamesystem lock* - a Java language ReentrantReadWriteLock) protects the namespace by grouping the NameNode's operations into read or write operations. The NameNode uses optimized data structures like multi-dimensional linked-lists for accessing blocks, replicas and DataNode information on which it is almost impossible to use fine-grained concurrency control techniques. The data structures are tightly coupled, and generally not indexed as memory access is fast and indexing would increase metadata storage requirements.

As the FSNamesystem lock is only acquired while updating metadata in memory, the lock is only held for a short duration. However, write operations also incur at least one network round-trip as they have to be persisted at a quorum of journal nodes. If writes were to hold FSNamesystem lock while waiting for the network round-trip to complete, it would introduce intolerable lock contention. So, writes release the FSNamesystem lock after applying updates in memory, while waiting for the updates to be persisted to the journal nodes. In addition to this, to improve network throughput to the journal nodes, writes are sent in batches [11] to journal nodes. When batched writes return, the thread waiting for the write operation returns to the client. However, thread scheduling anomalies at the NameNode can result in writes returning out-of-order, thus violating linearizability of metadata. As threads don't hold the FSNamesystem lock while waiting for edits to complete, it is even possible that thread scheduling anomalies could break sequential consistency semantics by returning a client's writes out-of-order. However, metadata operations also acquire leases while holding the FSNamesystem lock, thus making individual filesystem operations linearizable.

3 Problem Definition

We are addressing the problem of how to migrate HDFS' metadata to a relational model, while maintaining consistency semantics at least as strong as HDFS' NameNode currently provides. We assume that the database supporting the relational model provides support for transactions. While metadata consistency could be ensured by requiring that transactions' execute at a serializable isolation level, distributed relational databases typically demonstrate poor throughput when serializing all updates across partitions [18]. In HDFS, filesystem operations typically traverse the root directory, and the root inode is, therefore, a record that is frequently involved in many different transactions. As the root directory can only be located on one partition in a distributed database, transactions that take a lock on the root (and other popular directories) will frequently cross partitions. Thus, the root directory and popular directories become a synchronization bottleneck for transactions. A challenge is safely removing them from transactions' contention footprint, without having to give up on strong consistency for metadata. If we are to implement a consistency model at least as strong consistency as that provided for HDFS' metadata, we need transactions, and they need to support at least read-committed isolation level and row-level locks, so that we can implement stronger isolation levels when needed.

Another challenge we have is that, in the original HDFS, metadata operations, each executed in their own thread, do not read and write metadata objects in the same order. Some operations may first access blocks and then inodes, while other operations first access inodes and then blocks. If we encapsulate metadata operations in transactions, locking resources as we access them, cycles will be introduced resulting in deadlocks. Another problem, that is also an artifact of HDFS's NameNode design, is that many operations read objects first, and then update them later within the same metadata operation. When these operations are naively implemented as transactions, deadlock occurs due to transactions upgrading read locks to exclusive locks.

Finally, as we are moving the metadata to remote hosts, an excessive number of roundtrips from a NameNode to the database increases the latency of filesystem operation latencies and reduces throughput. Although we cannot completely avoid network roundtrips, we should avoid redundant fetching of the same metadata object during the execution of a transaction.

4   Hierarchical Concurrency Model

The goal of our concurrency model is to support as a high a degree of concurrent access to HDFS' metadata as possible, while preserving freedom from deadlock and livelock. Our solution is based on modelling the filesystem hierarchy as a *directed acyclic graph (DAG)*, and metadata operations that mutate the DAG are in a single transaction or that either commits or, in the event of partial failures in the distributed database, aborts. Aborted operations are transparently retried at NameNodes unless the error is not recoverable. Transactions pessimistically acquire locks on directory/file subtrees and file/block/replica subtrees, and these locks may be either explicit or implicit depending on the metadata operation. *Explicit locking* requires a transaction to take locks on all resources in the subtree. *Implicit locking*, on the other hand, only requires a transaction to take one explicit lock on the root of a subtree and it then implicitly acquires locks on all descendants in the subtree. There is a trade-off between overhead of taking too many locks with explicit locking over lower level of concurrency with implicit locking [8]. However, metadata operations not sharing any subtrees can be safely executed concurrently.

4.1   Building a DAG of Metadata Operations

After careful analysis of all metadata operations in the NameNode, we have classified them into three different categories based on the primary metadata object used to start the operation:

1. *path operations,*
2. *block operations,*
3. *lease operations.*

The majority of HDFS' metadata operations are path operations that take an absolute filesystem path to either a file or directory as their primary parameter. Path operations typically lock one or more inodes, and often lock block objects, lease paths and lease objects. Block operations, on the other hand, take a block identifier as their primary parameter and contain no inode information. An example block operation is *AddBlock*: when a block has been successfully added to a DataNode, the DataNode acknowledges that the block has been added to the NameNode that then updates the block's inode. Blocks are unique to inodes, as HDFS does not support block sharing between files. Lease operations also provide a filesystem path, but it is just a subpath that is used to find all the lease-paths for the files containing that subpath. In figure 1a, we can see how block and lease operations can mutate inodes, introducing cycles into the metadata hierarchy and, thus, deadlock.

Our solution to this problem, in figure (1b), is to break up both block operations and lease operations into two phases. In the first phase, we start a transaction that executes only read operations, resolving the inodes used by the operations at a read committed isolation level. This transaction does not introduce deadlock. In the second phase, we start a new transaction that acquires locks in a total order, starting from the root directory. This second transaction needs to validate data acquired in the first phase (such as inode id(s)). Now path, block and lease operations all start acquiring locks starting from the root inode.

We need to ensure that metadata operations do not take locks on inodes in a conflicting order. For example, if a metadata operation $operation(x, y)$ that take two inodes as parameters always takes a lock on the first inode x then on the second inode y, then the concurrent execution of $operation(a, b)$ and $operation(b, a)$ can cause deadlock. The solution to this problem is to define a total ordering on inodes, a *total order rule*, and ensure all transactions acquire locks on inodes using this global ordering. The total order follows the traversal of the file system hierarchy that depth-first search would follow, traversing first towards the leftmost child and terminating at the rightmost child. The first inode is the root inode, followed by directory inodes until the leftmost child is reached, then all nodes in that directory, then going up and down the hierarchy until the last inode is reached.

More formally, we use the hierarchy of the file system to map inodes to a partially ordered set of IDs. A transaction that already holds a lock for an inode with ID m can only request a lock on an inode with ID n if $n > m$. This mechanism also implements implicit locking, as directory inodes always have a lower ID than all inodes in its subtree.

Our total ordering is impossible for range queries (with or without indexes), because not all databases support ordered queries. We fix this issue by also taking implicit locks in such cases. As paths are parsed in a consistent order

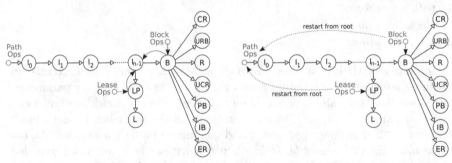

(a) HDFS' Directed Graph has cycles.   (b) Acyclic DAG. Ops start from root, locks taken in order from leftmost child.

I: *INode*, **B**: *BlockInfo*, **L**: *Lease*, **LP**: *LeasePath*, **CR**: *CorruptedReplica*, **URB**: *UnderRepliatedBlock*, **R**: *Replica*, **UCR**: *UnderConstructionReplica*, **PB**: *PendingBlock*, **IB**: *InvalidatedBlock*, **ER**: *ExcessReplica*

Fig. 1. Access graph of HDFS metadata

from the root to leaf inodes in the path, when we take an exclusive lock on a directory inode, we implicitly lock its subtree. This prevents concurrent access to the subtree, and thus reduces parallelism, but solves our problem. Fortunately, typical operations, such as getting blocks for a file and writing to a file do not require implicit locks at the directory level. However, we do take implicit locks at the file inode level, so when a node is writing to a file, by locking the inode, we implicitly lock all block and replica objects within that file.

4.2 Preventing Lock Upgrades

A naive implementation of our relational model would translate read and write operations on metadata in the existing NameNode to read and write operations directly on the database. However, assuming each metadata operation is encapsulated inside a single transaction, such an approach results in locks being upgraded, potentially causing deadlock. Our solution is to only acquire a lock once on each data item within a metadata operation, and we take the lock with the highest strength lock that will be required for the duration of that transaction.

4.3 Snapshotting

As we only want to acquire locks once for each data item, and we are assuming an architecture where the NameNode accesses a distributed database, it makes no sense for the NameNode to read or write the same data item more than once from the database within the context of a single transaction. For any given transaction, data items can be cached and mutated at a NameNode and only updated in the database when the transaction commits. We introduce a snapshotting mechanism for transactions that, at the beginning of each transaction, reads all the resources a transaction will need, taking locks at the highest strength that

---

Algorithm 1. Snapshotting taking locks in a total order.

1. snapshot.clear

2. **operation** doOperation
3.   tx.begin
4.   create-snapshot()
5.   performTask()
6.   tx.commit

7. **operation** create-snapshot
8.   S = total_order_sort(op.X)
9.   **foreach** x in S **do**
10.   **if** x is a parent **then** level = x.parent_level_lock
11.   **else** level = x.strongest_lock_type
12.   tx.lockLevel(level)
13.   snapshot += tx.find(x.query)
14.   **end for**

15. **operation** performTask
16.   //Operation Body, referring to transaction cache for data

---

will be required. On transaction commit or abort, the resources are freed. This solution enables NameNodes to perform operations on the *per-transaction cache* (or snapshot) of the database state during the transaction, thus reducing the number of roundtrips required to the database. Note, this technique is not implementing snapshot isolation [1], we actually support serializable transactions. An outline of our concurrency model for transactions, including total order locks and snapshotting, is given in algorithm 1.

5 Correctness Discussion

In our solution, transactions are serializable, meaning that transactions are sortable in the history of operations. Therefore, it is always true that at any moment in time, all readers get the final and unique view of the mutated data which is strongly consistent. We ensure that transactions that contain both a read and a modify filesystem operation for the same shared metadata object should be serialized based on the *serialization rule:*

- $\forall (w_i, w_j)$ *if* $X_{wi} \cap X_{wj} \neq \emptyset$ then transactions of (w_i, w_j) must be serialized;
- $\forall (r_i, w_j)$ *if* $X_{ri} \cap X_{wj} \neq \emptyset$ then transactions of (r_i, w_j) must be serialized.

First, we use the hierarchy of the file system to define a partial ordering over inodes. Transactions follow this partial ordering when taking locks, ensuring that the circular wait condition for deadlock never holds. Similarly, the partial ordering ensures that if a transaction takes an exclusive lock on a directory inode, subsequent transactions will be prevented from accessing the directory's subtree until the lock on the directory's lock is released. Implicit locks are required for operations such as creating files, where concurrent metadata operations could return success even though only one of them actually succeeded. For operations such as deleting a directory, explicit locks on all child nodes are required.

To show that our solution is serializable, we use an anomalies-based definition of isolation levels, and then we justify why none of these anomalies happen in our solution [1]. The list of anomalies that can arise in transactions are namely *Dirty Write, Dirty Read, Fuzzy Read, Lost Update, Read Skew, Write Skew,* and *Phantom Reads* [1]. Assuming well-formed locking [1], that is, we have no bugs in our locking code, then the system guarantees that it is never possible that two concurrent transactions could mutate the same data item. This prevents *Dirty Reads and Write*, as well as *Fuzzy Reads* and *Read Skew*. Similarly, *Lost Updates* only occur if we do not have well-formed locking. Similarly, *Write Skew* is impossible, as a reader and writer transactions require concurrent access to the same data item. Likewise for a single data item, predicates are also taken into account in our solution in the form of implicit locks. All predicates are also locked even if the metadata operation does not intend to change them directly, thus making *Phantom Reads* impossible. Finally, we only execute index scans when we have an implicit lock preventing the insertion of new rows that could be returned by that index scan. This means that, for example, when listing files in a directory we take an implicit lock on the directory so that no new files can be inserted in the directory while the implicit lock is held. Similarly, list all blocks for an inode only happens when we have an implicit lock on the inode.

6   Experiments

We used MySQL Cluster as the distributed relational database for metadata. In experiments the MySQL Cluster nodes and the NameNode run on machines each with 2 AMD 6 core CPUs (2.5 GHz clock speed, 512 KB cache size) connected with 1 GB Ethernet. The versions of our software were: MySQL Cluster 7.2.8, Java virtual machine 1.6 and ClusterJ 7.1.15a as the connector.

6.1   Capacity

Based on Shvachko in [16], HDFS files on average contain 1.5 blocks and, assuming a replication factor of 3, then 600 bytes of memory is required per file. Due to garbage collection effects, the upper limit on the size of the JVM heap for the NameNode is around 60GB, enabling the NameNode to store roughly 100 million files [16]. Existing clusters at Facebook have larger block sizes, up to 1 GB, and carefully configure and manage the JVM to scale the heap up to 100 GB, leading to larger clusters but not to significantly more files. For our NameNode, we estimate the amount of metadata consumed per file by taking into account that each INode, BlockInfo and Replica row in database require 148, 64 and 20 bytes, respectively. Per file, our system creates 1 INode, 2 BlockInfo and 6 Replica rows, which is 396 bytes. MySQL Cluster supports up to 48 datanodes and, in practice, each node can have up to 256GB of memory for storage.

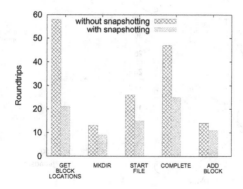

Fig. 2. Impact of snapshotting on database roundtrips

So in principle, a MySQL Cluster implementation can scale up to 12 TB in size, although the largest cluster we are aware of is only 4 TBs. If we conservatively assume that MySQL Cluster can support up to 3.072 TB for metadata, then with a replication factor of 2 for the metadata in MySQL cluster, our file system can store up to 4.1 billion files. This is a factor of 40 increase over Shvachko's estimate for HDFS from 2010.

6.2 Snapshots Reduce the Number of Roundtrips to the Database

Our snapshotting layer, or *Transaction Cache,* caches data items retrieved from the database in the local memory of the NameNode. This minimizes the number of roundtrips to the database and consequently the overall latency for the metadata operation. We wrote an experiment to analyze a number of popular metadata operations, counting the number of roundtrips to the database that our *Transaction Cache* saves for each metadata operation. GET_BLK_LOC is a metadata operation that returns the addresses of the DataNodes storing a replica of a given block. MKDIR creates directories recursively. START_FILE creates INodes for all the non-existent inodes, writes the owner of the lease and creates a new lease-path entry. COMPLETE, sent by the client after having successfully written the last block of a file, removes all the under-construction-replicas and marks the corresponding BlockInfo as complete. ADD_BLOCK adds a new BlockInfo and returns a list containing the location for its replicas. As can be seen in figure 2, GET_BLK_LOC, START_FILE, and COMPLETE reduce the number of roundtrips to the database by 60%, 40% and 50%.

6.3 Row-Level Lock in MySQL Cluster

To demonstrate the feasibility of our approach on a real database, we present a micro-benchmark on the performance of row-level locking in MySQL Cluster. In this setup, MySQL Cluster has 4 DataNodes, each running on a different host. In this experiment, we vary the number of threads and the lock type taken,

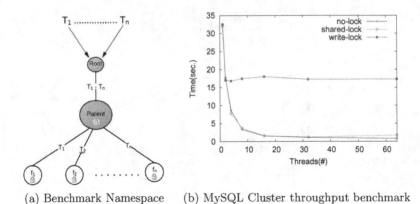

(a) Benchmark Namespace   (b) MySQL Cluster throughput benchmark

Fig. 3. Influence of locking on MySQL Cluster throughput

while we measure the total time for threads to read a set of rows of data in a pre-existing namespace. This experiment simulates the cost of a taking a lock on a parent directory and then reading the rows required to read in a file (inode, blocks, and replicas).

In the namespace structure in figure 3a, the root and a parent directory are shared between all threads while each thread is assigned just one file to read. All threads read the root directory without a lock (at read committed isolation level), but they each acquire a different type of lock on the parent directory. Threads that take write locks on the parent directory must be executed serially, while threads that take either a shared lock (read lock) or no lock can execute in parallel.

The results for 10,000 transactions are shown in the figure 3b. As the number of threads is increased, the time to perform 10,000 transactions decreases almost linearly for reading with shared lock until about 30 threads are run in parallel, then the time taken levels out, finally increasing slightly, starting from 50+ threads. We believe this increase is because of the extra overhead of acquiring/releasing locks at the data nodes in MySQL Cluster. For transactions that do not take any locks, the time taken decreases continually up to the 60 threads used in our experiments. However, for the write lock, we can see that the total time is halved for more than one thread but it doesn't decrease after that. This is because only one thread can acquire the write lock on the parent at a time, and the threads must wait until the lock is released before they can read the data.

6.4   System-Level vs Row-Level Locking

In order to compare the performance of Apache HDFS' NameNode using a system-level lock (*FSNamesystem lock*) with our NameNode that uses row-level locks, we implemented a NameNode benchmark as an extension of NNThroughputBenchmark [16]. In this benchmark, we measure the throughput of open and

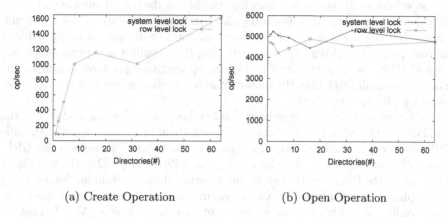

(a) Create Operation   (b) Open Operation

Fig. 4. Impact of the row-level lock on throughput

create operations on two different locking mechanisms with a constant 64 number of threads while increasing the number of directories (decreasing number of files per directory). The number of concurrent threads on each parent directory is a function of the number of directories. The modification we made to the NNThroughputBenchmark is that we allocated one directory per thread.

The result of a create operation for 16384 (2^{14}) files is depicted in figure 4a. As the diagram shows, the throughput for creating files under a single directory is the same for both the system-level lock in Apache's HDFS and our row-level lock. This is because all 64 threads try to acquire a write lock on the same directory in the NameNode. The advantage of row-level locking is seen when we increase the number of directories. Increasing the number of directories, we see that the throughput of our NameNode with row-level locking increases while for Apache's NameNode using a system-level lock, the throughput remains almost constant. For the *open* operation in figure 4b, row-level locking and system-level locking perform almost the same, since both row-level and system-level locks allow multiple read locks to be acquired simultaneously.

7 Related Work

Microsoft's WinFs [13] is an early attempt at building a distributed filesystem for a networked desktop environment with the goal of centrally managing updates to the distributed filesystem's metadata in a relational database. The database supported efficient searching and filtering of metadata. However, in contrast to our model clients mutated local copies of the filesystem and then used peer-to-peer synchronization with conflict resolution, resulting in a model where the metadata was eventually consistent.

HDFS v1 [2] follows the *single metadata server* model. Google's GFS [4], HDFS v2 [20] and TidyFs [3] have a highly available *master/slave replication model* for metadata, while Ceph [21] and Lustre [15] partition metadata across *distributed metadata servers*. However, in contrast to HDFS, Ceph and Lustre are object-based file systems, somewhat simplifying the partitioning of metadata. Google's successor to GFS, Collosus, also partitions metadata across many machines, but the mechanisms of how they maintain consistency across partitions are not public knowledge [12]. Similarly, MapR has built a new proprietary version of HDFS with partitioned metadata, although MapR have stated at the Hadoop Summit 2011 that the metadata is not replicated using a strongly consistent replication protocol.

GFS's replication scheme is based on batching operation log updates to the local disk of the primary server and replicating them to a remote server to handle failures by reconstructing state of the file system. TidyFs [3] supports flat URL-based files and replicates metadata using Paxos [9]. In Ceph [21], the main data structure is the Directory that stores information about its child inodes. By using a two phase commit algorithm, Ceph dynamically partitions the namespace tree and evenly distributes it over a cluster of metadata servers (MDS). Lustre's general object model stores both metadata and block data in a cluster of Object Storage Devices (OSD) [15], so for replication Lustre relies on the promises of the underlying OSD cluster, while its Distributed Lock Manager (DLM) library assures the consistency of the file system.

It is also worth mentioning that our approach is similar to multi-version concurrency control (MVCC), in that we take a copy of the data items, however, in contrast to MVCC, we only work on a single copy of the data items and we take pessimistic locks.

8   Conclusion and Future Work

In this paper, we introduced a new relational model for HDFS' metadata. We also showed how to migrate metadata from highly performant and in-memory data structures in Apache's HDFS to a relational representation that guarantees strong consistency for metadata. In particular, we demonstrated that how metadata operations could be made serializable and deadlock-free using pessimistic-locking concurrency control, requiring only locking and transactions that support a read-committed isolation level. The mechanisms we introduced to ensure freedom from deadlock were the representation of a logical DAG for the metadata, specifying a global order for acquiring locks on metadata objects, preventing lock upgrades, and using of implicit locks to lock subtrees. We showed that the performance of the database underlying our system is competitive, and that our NameNode architecture can potentially scale to store 40 times more metadata than Apache's NameNode.

In future work, we will extend our system to support a multiple NameNode architecture. Certain cluster-wide NameNode tasks, such as replication management, should only be executed by a single NameNode at a time. We are also working on optimizing our schemas for representing inodes, blocks, and replicas to reduce their footprint, and to support distribution aware transactions - we want to reduce the number of partitions that transactions for common operations must cross to help improve throughput.

References

1. Berenson, H., Bernstein, P., Gray, J., Melton, J., O'Neil, E., O'Neil, P.: A Critique of ANSI SQL Isolation Levels. ACM SIGMOD Record 24(2), 1–10 (1995)
2. Borthakur, D.: The Hadoop Distributed File System: Architecture and Design (2007), http://hadoop.apache.org/docs/r0.18.0/hdfs_design.pdf (accessed November 20, 2011)
3. Fetterly, D., Haridasan, M., Isard, M., Sundararaman, S.: TidyFS: A Simple and Small Distributed File System. In: Proc. of USENIXATC 2011, p. 34. USENIX Association (2011)
4. Ghemawat, S., Gobioff, H., Leung, S.-T.: The Google File System. In: Proc. of SOSP 2003, pp. 29–43. ACM (2003)
5. Gunawi, H.S., Rajimwale, A., Arpaci-Dusseau, A.C., Arpaci-Dusseau, R.H.: SQCK: A Declarative File System Checker. In: Proc. of OSDI 2008, pp. 131–146. USENIX Association (2008)
6. Herlihy, M.P., Wing, J.M.: Linearizability: A Correctness Condition for Concurrent Objects. ACM TPL 12(3), 463–492 (1990)
7. Hunt, P., Konar, M., Junqueira, F.P., Reed, B.: ZooKeeper: Wait-free Coordination for Internet-scale Systems. In: Proc. of USENIXATC 2010, p. 11. USENIX Association (2010)
8. Putzolu, G., Gray, J., Lorie, R., Traiger, I.: Granularity of Locks and Degrees of Consistency in a Shared Database. In: IFIP Working Conference on Modelling in Data Base Management Systems, pp. 365–394. IFIP (1976)
9. Lamport, L.: The Part-Time Parliament. ACM TOCS 1998 16(2), 133–169 (1998)
10. Lindholm, T., Yellin, F., Bracha, G., Buckley, A.: The Java Virtual Machine Specification. Addison-Wesley (2013)
11. Lipcon, T.: Quorum-Journal Design (2012), https://issues.apache.org/jira/browse/HDFS-3077 (online; accessed December 11, 2012)
12. McKusick, M.K., Quinlan, S.: GFS: Evolution on Fast-forward. ACM Queue 7(7), 10 (2009)
13. Novik, L., Hudis, I., Terry, D.B., Anand, S., Jhaveri, V., Shah, A., Wu, Y.: Peer-to-Peer Replication in WinFS. Technical ReportMSR-TR-2006-78, Microsoft Research (2006)
14. Ronström, M., Oreland, J.: Recovery Principles of MySQL Cluster 5.1. In: Proc. of VLDB 2005, pp. 1108–1115. VLDB Endowment (2005)
15. Schwan, P.: Lustre: Building a File System for 1000-node Clusters. In: Proc. of OLS 2003 (2003)
16. Shvachko, K.V.: HDFS Scalability: The limits to growth. Login 35(2), 6–16 (2010)
17. Stonebraker, M.: New Opportunities for New SQL. CACM 55(11), 10–11 (2012)
18. Thomson, A., Diamond, T., Weng, S.-C., Ren, K., Shao, P., Abadi, D.J.: Calvin: Fast Distributed Transactions for Partitioned Database Systems. In: Proc. of SIGMOD 2012, pp. 1–12. ACM (2012)
19. Valerio, J., Sutra, P., Rivière, É., Felber, P.: Evaluating the Price of Consistency in Distributed File Storage Services. In: Dowling, J., Taïani, F. (eds.) DAIS 2013. LNCS, vol. 7891, pp. 141–154. Springer, Heidelberg (2013)
20. Wang, F., Qiu, J., Yang, J., Dong, B., Li, X., Li, Y.: Hadoop High Availability Through Metadata Replication. In: Proc. CloudDB 2009, pp. 37–44. ACM (2009)
21. Weil, S.A., Brandt, S.A., Miller, E.L., Long, D.D.E., Maltzahn, C.: Ceph: A Scalable, High-Performance Distributed File System. In: Proc. of OSDI 2006, pp. 307–320. USENIX Association (2006)

Distributed Exact Deduplication
for Primary Storage Infrastructures

João Paulo and José Pereira

High-Assurance Software Lab (HASLab)
INESC TEC and University of Minho, Braga, Portugal
{jtpaulo,jop}@di.uminho.pt

Abstract. Deduplication of primary storage volumes in a cloud computing environment is increasingly desirable, as the resulting space savings contribute to the cost effectiveness of a large scale multi-tenant infrastructure. However, traditional archival and backup deduplication systems impose prohibitive overhead for latency-sensitive applications deployed at these infrastructures while, current primary deduplication systems rely on special cluster filesystems, centralized components, or restrictive workload assumptions.

We present DEDIS, a fully-distributed and dependable system that performs exact and cluster-wide background deduplication of primary storage. DEDIS does not depend on data locality and works on top of any unsophisticated storage backend, centralized or distributed, that exports a basic shared block device interface. The evaluation of an open-source prototype shows that DEDIS scales out and adds negligible overhead even when deduplication and intensive storage I/O run simultaneously.

Keywords: deduplication, storage systems, distributed systems, cloud computing.

1 Introduction

Deduplication is accepted as an efficient technique for reducing storage costs at the expense of some processing overhead, being increasingly sought in primary storage systems [18,5,14] and cloud computing infrastructures holding Virtual Machine (VM) volumes [7,4,12]. As static VM images are highly redundant, many systems avoid duplicates by storing unique Copy-on-Write (CoW) golden images and using snapshot mechanisms for launching identical VM instances [6,10]. Other systems also target the duplicates found in dynamic general purpose data from VMs volumes thus, increasing the space savings that, may range from 58% up to 80% for cluster-wide deduplication [4,11,18]. In fact, with the unprecedented growth of data in cloud computing services and the introduction of more expensive storage devices, as Solid State Drives (SSDs), these space savings are key to reduce the costs of cloud infrastructures [2].

Deduplication in a distributed infrastructure and across VMs primary volumes with dynamic and latency sensitive data raises, however, several challenges.

K. Magoutis and P. Pietzuch (Eds.): DAIS 2014, LNCS 8460, pp. 52–66, 2014.

Primary volumes have strict latency requirements that are not met by traditional *in-line* deduplication systems where data is shared before being stored thus, including deduplication processing overhead in the storage writes [17]. As a matter of fact, although some attempts were made to extend traditional deduplication algorithms to support file system semantics, none of these systems were able to handle efficiently random storage workloads [21,9,8].

As an alternative, *off-line* deduplication decouples aliasing from disk I/O operations and performs both asynchronously thus, minimizing the impact in storage writes [7,4]. As data is only aliased after being stored, off-line deduplication requires additional storage space when compared to the in-line approach. Also, since deduplication and storage requests are performed asynchronously, a CoW mechanism must be used to prevent updates on aliased data and possible data corruption. This mechanism increases the overhead in storage writes and the complexity of reference management and garbage collection, confining off-line deduplication to off-peak periods to avoid performance degradation [4]. Unfortunately, off-peak periods are scarce or inexistent in cloud infrastructures hosting VMs from several clients, giving deduplication a short time-window for processing the storage backlog and eliminating duplicates. Ideally, deduplication should run continuously and duplicates should be kept on disk for short periods of time to ensure a smaller storage size.

Distributed infrastructures raise additional challenges as deduplication must be performed across volumes belonging to VMs deployed on remote cluster servers [7,4]. Space savings are maximized when duplicates are found and eliminated globally across all volumes but this requires a more complex remote indexing mechanism, accessible by all cluster servers, that tracks unique storage content and is consulted for finding duplicates. Accessing this index in the storage path has prohibitive overhead for latency-sensitive applications thus, forcing distributed in-line deduplication systems to relax deduplication's accuracy and find only a subset of the duplicates across the cluster [19,12,18].

For clarity purposes, we use the term *chunks* as the units of deduplication, that usually are files, variable-sized blocks, or fixed-size blocks [17,1]. Also, most deduplication systems compare compact signatures of the chunks' content, referred to as *chunk signatures* or *digests*, instead of comparing the chunks' full content [17].

The combined challenges of primary storage and global deduplication are addressed with DEDIS, a fully-decentralized and dependable system that performs exact and cluster-wide off-line deduplication of VMs primary volumes. Unlike previous systems, it works on top of any storage backend, centralized or distributed, that exports an unsophisticated shared block device interface. This way, DEDIS does not rely on storage backends with built-in locking, aliasing, CoW, and garbage collection operations. Instead, deduplication is decoupled from a specific storage backend, avoiding performance issues of previous systems [7,4] and changing the system design thus favoring distinct optimizations, as discussed in Section 2. Moreover, DEDIS overhead and performance are independent from the storage workloads' spatial and temporal locality [18].

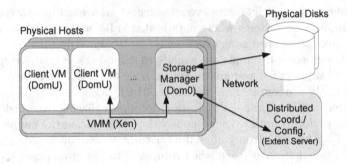

Fig. 1. Distributed storage architecture assumed by DEDIS

As the main contribution, we present a fully-distributed off-line deduplication mechanism. VMs I/O requests are intercepted and redirected to the correct storage locations, at the fixed block granularity, by a layer that also eliminates duplicate chunks asynchronously. This design excludes costly accesses to remote metadata, hash calculations and reference management from the storage path. Deduplication is performed globally and exactly across the cluster by using a sharded and replicated fault tolerant distributed service that maintains both the index of unique chunks signatures and the metadata for reference management. This service is key for achieving a fully-decentralized and scalable design. A persistent logging mechanism stores the necessary metadata, in a shared storage pool, for recovering and reassigning volumes of failed cluster to other nodes.

As other contributions, DEDIS leverages off-line deduplication to detect and avoid I/O hotspots thus, reducing the amount of CoW operations and their cost. Latency overhead is then further reduced with batch processing and caching that, also increase deduplication throughput. Moreover, DEDIS can withstand hash collisions in specific VM volumes by performing byte comparison of chunks before aliasing them, while keeping a small impact in both deduplication and storage performance. Finally, DEDIS prototype, implemented within the middleware Xen blktap driver, is evaluated in a distributed setting where it is shown that our design scales and introduces negligible overhead in storage requests while maintaining acceptable deduplication throughput and resource consumption.

The paper is structured as follows: Section 2 discusses DEDIS components, fault-tolerance considerations, design optimizations and implementation details. Section 3 evaluates DEDIS open-source prototype and, Section 4 distinguishes DEDIS from state of the art systems. Section 5 concludes the paper.

2 The DEDIS System

Figure 1 outlines the baseline distributed primary storage architecture assumed by DEDIS. A number of physical disks are available over a network to physical hosts running multiple VMs. Together with the hypervisor, storage manage- ment services provide logical volumes to VMs by translating *logical addresses* within each volume to *physical addresses* in arbitrary disks upon each block I/O operation. Since networked disks provide only simple block I/O primitives, a distributed coordination and configuration service is assumed to locate meta-information for logical volumes, free block extents and to ensure that a logical volume is mounted at any time by at most one VM. The main functionality is as follows:

Interceptor. A local module in each storage manager maps logical addresses of VMs to physical addresses, storing the physical location of each logical block in a persistent map structure (*logical-to-physical* map). In some LVM systems, VM snapshots are created by pointing multiple logical volumes to the same physical locations [10]. Shared blocks are then marked as CoW in the persistent map while, updates to these blocks require a free block to write the new content and updating the map to break aliasing.

Extent Server. A distributed coordination mechanism allocates free blocks from a common pool when a logical volume is created, or lazily when a block is written for the first time, or when an aliased block is updated (*i.e.*, copied on write). The overhead of remote calls is reduced by allocating storage extents with a large granularity that are then, within each physical host, used for local requests [10].

The architecture presented in Figure 1 is a logical architecture, as physical disks and even the *Extent* service itself can be contained within the same physical hosts. For simplicity, we assume that the Xen hypervisor is being used and we label payload VMs as DomU and the storage management VM as Dom0. However, the architecture is generic and can be implemented within other hypervisors, while using networked storage protocols distinct from ISCSI, which is the one used in DEDIS evaluation. Since we focus on the added functionality needed for deduplication, we do not target a specific map structure of logical to physical addresses. Also, DEDIS does not require built-in CoW functionalities, as we introduce our own operation. Finally, DEDIS uses fixed-size blocks because the *interceptor* module already processes fixed-size blocks and, generating variable-sized chunks would impose unwanted computation overhead [7,4].

2.1 Architecture

DEDIS architecture is depicted in Figure 2 and requires, in addition to the baseline architecture, a *distributed* module and two *local* modules, highlighted in the figure by the dashed rectangle.

Distributed Duplicates Index (DDI). Indexes unique content signatures of blocks belonging to the primary storage. Each entry maps a signature to the physical address of the corresponding storage block and to the number of logical addresses pointing to (sharing) that block, which allows aliasing duplicate blocks and performing garbage collection of unreferenced blocks. Index entries are persistent and are not assumed to be fully-loaded on RAM. Also, entries are sharded and replicated across several DDI nodes for scalability and fault

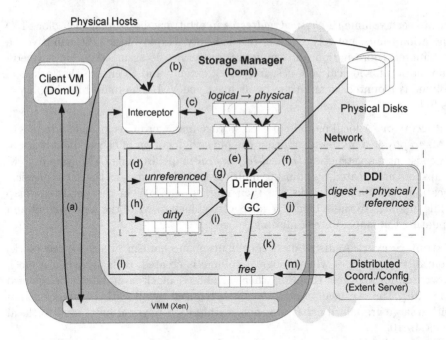

Fig. 2. Overview of the DEDIS storage manager

tolerance purposes. The size of each entry is small (few bytes) so, each node can index many blocks, thus allowing a small number of DDI nodes even in large infrastructures.

Duplicate Finder (D. Finder). Asynchronously collects addresses written by local *interceptors*, which are stored at the *dirty* queue, and matches the correspondent blocks with others registered at the DDI. Blocks processed by this module are preemptively marked as CoW in order to avoid concurrent updates and possible data corruption. This module is thus the main difference from a storage manager that does not support deduplication.

Garbage Collector (GC). Processes aliased blocks that were updated (copied on write) and are no longer being referenced by a specific logical address. Physical addresses of copied blocks are kept at the *unreferenced* queue, and the number of references to a specific block can be consulted and decremented at the DDI. Blocks are unused when the number of references reaches zero. Both *D. Finder* and *GC* modules free unused blocks by inserting their physical addresses in a local *free* blocks pool that provides blocks addresses for CoW operations.

2.2 I/O and DEDIS Operations

The operations executed by each DEDIS module are depicted in Figure 2. Bidirectional arrows mean that information is both retrieved and updated at the target resource. *GC* and *D. Finder* modules are included in the same process box because both run in distinct threads of the same process, within the Xen Dom0, and perform concurrent operations for each VM. The latency of I/O requests is reduced by finding and managing duplicates in a background thread. Each VM volume has an independent process running its own *interceptor*.

An I/O Operation in the Interceptor. The interceptor (a) gets read and write requests from local VMs, (c) queries the *logical-to-physical* map for the corresponding physical addresses and, (b) redirects them to a physical disk over the network. As potentially aliased blocks are marked in the map as CoW by *D. Finder*, writes to such blocks must first (l) collect a free address from the *free* pool, (b) redirect the write to the free block and update the map accordingly (c). Then, the physical address of the copied block is added to the *unreferenced* queue (d) and, processed later by *GC*. For both regular and CoW write operations, (h) the logical address of the written block is inserted in a *dirty* queue. I/O requests are acknowledged as completed to the VMs (a) after completing all these steps.

Sharing an Updated Block in D. Finder. This background module aliases duplicate blocks. Therefore, each logical address that was updated and inserted in the *dirty* queue is eventually picked up by the *D. Finder* module (i), that preemptively marks the address as CoW (e), reads its content from the storage (f), computes a signature and queries the DDI in search of an existing duplicate (j). This is done using a test-and-increment remote operation, that stores the block's information as a new entry at the DDI if a match is not found. If a match is found, the counter of logical addresses (references) pointing to the DDI entry is incremented while, locally (e), the *logical-to-physical* map is updated with the new physical address found at the DDI entry and (k) the physical address of the duplicate block is added to the *free* pool. Blocks are marked as CoW before reading their content because deduplication runs in parallel with I/O requests and updates to these blocks could originate data corruption.

Freeing an Unused Block in GC. This background module examines if a copied block, at the *unreferenced* queue (g), has become unreferenced. The block's content is read from the storage (f), its signature is calculated and then the DDI is queried (j) using a remote test-and-decrement operation that decrements the number of logical addresses pointing to the corresponding DDI entry. If the block is unused (zero references), its entry is removed from the DDI and, locally, the block address is added to the *free* pool (k). This pool keeps only the necessary addresses for local CoW operations, while the remainder is returned to the *extent* server (m). If the queue is empty, unused block addresses are requested from the *extent* server pool (m).

The latency-critical *interceptor* does not invoke any remote service and, only blocks if the local *free* pool becomes empty, which can be avoided by tuning the frequency of the *GC* execution. The *test-and-increment* and *test-and-decrement* operations and metadata stored in each DDI entry allow performing the lookup of unique block signatures and incrementing or decrementing the entry's logical references in a single round-trip to the DDI. Unlike in DDe and DeDe, this design combines aliasing and reference management in a single remote invocation, avoiding a higher throughput penalty and reducing metadata size [7,4]. VM volumes have an independent *D. Finder* and *GC* thread, as well as, a distinct *logical-to-physical* map, *dirty* queue and *unreferenced* queue. Only the *free* pool is shared across VMs in the same server thus, requiring mutual exclusion for concurrent acesses. Multiple updates to the same block between two *D. Finder* iterations count as a single one because only the latest written content is shared. Finally, the *interceptor* is able to collect writes from applications and from the operating system so, deduplication can be applied to both types of dynamic data.

2.3 Concurrent Optimistic Deduplication and Fault Tolerance

DEDIS removes deduplication processing overhead, including chunk signatures calculation, from the storage write path. However, contention still exists when the *D. Finder* and *interceptor* modules access shared metadata. To reduce contention and its penalty in storage latency, DEDIS uses an optimistic deduplication approach that only performs fine grained locking when *D. Finder* and *interceptor* operations access common metadata (e.g. *logical-to-physical* map), while avoiding remote invocations to the DDI and other time consuming operations in the mutual exclusion space. This decision leads to race conditions that are detected and processed accordingly, as explained in previous work that validates our algorithm with a model checker [15]. Also, since signatures are calculated asynchronously by *Share* and *GC* modules, an additional read to the storage backend is required for each processed block, whose overhead is accounted in our evaluation.

DEDIS is resilient to cluster nodes crashes and to lost and repeated requests by writing meta-information persistently. Transactional logs track changes to metadata structures and allow logical volumes of a crashed physical node to be recovered by another freshly booted node. To reduce the impact on storage latency, logging operations are performed outside the storage path with only two exceptions, namely, when a block is copied at the *interceptor* and when a block is preemptively marked as CoW by *D. Finder*. Logs and persistent metadata structures may be stored in a shared storage pool and the recovery of failed nodes is then ensured by the distributed coordination and configuration service that provides the *extent* server functionalities. DDI nodes have on-disk persistent entries and are fully replicated using the primary-backup approach with a virtually-synchronous group communication protocol. This way, DDI entries can be stored in the shared storage pool or in cluster nodes local disks. The overhead of all logging operations is contemplated in our evaluation.

2.4 Optimizations

The *D. Finder* module uses a hotspot detection mechanism for identifying storage blocks that are write hotspots. By not sharing blocks that are frequently rewritten, the amount of costly CoW operations is reduced. Namely, logical addresses in the *dirty* queue are only processed in the next *D. Finder* iteration if they were not updated during a certain period of time. For instance, in our evaluation, only the logical addresses at the *dirty* queue that were not updated between two consecutive *D. Finder* iterations (approximately 5 minutes) are shared. The time period can be tuned independently for each VM. This mechanism is essential for keeping low storage overhead because DEDIS preemptively marks written blocks as CoW so, without this mechanism, every re-write would generate a copy operation. In previous work, CoW is reduced by only marking a block when a duplicate is actually found at the storage, however, DEDIS does not assume a storage backend with locking capabilities so, implementing such strategy would require costly cross-host communication [4].

As other optimizations, a resilient in-memory cache of unused storage blocks addresses, from the persistent *free* pool, allows serving free blocks to CoW operations more efficiently. The throughputs of *D. Finder* and *GC* operations are improved by performing batch accesses to persistent logs, the DDI, the *extent* server and to the *free* pool, which allows using efficiently both disk and network resources. Moreover, the DDI nodes can serve batch requests efficiently without requiring the full index on RAM. Finally, although DEDIS implementation uses the SHA-1 hash function which has a negligible probability of collisions [17], the comparison of chunks bytes before aliasing them can be enabled independently for VM volumes persisting data from critical applications. This comparison requires reading the content of an extra block (referenced in the DDI entry) from the storage but it is performed outside the storage write path.

2.5   Implementation

DEDIS prototype is implemented within Xen and uses the Blktap mechanism for building the *interceptor* module. Blktap exports an user-level disk I/O interface that replaces the commonly used loopback drivers while providing better scalability, fault-tolerance and performance [3]. Each VM volume has an independent process intercepting VM disk requests with a fixed block size of 4KB, which is also the block size used in DEDIS.

The goal of the current implementation is to highlight the impact of deduplication, and not to re-invent a LVM system or the DDI. Simplistic implementations have thus been used for metadata and log structures. Namely, both the *logical-to-physical* map, *dirty* queue and *free* blocks queue cache are implemented as arrays fully loaded in memory, accessible by both *interceptor* and *D. Finder* modules. The *unreferenced* and *free* queues are implemented as persistent queues. The DDI is a slightly modified version of the Accord replicated, transactional and fully-distributed key-value store that supports atomic test-and-increment and test-and-decrement operations [20]. The *extent* server is implemented as a remote service with a persistent queue of unused storage blocks.

Despite being simplistic, all these structures are usable in a real implementation, so the resource utilization (*i.e.*, CPU, RAM, disk and network) in our evaluation is realistic. In fact, this implementation presents a worst-case scenario for the storage and RAM space occupied by metadata and persistent logs as more space-efficient structures could have been used instead.

3   Evaluation

This section validates the following properties of DEDIS. First, that an acceptable deduplication throughput is achievable and, the size needed for VM volumes is reduced. Then, that deduplication does not overly impact write I/O latency even with deduplication and I/O intensive workloads running simultaneously. Finally, that DEDIS scales out for several cluster machines.

Tests ran in cluster nodes equipped with a 3.1 GHz Dual-Core Intel i3 Core Processor, 4GB of RAM and a 7200 RPMs SATA disk. The VMs were configured with 2GB of RAM and two disk volumes: a 16GB volume holding the Operating System (OS) and a 4GB data volume. Two fully-replicated DDI instances ran, for all tests, in isolated cluster nodes thus, including the overhead of remote calls and replication. The *extent* server ran together with one of the DDI instances. DEDIS, DDI and *extent* server persistent metadata and logs were stored in the local disks of cluster nodes to have a distinct storage pool for the logs and exclude their overhead from the VM data volumes. Similarly, OS volumes were stored in local disks and left out of this evaluation to avoid an unknown number of duplicates originating from OS images, and ensure that duplicate chunks are introduced in a controllable way by the benchmark.

As DEDIS targets dynamic data, static traces of VM images are not suitable for its evaluation, so the open-source DEDISbench disk micro-benchmark was used, in each VM, to assess the storage performance [16]. DEDISbench simulates realistic content for written blocks by following a content distribution extracted from real data sets that mimics the percentage and distribution of duplicates per block. Our tests used an workload that simulates the content of a primary storage, with ≈1.5 TB and 25% of duplicates, which fits our storage environment. DEDISbench also supports an access pattern based on the TPC-C NURand function that simulates a random I/O workload where few blocks are hotspots and most blocks are accessed sporadically. Moreover, to clearly understand the latency introduced by deduplication in storage requests, the *fsync* primitive was enabled in the benchmark to ensure synchronous storage writes.

I/O operations were measured at the VM (DomU) while, deduplication, CPU, metadata, RAM and network utilization were measured at the host (Dom0). Measurements were taken for stable and identical periods of the workloads, excluding ramp up and cool down periods, and, include the overhead of all DEDIS modules, both local and remote, as well as, the overhead of persistent logging.

3.1   Deduplication Results

Deduplication's overhead and performance were measured in a *single node setting* with one VM deployed on a single cluster node. VM data volumes, with 4GB, were stored in a HP StorageWorks 4400 Enterprise Virtual Array (EVA4400). As our cluster nodes could not directly access the EVA storage, volumes were exported via iSCSI and over a gigabit link by a server equipped with an AMD Opteron(tm) Processor 6172, 24 cores and 128 GB of RAM.

Table 1. Deduplication gain and throughput (Thr)

	DEDIS hash	DEDIS byte
Space shared (MB)	696	684
% VM data volume size reduced	17%	17%
Average Thr (MB/s)	4.78	4.55
Required continuous Thr (MB/s)	0,76	0,75

Table 1 shows deduplication space savings and throughput for a 90 minutes run of DEDISbench performing hotspot random writes (with a block size of 4K) and for the subsequent 30 minutes, where deduplication ran isolated from the I/O workload. 5 minutes were chosen as the interval between *D. Finder* iterations to obtain several iterations of the module during the test ($\approx$16).

Tests ran for DEDIS prototype with hash (DEDIS hash) and byte (DEDIS byte) comparison enabled. As expected, DEDIS byte has a slightly lower deduplication throughput and, consequently, smaller space savings due to the extra computation for comparing the content of the blocks. DEDIS hash processes in average 4.78 MB/s and, this value is identical when *D. Finder* is processing requests simultaneously or isolated from the I/O workload.

We also calculated the minimum continuous deduplication throughput needed to keep up with this workload, for an unbounded amount of time, without accumulating unprocessed duplicate storage backlog. The value is $\approx$0,76 MB/s and DEDIS is able to accomplish it.

Some writes are not processed by the *D. Finder*. First, multiple updates to the same block, between two iterations, originate a single share operation for the latest content written. Also, the hotspot avoidance mechanism avoids sharing frequently updated blocks. In this run, the *D. Finder* only processed 1 million blocks while the benchmark wrote $\approx$13G. Both DEDIS versions deduplicated approximately 17% of the original data volume size (4GB), which is smaller than the 25% of duplicates simulated by DEDISbench workload. However, as explained in the benchmark's paper, the algorithm only converges to the expected percentage of duplicates for higher volumes of written data.

3.2 Performance and Resources Consumption Results

To assess DEDIS's performance we compared it with the default Blktap driver for asynchronous I/O, Tap:aio, that was the base to implement DEDIS *interceptor* and does not perform deduplication [3]. This comparison ensures that the overhead is a direct consequence of DEDIS deduplication. Unfortunately, a direct comparison with DDE or DeDe systems was not possible as they are not publicly available. The tests' setup was identical to the previous one and the Tap:aio VM data volumes were also stored on the EVA storage. DEDIS and the I/O benchmark ran simultaneously to evaluate the impact of deduplication and garbage collection in peak hours. A 5 minute interval between *D. Finder* and *GC* iterations was chosen to assess the benefits of the hotspot avoidance mechanism,

Table 2. DEDIS overhead (o/h) in VMs storage latency (Lat) and throughput (Thr) with concurrent storage writes and deduplication

	AIO	DEDIS w/o hspot	o/h	DEDIS hash	o/h	DEDIS byte	o/h
Thr (IOps)	720.528 ±13.730	636.031 ±14.403	11.73%	688.844 ±15.383	4,40%	662.863 ±22.316	8.00%
Lat (ms)	5.575 ±0,106	6.470 ±0,130	16.05%	5.850 ±0,155	4.93%	6.094 ±0,289	9.31%
% CoWs avoided	-	0	-	73.33%	-	72.89%	-

which was configured to share blocks that were not written or re-written in the interval comprehending the current and previous *D. Finder* iterations.

Table 2 shows the results of performing hotspot random writes, during 30 minutes, for Tap:aio and three DEDIS versions. The first, (DEDIS w/o hspot) is the only that does not use hotspot avoidance. The second, (DEDIS hash) uses hash comparison while, the other (DEDIS byte) performs byte comparison. As expected, DEDIS introduces overhead in both storage throughput and latency, however, this value is small when compared to previous systems [4] and, accounts the impact of *D. Finder*, *GC*, *DDI*, *extent* server and corresponding persistent logging mechanisms while running in parallel with the I/O workload.

A significant amount of this overhead is due to CoW operations. In DEDIS each operations requires ≈7ms to be executed. This is already an improvement over previous systems where CoW requires 10ms in servers with more computational resources than ours [4]. This is possible because DEDIS uses a memory cache that provides free blocks for CoW and, performs batch insertions in the *unreferenced* pool, which is a time consuming operation in the critical I/O path. However, as shown in Table 2, the overhead without the hotspot avoidance mechanism is still significant while, with this mechanism, DEDIS performs 70% less CoW operations (≈210,000 less), which enables a clear reduction in I/O latency.

We compared the resource consumptions of DEDIS and Tap:aio for the run described in Section 3.1. DEDIS local modules have a CPU usage of ≈ 14%, only 5% more than Tap:aio, which is a consequence of performing background deduplication. Moreover, DEDIS modules use less than 1% of the node's total RAM and require ≈75 MB to store persistent logs and metadata.

The DDI service uses less than 5% of CPU, 0,35% of the nodes' RAM while, requiring 80MB of disk space and ≈2.2 KB/s of average network usage. These values include the costs of indexing and persisting signatures of 4KB blocks in a replicated fashion. As shown in Section 3.1, the disk usage is nevertheless compensated by the deduplicated space, ≈700 MB.

Finally, the *extent* server uses less than 1Mb of RAM and has a negligible CPU usage since, in these tests, it is only called for the initial allocation of blocks to the local *free* pool. The *extent* queue requires ≈5 MB of storage space for indexing ≈11 GB of unused addresses.

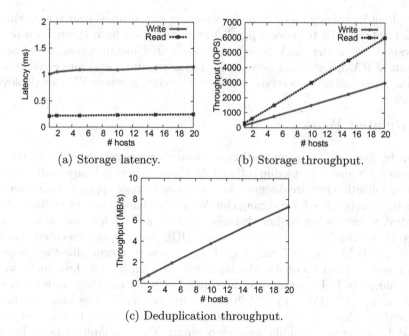

(a) Storage latency.

(b) Storage throughput.

(c) Deduplication throughput.

Fig. 3. DEDIS results for up to 20 cluster nodes with mixed storage writes and reads

3.3   Scalability Results

Scalability was assessed in a *distributed setting* with up to 20 cluster nodes. After performing some tests, we observed that the EVA storage was having a significant latency degradation when handling I/O requests from all the nodes, even with the Tap:aio baseline. Therefore, data volumes were exported by a 110GB RAMdisk ISCSI device, in our AMD server, which increased significantly the load supported by the storage backend.

A mixed load of write and read requests was used to test the performance of both I/O operations in parallel with DEDIS performing hash comparison. To ensure that the the network link supporting the iSCSI protocol would not be overloaded by the aggregated throughput of the 20 cluster nodes, the throughput of DEDISbench was limited to 300 reads/s and 150 writes/s, per VM. Tap:aio baseline was not evaluated in this test since the goal was to prove that DEDIS scales for several nodes. DEDISbench ran for 30 minutes in each VM and the subsequent 20 minutes were used to observe DEDIS behavior without I/O load. Tests ran for 1,2,5,10,15 and 20 cluster nodes hosting a single VM. Finally, deduplication throughput, in each node, was limited to 100 ops/s to have an uniform throughput over the entire cluster, *i.e.*, up to 20× more.

As depicted in Figures 3(a) and 3(b), the throughput for both read and write requests scales linearly up to 20 nodes. There is a slight increase in the latency of writes and reads when nodes are added, which is a consequence of having more load in the centralized storage. Figure 3(c) shows the aggregated deduplication throughput increasing up to 20 nodes which, in our setup, is near the maximum capacity of the DDI to process parallel requests with a fixed throughput of 100 requests/s. As in the single server tests, each DDI instance consumes a small amount of RAM, CPU and network so, infrastructure costs can be reduced by running these instances in servers with other services or where VMs are deployed.

4   Related Work

Recently, live volume deduplication in cluster and enterprise scale systems is becoming popular. Opendedup [13] and ZFS [14] support primary multi-host in-line deduplication but are designed for enterprise storage appliances, and require large RAM capacities for indexing chunks and to enable efficient deduplication.

Primary distributed off-line deduplication for a SAN file system was introduced in the Duplicate Data Elimination (DDE) system, implemented over the distributed IBM Storage Tank [7]. DDE has, however, a centralized single-point of failure metadata server for sharing duplicate chunks asynchronously, which was removed in DeDe, an off-line distributed deduplication system for VM volumes on top of VMWares's VMFS cluster file system [4]. The index of chunks is stored on VMFS and is accessible to all nodes while, index lookups are made in batch to increase deduplication throughput. VMFS simplifies deduplication as it already has explicit locking, block aliasing, CoW, and reference management, which are not present in most cluster file systems. These primitives are combined to implement the atomic share function that replaces two duplicate fixed-size blocks with a CoW block. However, this dependency leads to alignment issues between the block size used in VMFS and DeDe, implying additional translation metadata and, consequently, an impact in storage requests latency. Also, the overhead of CoW operations in storage I/O is significant, forcing DeDe deduplication to run only in periods of low I/O load. CoW overhead may, however, be reduced by deduplicating selectively files that meet a specific policy such as, file age superior to a certain threshold, as suggested in Microsoft Windows Server 2012 centralized off-line deduplication system [5].

DDE and DeDe are the systems that most resemble DEDIS, however, DEDIS is fully-decentralized and does not dependent on a specific cluster file system. This way, there are no single point of failures and an unsophisticated storage implementation, centralized or distributed, can be used as backend as long as a shared block device interface is provided for the storage pool. Decoupling deduplication from the storage backend changes significantly DEDIS's design, allows exploring novel optimizations and avoids DeDe alignment issues. In fact, and as explained in this paper, these design changes and optimizations are key for having a scalable design and for running deduplication and I/O intensive workloads simultaneously with low overhead, which is not possible in previous systems.

5   Conclusions

We presented DEDIS, a dependable and distributed system that performs cluster-wide off-line deduplication across primary storage volumes. The design is fully-decentralized avoiding any single point of failure or contention thus, safely scaling-out. Also, it is compatible with any storage backend, distributed or centralized, that exports a shared block device interface.

The evaluation of a Xen-based prototype in up to 20 nodes shows that by relying on an optimistic deduplication algorithm and on several optimizations, deduplication and primary I/O workloads can run simultaneously in a scalable system. In fact, DEDIS introduces less than 10% of latency overhead while maintaining a baseline single-server deduplication throughput of 4.78 MB/s with low-end hardware. This is key for performing efficient deduplication and reducing the storage backlog of duplicates in infrastructures with scarce off-peak periods. Also, even with a trivial implementation of a LVM system, deduplication space savings compensate metadata overhead, while maintaining an acceptable consumption of CPU, RAM and network resources.

As future work, we would like to evaluate DEDIS in a scalable distributed storage environment, where both DEDIS metadata and VMs volumes would be stored, and with other primary storage workloads with higher duplication ratios.

6   Availability

DEDIS system is open-source and is publicly available at http://www.holeycow. org for anyone to deploy and benchmark.

Acknowledgments. This work is funded by ERDF - European Regional Development Fund through the COMPETE Programme (operational programme for competitiveness) and by National Funds through the FCT - Fundação para a Ciência e a Tecnologia (Portuguese Foundation for Science and Technology) within project FCOMP 01-0124-FEDER-022701 and FCT by Ph.D scholarship SFRH-BD-71372-2010.

References

1. Bolosky, W.J., Corbin, S., Goebel, D., Douceur, J.R.: Single Instance Storage in Windows 2000. In: Proceedings of USENIX Windows System Symposium, WSS (2000)
2. Chute, C., Manfrediz, A., Minton, S., Reinsel, D., Schlichting, W., Toncheva, A.: The Diverse and Exploding Digital Universe: An updated forecast of worldwide information growth through 2011. IDC White Paper - sponsored by EMC (2008), http://www.emc.com/collateral/analyst-reports/diverse-exploding-digital-universe.pdf
3. Citrix. Blktap page (January 2014), http://wiki.xen.org/wiki/Blktap2
4. Clements, A.T., Ahmad, I., Vilayannur, M., Li, J.: Decentralized Deduplication in SAN Cluster File Systems. In: Proceedings of USENIX Annual Technical Conference, ATC (2009)

5. El-Shimi, A., Kalach, R., Kumar, A., Oltean, A., Li, J., Sengupta, S.: Primary Data Deduplication Large Scale Study and System Design. In: Proceedings of USENIX Annual Technical Conference, ATC (2012)
6. Hewlett-Packard Development Company, L.P. Complete storage and data protection architecture for vmware vsphere. White Paper (2011)
7. Hong, B., Long, D.D.E.: Duplicate Data Elimination in a San File System. In: Proceedings of Conference on Mass Storage Systems, MSST (2004)
8. Lessfs. Lessfs page (January 2014), http://www.lessfs.com/wordpress/
9. Liguori, A., Van Hensbergen, E.: Experiences with Content Addressable Storage and Virtual Disks. In: Proceedings of USENIX Workshop on I/O Virtualization, WIOV (2008)
10. Meyer, D.T., Aggarwal, G., Cully, B., Lefebvre, G., Feeley, M.J., Hutchinson, N.C., Warfield, A.: Parallax: Virtual Disks for Virtual Machines. In: Proceedings of European Conference on Computer Systems, EuroSys (2008)
11. Meyer, D.T., Bolosky, W.J.: A Study of Practical Deduplication. In: Proceedings of USENIX Conference on File and Storage Technologies, FAST (2011)
12. Ng, C.-H., Ma, M., Wong, T.-Y., Lee, P.P.C., Lui, J.C.S.: Live Deduplication Storage of Virtual Machine Images in an Open-Source Cloud. In: Kon, F., Kermarrec, A.-M. (eds.) Middleware 2011. LNCS, vol. 7049, pp. 81–100. Springer, Heidelberg (2011)
13. Opendedup. Opendedup page (January 2014), http://opendedup.org
14. OpenSolaris. Zfs documentation (January 2014), http://www.freebsd.org/doc/en/books/handbook/filesystems-zfs.html
15. Paulo, J., Pereira, J.: Model checking a decentralized storage deduplication protocol. In: Fast Abstract in Latin-American Symposium on Dependable Computing (2011)
16. Paulo, J., Reis, P., Pereira, J., Sousa, A.: Towards an Accurate Evaluation of Deduplicated Storage Systems. International Journal of Computer Systems Science and Engineering 29 (2013)
17. Quinlan, S., Dorward, S.: Venti: A New Approach to Archival Storage. In: Proceedings of USENIX Conference on File and Storage Technologies, FAST (2002)
18. Srinivasan, K., Bisson, T., Goodson, G., Voruganti, K.: iDedup: Latency-aware, Inline Data Deduplication for Primary Storage. In: Proceedings of USENIX Conference on File and Storage Technologies, FAST (2012)
19. Tsuchiya, Y., Watanabe, T.: DBLK: Deduplication for Primary Block Storage. In: Proceedings of Conference on Mass Storage Systems, MSST (2011)
20. Tsuyoshi, O., Kazutaka, M.: Accord page (January 2014), http://www.osrg.net/accord/
21. Ungureanu, C., Atkin, B., Aranya, A., Gokhale, S., Rago, S., Calkowski, G., Dubnicki, C., Bohra, A.: HydraFS: A High-Throughput File System for the HYDRAstor Content-Addressable Storage System. In: Proceedings of USENIX Conference on File and Storage Technologies, FAST (2010)

Scalable and Accurate Causality Tracking
for Eventually Consistent Stores

Paulo Sérgio Almeida[1], Carlos Baquero[1],
Ricardo Gonçalves[1], Nuno Preguiça[2], and Victor Fonte[1]

[1] HASLab, INESC Tec & Universidade do Minho
{psa,cbm,tome,vff}@di.uminho.pt
[2] CITI/DI, FCT, Universidade Nova de Lisboa
nuno.preguica@fct.unl.pt

Abstract. In cloud computing environments, data storage systems often rely on optimistic replication to provide good performance and availability even in the presence of failures or network partitions. In this scenario, it is important to be able to accurately and efficiently identify updates executed concurrently. Current approaches to causality tracking in optimistic replication have problems with concurrent updates: they either (1) do not scale, as they require replicas to maintain information that grows linearly with the number of writes or unique clients; (2) lose information about causality, either by removing entries from client-id based version vectors or using server-id based version vectors, which cause false conflicts. We propose a new logical clock mechanism and a logical clock framework that together support a traditional key-value store API, while capturing causality in an accurate and scalable way, avoiding false conflicts. It maintains concise information per data replica, only linear on the number of replica servers, and allows data replicas to be compared and merged linear with the number of replica servers and versions.

1 Introduction

Amazon's Dynamo system [5] was an important influence to a new generation of databases, such as Cassandra [10] and Riak [9], focusing on partition tolerance, write availability and eventual consistency. The underlying rationale to these systems stems from the observation that when faced with the three concurrent goals of *consistency*, *availability* and *partition-tolerance* only two of those can be achievable in the same system [3,6]. Facing geo-replication operation environments where partitions cannot be ruled out, consistency requirements are inevitably relaxed in order to achieve high availability.

These systems follow a design where the data store is always writable: replicas of the same data item are allowed to temporarily diverge and to be repaired later on. A simple repair approach followed in Cassandra, is to use wall-clock timestamps to know which concurrent updates should prevail. This last writer wins (lww) policy may lead to lost updates. An approach which avoids this, must be able to represent and maintain causally concurrent updates until they can be reconciled.

Accurate tracking of concurrent data updates can be achieved by a careful use of well established causality tracking mechanisms [11,14,20,19,2]. In particular, for data

K. Magoutis and P. Pietzuch (Eds.): DAIS 2014, LNCS 8460, pp. 67–81, 2014.

storage systems, version vectors (vv) [14] enable the system to compare any pair of replica versions and detect if they are equivalent, concurrent or if one makes the other obsolete. However, as we will discuss in Section 3, vv lack the ability to accurately represent concurrent values when used with server ids, or are not scalable when used with client ids.

We present a new and simple causality tracking solution, Dotted Version Vectors (briefly introduced in [16]), that overcomes these limitations allowing both scalable (using server ids) and fully accurate (representing same server concurrent writes) causality tracking. It achieves this by explicitly separating a new write event identifier from its causal past, which has the additional benefit of allowing causality checks between two clocks in constant time (instead of linear with the size of version vectors).

Besides fully describing Dotted Version Vectors (dvv), in this paper we make two novel contributions. First, we propose a new container (DVV Sets or dvvs) that efficiently compacts a set of concurrent dvv's in a single data structure, improving on two dvv limitations: (1) dvvs representation is independent of the number of concurrent values, instead of linear; (2) comparing and synchronizing two replica servers w.r.t. a single key is linear with the number of concurrent values, instead of quadratic.

Our final contribution is a general framework that clearly defines a set of functions that logical clocks need to implement to correctly track causality in eventually consistent systems. We implement both dvv and dvvs using this framework.

The rest of this paper is organized as follows. Section 2 presents the system model for the remaining paper. We survey and compare current mechanisms for causality tracking in Section 3. In Section 4, we present our mechanism dvv, followed by its compact version dvvs, in Section 5. We then propose in Section 6 a general framework for logical clocks and its implementation with both dvv and dvvs. In Section 7 we present the asymptotic complexities for both the current and proposed mechanisms, as well as an evaluation of dvvs. Additional techniques are briefly discussed in Section 8. We conclude in Section 9.

2   System Model and Data Store API

We consider a standard Dynamo-like key-value store interface that exposes two operations: get(*key*) and put(*key, value, context*). get returns a pair (*value(s), context*), i.e., a value or set of causally concurrent values, and an opaque context that encodes the causal knowledge in the value(s). put submits a single value that supersedes all values associated to the supplied context. This context is either empty if we are writing a new value, or some opaque data structure returned to the client by a previous get, if we are updating a value. This context encodes causal information, and its use in the API serves to generate a *happens-before* [20] relation between a get and a subsequent put.

We assume a distributed system where nodes communicate by asynchronous message passing, with no shared memory. The system is composed by possibly many (e.g., thousands) clients which make concurrent get and put requests to server nodes (in the order of, e.g., hundreds). Each key is replicated in a typically small subset of the server nodes (e.g., 3 nodes), which we call the replica nodes for that key. These different orders of magnitude of clients, servers and replicas play an important role in the design of a scalable causality tracking mechanism.

We assume: no global distributed coordination mechanism, only that nodes can perform internal concurrency control to obtain atomic blocks; no sessions or any form of client-server affinity, so clients are free to read from a replica server node and then write to a different one; no byzantine failures; server nodes have stable storage; nodes can fail without warning and later recover with their last state in the stable storage.

As we do not aim to track causality between different keys, in the remainder we will focus on operations over a single key, which we leave implicit; namely, all data structures in servers that we will describe are per key. Techniques as in [13] can be applied when considering groups of keys and could introduce additional savings; this we leave for future work.

3   Current Approaches

To simplify comparisons between different mechanisms, we will introduce a simple execution example between clients Mary and Peter, and a single replica node. In this example, presented in Figure 1, Peter starts by writing a new object version v_1, with an empty context, which results in some server state A. He then reads server state A, returning current version v_1 and context ctx_A. Meanwhile, Mary writes a new version v_2, with an empty context, resulting in some server state B. Since Mary wrote v_2 without reading state A, state B should contain both v_1 and v_2 as concurrent versions, if causality is tracked. Finally, Peter updates version v_1 with v_3, using the previous context ctx_A, resulting in some state C. If causal relations are correctly represented, state C we should only have v_2 and v_3, since v_1 was superseded by v_3 and v_2 is concurrent with v_3. We now discuss how different causality tracking approaches address this example, which are summarized in Table 1.

Last Writer Wins (lww). In systems that enforce a lww policy, such as Cassandra, concurrent updates are not represented in the stored state and only the last update prevails. Under lww, our example would result in the loss of v_2. Although some specific application semantics are compatible with a lww policy, this simplistic approach is not adequate for many other application semantics. In general, a correct tracking of concurrent updates is essential to allow all updates to be considered for conflict resolution.

Causal Histories (ch). Causal Histories [20] are simply described by sets of unique write identifiers. These identifiers can be generated with a unique identifier and a monotonic counter. In our example, we used server identifiers r, but client identifiers could be used as well. The crucial point is that identifiers have to be globally unique to correctly represent causality. Let id_n be the notation for the nth event of the entity represented by id. The partial order of causality can be precisely tracked by comparing these sets under set inclusion. Two ch are concurrent if neither includes the other: $A \parallel B$ iff $A \nsubseteq B$ and $B \nsubseteq A$. ch correctly track causality relations, as can be seen in our example, but have a major drawback: they grow linearly with the number of writes.

Version Vectors (vv). Version Vectors are an efficient representation of ch, provided that the ch has no gaps in each id's event sequence. A vv is a mapping from identifiers

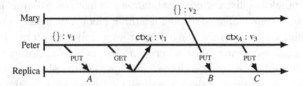

Fig. 1. Example execution for one key: Peter writes a new value v_1 (A), then reads from Replica (ctx_A). Next, Mary writes a new value v_2 (B) and finally Peter updates v_1 with v_3 (C).

Table 1. The table shows the replica (r) state after write from Peter (p) and Mary (m), and the context returned by Peter's read. We use the *metadata* : *value*(s) notation, except for dvvs which has its own internal structure.

	lww	ch	vv$_\text{client}$	vv$_\text{server}$	dvv	dvvs
A	17h00 : v_1	$\{r_1\}$: v_1	$\{(p,1)\}$: v_1	$\{(r,1)\}$: $\{v_1\}$	$((r,1),\{\})$: v_1	$\{(r,1,[v_1])\}$
ctx_A	$\{\}$	$\{r_1\}$	$\{(p,1)\}$	$\{(r,1)\}$	$\{(r,1)\}$	$\{(r,1)\}$
B	17h03 : v_2	$\{r_1\}$: v_1	$\{(p,1)\}$: v_1	$\{(r,2)\}$:	$((r,1),\{\})$: v_1	$\{(r,2,[v_2,v_1])\}$
		$\{r_2\}$: v_2	$\{(m,1)\}$: v_2	$\{v_1,v_2\}$	$((r,2),\{\})$: v_2	
C	17h07 : v_3	$\{r_2\}$: v_2	$\{(m,1)\}$: v_2	$\{(r,3)\}$:	$((r,2),\{\})$: v_2	$\{(r,3,[v_3,v_2])\}$
		$\{r_1,r_3\}$: v_3	$\{(p,2)\}$: v_3	$\{v_1,v_2,v_3\}$	$((r,3),\{(r,1)\})$: v_3	

to counters, and can be written as a set of pairs $(id, counter)$; each pair represents a set of ch events for that id: $\{id_n \mid 0 < n \leq counter\}$. In terms of partial order, $A \leq B$ iff $\forall(i,c_a) \in A \cdot \exists(i,c_b) \in B \cdot c_a \leq c_b$. Again, $A \parallel B$ iff $A \not\leq B$ and $B \not\leq A$. Whether client or server identifiers are used in vv has major consequences, as we'll see next.

Version Vectors with Id-per-Client (vv$_\text{client}$). This approach uses vv with clients as unique identifiers. An update is registered in a server by using the client identification issued in a put. This provides enough information to accurately encode the concurrency and causality in the system, since concurrent client writes are represented in the vv$_\text{client}$ with different ids. However, it sacrifices scalability, since vv$_\text{client}$ will end up storing the ids of all the clients that ever issued writes to that key. Systems like Dynamo try to compensate this by *pruning* entries in vv$_\text{client}$ at a specific threshold, but it typically leads to false concurrency and further need for reconciliation. The higher the degree of pruning, the higher is the degree of false concurrency in the system.

Version Vectors with Id-per-Server (vv$_\text{server}$). If causality is tracked with vv$_\text{server}$, i.e., using vv with server identifiers, it is possible to correctly detect concurrent updates that are handled by different server nodes. However, if concurrent updates are handled by the same server, there is no way to *express* the concurrent values — *siblings* — separately. To avoid overwriting siblings and losing information (as in lww), a popular solution to this, is to group all siblings under the same vv$_\text{server}$, losing individual causality information. This can easily lead to false concurrency: either a write's context causally dominates the server vv$_\text{server}$, in which case all siblings are deemed obsolete and replaced by the new value; or this new value must be added to the current siblings, even if some of them were in its causal past.

Using our example, we finish the execution with all three values $\{v_1, v_2, v_3\}$, when in fact v_3 should have obsoleted v_1, like the other causally correct mechanisms in Table 2 (expect for lww).

With vv$_{server}$, false concurrency can arise whenever a client *read-write cycle* is interleaved with another concurrent write on the same server. This can become especially problematic under heavy load with many clients concurrently writing: under high latency, if a read-write cycle cannot be completed without interleaving with another concurrent write, the set of siblings will keep on growing. This will make messages grow larger, the server load heavier, resulting in a positive feedback loop, in what can be called a *sibling explosion*.

4 Dotted Version Vectors

We now present an accurate mechanism that can be used as a substitute for classic version vectors (vv) in eventually consistent stores, while still using only one *Id* per replica node. The basic idea of *Dotted Version Vectors* (dvv) is to take a vv and add the possibility of representing an individual causal event — *dot* — separate from the rest of the contiguous events. The dot is kept separate from the causal past and it globally and uniquely identifies a write. This allows representing concurrent writes, on the same server, by having different dots.

In our example from Figure 1, we can see that state B is represented with a unique dot for both v_1 and v_2, even-though they both were written with an equally empty context. This distinction in their dots is what enables the final write by Peter to correctly overwrite v_1, since the context supersedes its dot (and dvv), while maintaining v_2 which has a newer dot than the context. In contrast, vv$_{server}$ loses this distinction gained by separating dots by grouping every sibling in one vv and thus cannot know that v_1 is outdated by v_3.

4.1 Definition

A dvv consists in a pair (d, v), where v is a traditional vv and the dot d is a pair (i, n), with i as a node identifier and n as an integer. The dot uniquely represents a write and its associated version, while the vv represents the causal past (i.e. its context). The causal events (or dots) represented by a dvv can be generated by a function toch that translates logical clocks to causal histories (ch can be viewed as sets of dots):

$$\mathsf{toch}(((i,n),v)) = \{i_n\} \cup \mathsf{toch}(v),$$
$$\mathsf{toch}(v) = \bigcup_{(i,n)\in v} \{i_m \mid 1 \le m \le n\},$$

where i_n denotes the nth dot generated by node i, and toch(v) is the same function but for traditional vv. With this definition, the ch $\{a_1, b_1, b_2, c_1, c_2, c_4\}$ that cannot be represented by vv, can now be represented by the dvv $((c,4), \{(a,1),(b,2),(c,2)\})$.

4.2 Partial Order

The partial order on dvv can be defined in terms of inclusion of ch; i.e.:

$$X \leq Y \Longleftrightarrow \text{toch}(X) \subseteq \text{toch}(Y),$$

Given that each dot is generated as a globally unique event — using the notational convenience $v[i] = n$, for $(i,n) \in v$ and $v[i] = 0$ for any non mapped id — the partial order on possible dvv values becomes:

$$((i,n),u) < ((j,m),v) \Longleftrightarrow n \leq v[i] \wedge u \leq v,$$

where the traditional point-wise comparison of vv is used: $u \leq v \Longleftrightarrow \forall_{(i,n)\in u}. n \leq v[i]$.

An important consequence of keeping the dot separate from the causal past is that, if the dot in X is contained in the causal past of Y, it means that Y was generated causally after X, thus Y also contains the causal past of X. This means that there is no need for the comparison of the vv component and the order can be computed as an $O(1)$ operation (assuming access to a map data structure in effectively constant time), simply as:

$$((i,n),u) < ((j,m),v) \Longleftrightarrow n \leq v[i].$$

5 Dotted Version Vector Sets

Dotted Version Vectors (dvv), as presented in the previous section, allow an accurate representation of causality using server-based ids. Still, a dvv is kept for each concurrent version: $\{(dvv_1,v_1),(dvv_2,v_2),\ldots\}$. We can go further in exploring the fact that operations will mostly handle sets of dvv, and not single instances.

We propose now that the set of $(dvv, version)$ for a given key in a replica node is represented by a single instance of a container data type, a *Dotted Version Vector Set* (dvvs), which describes causality for the whole set. dvvs factorizes out common knowledge for the set of dvv described, and keeps only the strictly relevant information in a single data structure. This results in not only a very succinct representation, but also in reduced time complexity of operations: the concurrent values will be indexed and ordered in the data structure, and traversal will be efficient.

5.1 From a Set of Clocks to a Clock for Sets

To obtain a logical clock for a set of versions, we will explore the fact that at each node, the set of dvv as a whole can be represented with a compact vv. Formally this invariant means that, for any set of dvv S, for each node id i, *all* dots for i in S form a contiguous range up to some dot. Note that we can only assume to have this invariant, if we follow some protocol rules enforced by our framework, described in detail in section 6.3.

Assuming this invariant, we obtain a logical clock for a set of $(dvv, version)$ by performing a two-step transformation of the sets of versions. In the *first step*, we compute a single vv for the whole set — the *top vector* — by the pointwise maximum of the dots and vv in the dvv's; additionally, for each dvv in the set, we discard the vv component. As an example, the following set:

$$\{(((r,4),\{(r,3),(s,5)\}),v_1),(((r,5),\{(r,2),(s,3)\}),v_2),(((s,7),\{(r,2),(s,6)\}),v_3)\},$$

generates the top vector $\{(r,5),(s,7)\}$ and is transformed to a set of *(dot, version)*:

$$\{((r,4),v_1),((r,5),v_2),((s,7),v_3)\}.$$

This first transformation has incurred in a loss of knowledge: the specific causal past of each version. This knowledge is not, however, needed for our purposes. The insight is that, to know whether to discard or not a pair (dot,version) (d,v) from some set when comparing with another set of versions S, we do not need to know exactly *which* version in S dominates d, but only that *some* version does; if version v is not present in S, but its dot d is included in the causal information of the whole S (which is now represented by the top vector), then we know that v was obsolete and can be removed.

In the *second step*, we use the knowledge that all dots for each server id, form a contiguous sequence up to the corresponding top vector entry. Therefore, we can associate a list of versions (siblings) to each entry in the top vector, where each dot is implicitly derived by the corresponding version position in the list. In our example, the whole set is then simply described as:

$$\{(r,5,[v_2,v_1]),(s,7,[v_3])\},$$

where the head of each list corresponds to the more recently generated version at the corresponding node. The first version has the dot corresponding to the maximum of the top vector for that entry, the second version has the maximum minus one, and so on.

5.2 Definition

A dvvs is a set of triples (i,n,l), each containing a server id, an integer, and a list of concurrent versions. It describes a set of versions and their dots, implicitly given by the position in the list. It also describes only the knowledge about the collective causal history, as given by the vv derived from the pairs (i,n).

6   Using dvv and dvvs in Distributed Key-Value Stores

In this section we show how to use logical clocks — in particular dvv and dvvs— in modern distributed key-value stores, to accurate and efficiently track causality among writes in each key. Our solution consists in a general workflow that a database must use to serve get and put requests. Towards this, we define a kernel of operations over logical clocks, on top of which the workflow is defined. We then instantiate these operations over the logical clocks that we propose, first dvv and then dvvs.

We support both get and put operations, performing possibly several steps, as sketched in Figure 2. Lets first define our kernel operations.

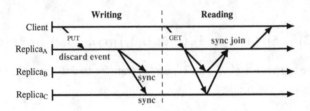

Fig. 2. Generic execution paths for operations get and put

Function sync. The function sync takes two sets of clocks, each describing a set of siblings, and returns the set of clocks for the siblings that remain after removing obsolete ones. It can have a general definition only in terms of the partial order on clocks, regardless of their actual representation: Equation 1.

Function join. The join function takes a set of clocks and returns a single clock that describes the collective causal past of all siblings in the set received. An actual implementation of join is any function that corresponds to performing the union of all the events (dots) in the ch corresponding to the set, i.e., that satisfies Equation 2.

Function discard. The discard function takes a set of clocks S (representing siblings) and a clock C (representing the context), and discards from S all siblings that are obsolete because they are included in the context C. Similar to sync, discard has a simple general definition only in terms of the partial order on clocks: Equation 3.

Function event. The event function takes a set of clocks S (representing siblings) and a clock C (representing the context) and a replica node identifier r; it returns a new clock to represent a new version, given by a new unique event (dot) generated at r, and having C in the causal past. An implementation must respect Equation 4.

$$\mathsf{sync}(S_1, S_2) = \{x \in S_1 \mid \nexists y \in S_2 . x < y\} \cup \{x \in S_2 \mid \nexists y \in S_1 . x < y\}. \quad (1)$$

$$\mathsf{toch}(\mathsf{join}(S)) = \bigcup\{\mathsf{toch}(x) \mid x \in S\}. \quad (2)$$

$$\mathsf{discard}(S, C) = \{x \in S \mid x \not\leq C\}. \quad (3)$$

$$\mathsf{toch}(\mathsf{event}(C, S, r)) = \mathsf{toch}(C) \cup \{\mathsf{next}(C, S, r)\}, \quad (4)$$

where next denotes the next new unique event (dot) generated with r, which can be deterministically defined given C, S and r.

6.1 Serving a get

Functions sync and join are used to define the get operation: when a server receives a get request, it may ask to a subset of replica nodes for their set of versions and clocks for that key, to be then "merged" by applying sync pairwise; however, the server can skip this phase if it deems it unnecessary for a successful response. Having the necessary information ready, it is returned to the client both the values stripped from causality information and the context as a result of applying join to the clocks. sync can also be used at other times, such as anti-entropy synchronization between replica nodes.

6.2 Serving a put

When a put request is received, the server forwards the request to a replica node for the given key, unless the server is itself a replica node. A non-replica node for the key being written can coordinate a put request using vv_{client} for example, because it can use the *client Id* to update the clock and then propagate the result to the replica nodes. However, clocks using *server Ids* like vv_{server}, dvv and dvvs need the coordinating node to generate an unique event in the clock, using its own *Id*. Not forwarding the request to replica node, would mean that non-replica nodes Ids would be added to clocks, making them linear with the total number of servers (e.g. hundreds) instead of only the replica nodes (e.g. three).

When a replica node r, containing the set of clocks S_r for the given key, receives a put request, it starts by removing obsolete versions from S_r, using function discard, resulting in S'_r; it also generates a new clock u for the new version with event; finally, u is added to the set of non- obsolete versions S'_r, resulting in S''_r.

The server can then save S''_r locally, propagate it to other replica nodes and success-fully inform the client. The order of these three steps depends on the system's durability and replication parameters. Each replica node that receives S''_r, uses function sync to apply it against its own local versions.

For each key, the steps at the coordinator (discarding versions, generating a new one and adding it to the non-obsolete set of versions) must be performed atomically when serving a given put. This can be trivially obtained by local concurrency control, and does not prevent full concurrency between local operations on different keys. For operations over the same key, a replica can pipeline the steps of consecutive put for maximizing throughput (note that some steps already need to be serialized, such as writing versions to stable storage).

6.3 Maintaining Local Conciseness

As previously stated, both dvv and dvvs have an crucial invariant that servers must maintain, in order to preserve their correctness and conciseness:

Invariant 1 (Local Clock Conciseness). *Every key at any server has locally associated with it a set of version(s) and clock(s), that collectively can be logically represented by a contiguous set of causal events (e.g. represented as a vv).*

To enforce this invariant, we made two design choices: *(rule 1)* a server cannot respond to a get with a subset of the versions obtained locally and/or remotely, only the entire set should be sent; *(rule 2)* a coordinator cannot replicate the new version to remote nodes, without also sending all local concurrent versions (siblings).

Without the first rule, clients could update a key by reading and writing back a new value with a context containing arbitrary gaps in its causal history. Neither dvv nor dvvs would be expressive enough to support this, since dvv only supports one gap (between the contiguous past and the dot) and dvvs does not support any.

Without the second rule, dvvs would clearly not work, since writes can create siblings, which cannot be expressed separately with this clock. It could work with dvv, however it would eventually result in some server not having a local concise representation for a key (e.g. the network lost a previous sibling), which in turn would make this server unable to respond to get without contacting other servers (see *rule 1*); it would degrade latency and in case of partitions, availability could also suffer.

6.4 Dotted Version Vectors

Functions sync and discard for dvv can be trivially implemented according to their general definitions, by using the partial order for dvv, already defined in Section 4.2.

We will make use of some two functions: function ids returns the set of identifiers of a pair from a vv, a dvv or a set of dvv; the maxdot function takes a dvv or set of dvv and a server id and returns the maximum sequence number of the events from that server:

$$ids((i,\_)) = \{i\},$$
$$ids(((i,\_),v)) = \{i\} \cup ids(v),$$
$$ids(S) = \bigcup_{s \in S} ids(s).$$
$$maxdot(r,((i,n),v)) = max(\{n \mid i = r\} \cup \{v[r]\}),$$
$$maxdot(r,S) = max(\{0\} \cup \{maxdot(r,s) \mid s \in S\}).$$

Function join returns a simple vv, which is enough to accurately express the causal information. Function event can be defined as simply generating a new dot and using the context C, which is already a vv, for the causal past.

$$join(S) = \{(i,maxdot(i,S)) \mid i \in ids(S)\}.$$
$$event(C,S,r) = ((r,max(maxdot(r,S),C[r])+1),C).$$

6.5 Dotted Version Vector Sets

With dvvs, we need to make slight interface changes: functions now receive a single dvvs, instead of a set of clocks; and event now inserts the newly generated version directly in the dvvs.

For clarity and conciseness, we will assume R to be the complete set of replica nodes ids, and any absent id i in a dvvs, is promoted implicitly to the element $(i,0,[])$. We will make use of the functions: first(n,l), that returns the first n elements of list l (or the whole list if it has less than n elements, or an empty list for non-positive n); $|l|$ for the number of elements in l, $[x \mid l]$ to append x at the head of list l; and function merge:

$$merge(n,l,n',l') = \begin{cases} first(n-n'+|l'|,l), & \text{if } n \geq n', \\ first(n'-n+|l|,l'), & \text{otherwise.} \end{cases}$$

Table 2. Space and time complexity, for different causality tracking mechanisms. U: updates; C: writing clients; R: replica servers; V: (concurrent) versions; S_r and S_w: number of servers involved in a GET and PUT, respectively.

		lww	ch	VV$_{client}$	VV$_{server}$	dvv	dvvs
Space		$\tilde{O}(1)$	$\tilde{O}(U)$	$\tilde{O}(C{\times}V)$	$\tilde{O}(R{+}V)$	$\tilde{O}(R{\times}V)$	$\tilde{O}(R{+}V)$
Time	event	–	$\tilde{O}(1)$	$\tilde{O}(1)$	$\tilde{O}(1)$	$\tilde{O}(V)$	$\tilde{O}(R)$
	join	–	$\tilde{O}(U{\times}V)$	$\tilde{O}(C{\times}V)$	$\tilde{O}(1)$	$\tilde{O}(R{\times}V)$	$\tilde{O}(R)$
	discard	–	$\tilde{O}(U{\times}V)$	$\tilde{O}(C{\times}V)$	$\tilde{O}(R)$	$\tilde{O}(V)$	$\tilde{O}(R{+}V)$
	sync	–	$\tilde{O}(U{\times}V^2)$	$\tilde{O}(C{\times}V^2)$	$\tilde{O}(R{+}V)$	$\tilde{O}(V^2)$	$\tilde{O}(R{+}V)$
	PUT	$\tilde{O}(1)$	$\tilde{O}(S_w{\times}U{\times}V^2)$	$\tilde{O}(S_w{\times}C{\times}V^2)$	$\tilde{O}(S_w{\times}(R{+}V))$	$\tilde{O}(S_w{\times}V^2)$	$\tilde{O}(S_w{\times}(R{+}V))$
	GET	$\tilde{O}(1)$	$\tilde{O}(S_r{\times}U{\times}V^2)$	$\tilde{O}(S_r{\times}C{\times}V^2)$	$\tilde{O}(S_r{\times}(R{+}V))$	$\tilde{O}(R{\times}V{+}S_r{\times}V^2)$	$\tilde{O}(S_r{\times}(R{+}V))$
Causally Correct		✗	✓	✓	✗	✓	✓

Function discard takes a dvvs S and a vv C, and discards values in S obsoleted by C. Similarly, sync takes two dvvs and removes obsolete values. Function join simply returns the top vector, discarding the lists. Function event is now adapted to not only produce a new event, but also to insert the new value, explicitly passed as parameter, in the dvvs. It returns a new dvvs that contains the new value v, represented by a new event performed by r and, therefore, appended at the head of the list for r. The context is only used to propagate causal information to the top vector, as we no longer keep it per version.

$$\mathrm{sync}(S, S') = \{(r, \max(n, n'), \mathrm{merge}(n, l, n', l')) \mid r \in R, (r, n, l) \in S, (r, n', l') \in S'\},$$
$$\mathrm{join}(C) = \{(r, n) \mid (r, n, l) \in C\},$$
$$\mathrm{discard}(S, C) = \{(r, n, \mathrm{first}(n - C(r), l)) \mid (r, n, l) \in S\},$$
$$\mathrm{event}(C, S, r, v) = \{(i, n+1, [v \mid l]) \mid (i, n, l) \in S \mid i = r\} \cup$$
$$\{(i, \max(n, C(i)), l) \mid (i, n, l) \in S \mid i \neq r\}$$

7 Complexity and Evaluation

Table 2 shows space and time complexities of each causality tracking mechanism, for a single key. Lets consider U the number of updates (writes), C the number of writing clients, R the number of replica servers, V the number of concurrent versions (siblings) and S_w and S_r the number of replicas nodes involved in a put and get, respectively. Note that U and C are generally several orders of magnitude larger than R and V. The complexity measures presented assume effectively constant time in accessing or updating maps and sets. We also assume ordered maps/sets that allow a pairwise traversal linear on the number of entries.

lww is constant both in time and space, since it does not track causality and ignores siblings. Space-wise, ch and vv$_{client}$ do not scale well, because they grow linearly with writes and clients, respectively. dvv scales well given that typically there is little concurrency per key, but it still needs a dvv per sibling. From the considered clocks, dvvs and vv$_{server}$ have the best space complexity, but the latter is not causally accurate.

Following our framework (Section 6), the time complexities are[1]:

- put is $\tilde{O}(discard + event + S_w \times sync)$ and get is $\tilde{O}(join + S_r \times sync)$;
- *event* is effectively $\tilde{O}(1)$ for ch, vv$_{client}$ and vv$_{server}$; is linear with V for dvv, because it has to check each value's clock; and is $\tilde{O}(R)$ for dvvs because it also merges the context to the local clock;
- *join* is constant for vv$_{server}$, since there is already only one clock; for ch, vv$_{client}$ and dvv it amounts to merging all their clocks into one; for dvvs, *join* simply extracts the top vector from the clock;
- *discard* is only linear with V in dvv, because it can check the partial order of two clocks in constant time; as for ch and vv$_{client}$, they have to compare the context to every version's clock; vv$_{server}$ and dvvs always compare the context to a single clock, and in addition, dvvs has to traverse lists of versions;
- *sync* resembles *discard*, but instead of comparing a set of versions to a single context, it compares two sets of versions. Thus, ch, vv$_{client}$ and dvv complexities are similar to *discard*, but quadratic with V instead of linear. Since vv$_{server}$ and dvvs have only one clock, the complexity of *sync* is linear on V.

7.1   Evaluation

We implemented both dvv and dvvs in Erlang, and integrated it with our fork of the NoSQL Riak datastore[2]. To evaluate the causality tracking accuracy of dvvs, and its ability to overcome the sibling explosion problem, we setup two equivalent 5 node Riak clusters, one using dvvs and the other vv$_{server}$.

We then ran a script[3] equivalent to the following: Peter (P) and Mary (M) write and read 50 times each to the same key, with read-write cycles interleaved (P writes then reads, next M writes then reads, in alternation). Figure 3 shows the growth in the number of siblings with every new write. The cluster with vv$_{server}$ had an explosion of false concurrency: 100 concurrent versions after 100 writes. Every time a client wrote with the its latest context, the clock in the server was already modified, thus generating and adding a sibling. However, with dvvs, although each write still conflicted with the latest write from the other client, it detected and removed siblings that were causally older (all the siblings present at the last read by that client). Thus, the cluster with dvvs had only two siblings after the same 100 writes: the last write from each client.

Finally, dvvs has already seen early adoption in the industry, namely in Riak, where it is the default logical clock mechanism in the latest release. As expected, it overcame the sibling explosion problem that was affecting real world Riak deployments, when multiple clients wrote on the same key.

---

[1] For simplicity of notation, we use the big O variant: $\tilde{O}$, that ignores logarithmic factors in the size of integer counters and unique ids.

[2] https://github.com/ricardobcl/Dotted-Version-Vectors

[3] https://gist.github.com/ricardobcl/4992839

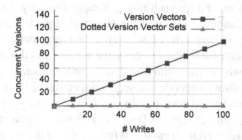

Fig. 3. Results of running two interleaved clients with 50 writes each

8 Related Work

The role of causality in distributed systems was introduced by Lamport [11], establishing the foundation for the subsequent mechanisms and theory [11,14,20,19,2,4]. In Section 3 we discussed the problems of solutions commonly used in eventually consistent stores. In this section, we discuss other related work.

Variability in the Number of Entities. The basic vector based mechanisms can be generalized to deal with a variable number of nodes or replicas. The common strategy is to map identifiers to counters and handle dynamism in the set of identifiers. Additions depend on the generation of unique identifiers. Removals can require communication with several other servers [7], or to a single server [15,1]. While dvv and dvvs avoid identifier assignment to clients, these techniques could support changes in the set of servers.

Exceptions on Conflicts. Some systems just detect the concurrent PUT operations from different clients and reject the update (e.g. version control systems such as CVS and subversion) or keep the updates but do not allow further accesses until the conflict is solved (e.g. original version of Coda [8]); in these cases, using version vectors (vv) with one entry per server is sufficient. However, these solutions sacrifice write availability which is a key "feature" of modern geo-replicated databases.

Compacting the Representation. In general, using a format that is more compact than the set of independent entities that can register concurrency, leads to lossy representation of causality [4]. Plausible clocks [21] condense event counting from multiple replicas over the same vector entry, resulting in false concurrency. Several approaches for removing entries that are not necessary have been proposed, some being safe but requiring running consensus (e.g. Roam [18]), and others fast but unsafe (e.g. Dynamo [5]) potentially leading to causality errors.

Extensions and Added Expressiveness. In Depot [12], the vv associated with each update only includes the entries that have changed since the previous update in the same node. However, each node still needs to maintain vv that include entries for all clients and servers; in a similar scenario, the same approach could be used as a complement to our solution. Other systems explore the fact that they manage a large number of objects to maintain less information for each object. WinFS [13] maintains a base vv for all objects is the file system, and for each object it maintains only the difference for the base in a concise vv. Cimbiosys [17] uses the same technique in a peer-to-peer system. These systems, as they maintain only one entry per server, cannot generate two vv for tagging concurrent updates submitted to the same server from different clients, as discussed in Section 3 with vv_{server}. WinFS includes a mechanism to deal with disrupted synchronizations that allow to encode non sequential causal histories by registering exceptions to the events registered in vv; e.g. $\{a_1, a_2, b_1, c_1, c_2, c_4, c_7\}$ could be represented by $\{(a,2),(b,1),(c,7)\}$ plus exceptions $\{c_3, c_5, c_6\}$. However, using dvv with its system workflow, at most a single update event that is outside the vv is needed, and thus a single *dot* per version is enough. dvvs goes further, by condensing all causal information in a vv, while being able to keep multiple implicit *dots*. This ensures just enough expressiveness to allow any number of concurrent clients and still avoids the size complexity of encoding a generic non sequential ch. Wang et. al. [22] have proposed a variant of vv with $O(1)$ comparison time (like dvv), but the vv entries must be kept ordered which prevents constant time for other operations. Furthermore, it also incurs in the problems associate with vv_{server}, which we solved with dvvs.

9 Closing Remarks

We have presented in detail Dotted Version Vectors, a novel solution for tracking causality among update events. The base idea is to add an extra isolated event over a causal history. This is sufficiently expressive to capture all causality established among concurrent versions (siblings), while keeping its size linear with the number of replicas.

We then proposed a more compact representation — Dotted Version Vector Sets — which allows for a single data structure to accurately represent causal information for a set of siblings. Its space and time complexity is only linear with the number of replicas plus siblings, better than all current mechanisms that accurately track causality.

Finally, we introduced a general workflow for requests to distributed data stores. It abstracts and factors the essential operations that are necessary for causality tracking mechanisms. We then implemented both our mechanisms using those kernel operations.

Acknowledgements. This research was partially supported by FCT/MCT projects PEst-OE/EEI/UI0527/2014 and PTDC/EEI-SCR/1837/2012; by the European Union Seventh Framework Programme (FP7/2007-2013) under grant agreement n° 609551, SyncFree project; by the ERDF - European Regional Development Fund through the COMPETE Programme (operational programme for competitiveness) and by National Funds through the FCT – Fundação para a Ciência e a Tecnologia (Portuguese Foundation for Science and Technology) within project FCOMP-01-0124-FEDER-037281.

References

1. Almeida, P.S., Baquero, C., Fonte, V.: Interval tree clocks. In: Baker, T.P., Bui, A., Tixeuil, S. (eds.) OPODIS 2008. LNCS, vol. 5401, pp. 259–274. Springer, Heidelberg (2008)
2. Birman, K.P., Joseph, T.A.: Reliable communication in the presence of failures. ACM Trans. Comput. Syst. 5(1), 47–76 (1987)

3. Brewer, E.A.: Towards robust distributed systems (abstract). In: Proceedings of the Nineteenth Annual ACM Symposium on Principles of Distributed Computing, PODC 2000, p. 7. ACM, New York (2000)
4. Charron-Bost, B.: Concerning the size of logical clocks in distributed systems. Information Processing Letters 39, 11–16 (1991)
5. DeCandia, G., Hastorun, D., Jampani, M., Kakulapati, G., Lakshman, A., Pilchin, A., Sivasubramanian, S., Vosshall, P., Vogels, W.: Dynamo: amazon's highly available key-value store. In: Proceedings of Twenty-First ACM SIGOPS SOSP, pp. 205–220. ACM (2007)
6. Gilbert, S., Lynch, N.: Brewer's conjecture and the feasibility of consistent available partition-tolerant web services. ACM SIGACT News, 2002 (2002)
7. Golding, R.A.: A weak-consistency architecture for distributed information services. Computing Systems 5(4), 379–405 (1992)
8. Kistler, J.J., Satyanarayanan, M.: Disconnected operation in the Coda file system. In: Thirteenth ACM Symposium on Operating Systems Principles, vol. 25, pp. 213–225. Asilomar Conference Center, Pacific Grove (1991)
9. Klophaus, R.: Riak core: building distributed applications without shared state. In: ACM SIGPLAN Commercial Users of Functional Programming, CUFP 2010, p. 14:1. ACM, New York (2010), http://doi.acm.org/10.1145/1900160.1900176
10. Lakshman, A., Malik, P.: Cassandra: a decentralized structured storage system. SIGOPS Oper. Syst. Rev. 44, 35–40 (2010)
11. Lamport, L.: Time, clocks and the ordering of events in a distributed system. Communications of the ACM 21(7), 558–565 (1978)
12. Mahajan, P., Setty, S., Lee, S., Clement, A., Alvisi, L., Dahlin, M., Walfish, M.: Depot: Cloud storage with minimal trust. In: OSDI 2010 (October 2010)
13. Malkhi, D., Terry, D.: Concise version vectors in winFS. In: Fraigniaud, P. (ed.) DISC 2005. LNCS, vol. 3724, pp. 339–353. Springer, Heidelberg (2005)
14. Parker, D.S., Popek, G., Rudisin, G., Stoughton, A., Walker, B., Walton, E., Chow, J., Edwards, D., Kiser, S., Kline, C.: Detection of mutual inconsistency in distributed systems. Transactions on Software Engineering 9(3), 240–246 (1983)
15. Petersen, K., Spreitzer, M.J., Terry, D.B., Theimer, M.M., Demers, A.J.: Flexible update propagation for weakly consistent replication. In: Sixteen ACM Symposium on Operating Systems Principles, Saint Malo, France (October 1997)
16. Preguiça, N., Baquero, C., Almeida, P.S., Fonte, V., Gonçalves, R.: Brief announcement: Efficient causality tracking in distributed storage systems with dotted version vectors. In: Proceedings of the 2012 ACM Symposium on PODC, pp. 335–336. ACM (2012)
17. Ramasubramanian, V., Rodeheffer, T.L., Terry, D.B., Walraed-Sullivan, M., Wobber, T., Marshall, C.C., Vahdat, A.: Cimbiosys: a platform for content-based partial replication. In: Proceedings of the 6th USENIX Symposium on NSDI, Berkeley, CA, USA, pp. 261–276 (2009)
18. Ratner, D., Reiher, P.L., Popek, G.J.: Roam: A scalable replication system for mobility. MONET 9(5), 537–544 (2004)
19. Raynal, M., Singhal, M.: Logical time: Capturing causality in distributed systems. IEEE Computer 30, 49–56 (1996)
20. Schwarz, R., Mattern, F.: Detecting causal relationships in distributed computations: In search of the holy grail. Distributed Computing 3(7), 149–174 (1994)
21. Torres-Rojas, F.J., Ahamad, M.: Plausible clocks: constant size logical clocks for distributed systems. Distributed Computing 12(4), 179–196 (1999)
22. Wang, W., Amza, C.: On optimal concurrency control for optimistic replication. In: Proc. ICDCS, pp. 317–326 (2009)

Cooperation across Multiple Healthcare Clinics on the Cloud⋆

Neil Donnelly[1], Kate Irving[2], and Mark Roantree[3]

[1] School of Computing, Dublin City University
[2] School of Nursing and Human Sciences, Dublin City University
[3] Insight: Centre for Data Analytics, Dublin City University,
Glasnevin, Dublin 9, Ireland

Abstract. Many healthcare units are creating cloud strategies and migration plans in order to exploit the benefits of cloud based computing. This generally involves collaboration between healthcare specialists and data management researchers to create a new wave of healthcare technology and services. However, in many cases the technology pioneers are ahead of government policies as cloud based storage of healthcare data is not yet permissible in many jurisdictions. One approach is to store anonymised data on the cloud and maintain all identifying data locally. At login time, a simple protocol can be developed to allow clinicians to combine both sets of data for selected patients for the current session. However, the management of off-cloud identifying data requires a framework to ensure sharing and availability of data within clinics and the ability to share data between users in remote clinics. In this paper, we introduce the PACE healthcare architecture which uses a combination of Cloud and Peer-to-Peer technologies to model healthcare units or clinics where off-cloud data is accessible to all, and where exchange of data between remote healthcare units is also facilitated.

1 Introduction

Healthcare operations in many countries are examining cloud-migration plans in order to exploit the benefits of cloud based computing. While standards such as HL7 [9] sought to create a common healthcare record, the storage and management of these records using a cloud-based strategy is now in focus, including in the area of dementia. Dementia is a serious loss of cognitive ability beyond what might be expected from normal ageing. While dementia is a chronic and progressive illness with no known cure, there is now strong evidence that dementia can potentially be delayed by adopting midlife lifestyle changes aimed at improving areas such as cardiovascular health, poor diet and cognitive activity. Given the huge social and economic costs of dementia, even a delay of one year would make such interventions cost-effective [3]. The Dementia Elevator project represents a

⋆ This work is part of the Dementia Elevator Project and funded by HSE Ireland and Atlantic Philanthropies.

K. Magoutis and P. Pietzuch (Eds.): DAIS 2014, LNCS 8460, pp. 82–88, 2014.

collaboration with experts in dementia, which is seeking to build a new cloud-based data management system for dementia patients. Elevator is funded by the Irish healthcare system (the HSE) and The Atlantic Philanthropies.

Healthcare systems and research projects are numerous. In recent years, the trend has been towards personal health based systems where sensor devices can capture and monitor heart rate [11] with systems that generate large volumes of data. These types of systems were also used in projects looking at sports and performance data in personal heath systems [12]. Both of these types of projects produce large sets of data that can be easily managed in cloud-based architectures. However, there are problems associated with using purely cloud-based systems, as summarised in [13]. Trust was one of the biggest issues listed. Users and governments are reluctant trust that healthcare records are secure on the Cloud. Our approach is to use cloud-based technology to store anonymised healthcare data in while using a P2P approach to facilitate the storage and sharing of personal patient data between users. While this provides a level of security on top of the cloud, we do not focus specifically on security and assume that approaches such as [6] can be used in conjunction with the PACE system.

Paper Structure. In §2, we introduce the PACE system and provide a brief over of components; in §3, we provide a detailed discussion of the peer-based setup and how communication is provided; in §4, our evaluation is presented; in §5, a discussion of the similar healthcare approaches is provided; and finally in §6, we provide some conclusions.

2   The PACE System and Clients

The PACE (Peer-to-peer Architecture for Cloud based EHealth) system uses modern web technologies and a decentralised hybrid P2P topology, as described in [1], to enable the sharing of confidential patient data between healthcare professionals. The cloud portion of the system maintains the anonymised patient data on a SQL database and manages the super-peers. Each PACE user acts as a peer, is connected to a super-peer and can transfer patient data with other peers over a P2P connection. Figure 1 demonstrates the design of the PACE system, which has four main components (P1 - P4) which will now be described.

Client Interface (P1). The Client Interface component is the primary interface between the PACE system and the user. There is a basic set of functionality at this level and these are mostly mapped to functions in the backend processes.

- Authenticate. This function authorises users signing in and also informs the super-peer that a peer has logged on and is available to share data.
- Search. The search function is the first step in the P2P sharing protocol described in Section 3. The function uses the Clinic Connector (P2) to locate a patient's private data using an ID and initiate a P2P connection.

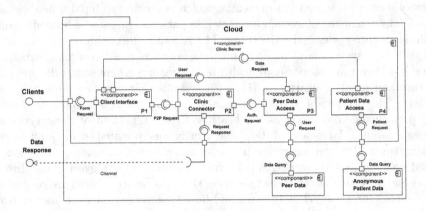

Fig. 1. PACE Components and Interaction

- **Retrieve.** This function uses the Patient Data Access (P3) component to find and retrieve patient data stored on the cloud using a patient ID.
- **Update.** The Update function uses the Patient Data Access (P4) to either update or add a patient's record on the cloud. When a new patient is added the Client Interface uses P2 and P3 to synchronise data between peers.

Peer Data Access (P3). The Peer Data Access component is responsible for the overlay network of the peers and super-peers. It manages the data on the users (peers) and clinics (super-peers). This is described in detail in Section 3. Each super-peer manages a list of peers; the users of the system. In typical super-peer systems [2], peers may join or leave the network at any time while super-peers are responsible for managing their own grouping and for communicating with other super-peers.

Patient Data Access (P4). The goal for the Patient Data Access component is to manage all the anonymised patient data stored on the cloud. All functions are called by related functions in P1.

- **Patient_Search.** This function locates specific patients based on a unique identifier and optionally a clinic identifier to reduce the dataset to search.
- **Query_Search.** This function provides the ability to use SQL-like queries to retrieve multiple patient records matching criteria specified in the query.
- **Update.** This function updates a patient in the database, or if the patient does not currently exist, it adds the the new patient's records.

Clinic Connector (P2). The Clinic Connector service locates and connects peers. It acts as a handshake mechanism that introduces clients in order to initiate a transient P2P connection. This has two scenarios: when a peer has been found to be missing patient information; and when a user requests data from another clinic. If a peer is missing information from the clinic, the Clinic

Connector simply introduces the peer the clinic's other peers. If the clinician makes a request for a patient from another clinic, the Clinic Connector instead communicates with other super-peers to locate the data. It does with the help of the Peer Data Access (P3) service.

3 Cooperation across Super-Peers

As users and clinics are modelled as peers and super-peers respectively, this section begins with a description of our model constructs, followed by a description of how data is found and shared. As private patient data cannot be stored on the cloud and must remain in local storage, sharing data across clinics becomes an important goal. This section explains in detail how this is achieved.

3.1 PACE Model Constructs

With peers randomly connecting to the system and individually creating data, all peers (end-users) are organised into peer groups (the clinics). As each user of the system belongs to a single clinic, peers were organised within a single group, managed by the super-peer. The following are the constructs of the PACE system in terms of their attributes and functionality.

- Peer. The attributes of the Peer are its ID, Peer Context, and the super-peer group in which it belongs. Its functions include: getPatient() which sends a request to the super-peer for a particular patient's data; Connect(Peer) creates a P2P connection with another peer; sendPatient() which sends requested patient data across an established P2P connection.
- Peer Context. This construct models the user of the system. It contains the name of the user and the list of private patient data it has stored.
- Super-peer. The construct attributes are a Super-peer Context and a list of clinic's peers. The functions of the super-peer are: introduce(Peer, Peer), which begins the protocol needed to introduce two peers to set up a P2P connection; peerConnect() requests information from a peer; and spConnect() creates a connection to another super peer.
- Super-peer Context. This construct represents a clinic with attributes such as the clinic's name.

3.2 Communication Method

We now describe the five steps involved in peers sharing data.

1. Patient Data Request. The PACE client sends a patient request using the peer's getPatient function.
2. Patient Request. The client interface forwards this to the Clinic Connector.
3. Data Location Request. The Clinic Connector requests a peer holding this information from the Peer Data Access using spConnect.

4. Return Data Location. The super-peer returns the a peer holding the data.
5. Introduce Peers. The Clinic Connector can now attempt to introduce the requestor to the prospective host:
   (a) The Clinic connector sends a request to the host peer using `peerConnect`.
   (b) Hosting peer confirms it has the requested patient data.
   (c) Clinic Connector sends hosts addressing information to requestor.
6. P2P Data Request. The requesting peer establishes a P2P connection with the host using the `Connect` function with the received address.
7. Private Patient Data Response. The host of the data uses `sendPatient` to transfer data to the requesting peer.

4 Experiments and Evaluation

The PACE server was run using Google's App Engine [7] platform. The machines ranged from a 3.4GHz Intel i7 with 8GB of RAM to a 3.2GHz Intel i5 with 8GB of RAM. All machines had the Windows 7 operating system. Each machine ran the client on Google's Chrome browser and acted as a peer for the experiment.

For the experiment, we encapsulated the super-peers within the cloud. This design ensured the availability of super-peers for the evaluation. The super-peers operated as autonomous peers in the overlay network but were provided on a cloud platform. For this experiment, two clinics and six peers were used.

The experiment aimed to demonstrate that the PACE system could successfully manage multiple healthcare workers across different clinics and facilitate data sharing between peers. In order to do this, we needed to prove: patient data could be shared over a P2P connection; a peer's patient records is updated on sign in; and every peer is updated when a new patient is added. The patient data to be kept by the peers included four Strings representing a name, an address, a phone number and a nine character ID. While the data stored online was a series of random boolean values representing medical records.

Once a peer entered the system, the supper-peer would update it's patient records by introducing it to other peers. A user could also search for a patient using a patient ID. The super-peer can then locate a peer that holds this data and introduce the peers. For our evaluation, we sought to test adding patients; updating patients; accessing peer data; and synchronisation. As timing for functions such as synchronisation was important, we set timers on all operations.

Time to Upload 10 Patients:	7490ms
Time to Upload 50 Patients:	36123ms
Time to Synchronise 10 Patients:	2876ms
Time to Synchronise 50 Patients:	12407ms
Time to Find and Receive a Patient:	478ms

Fig. 2. PACE Experiment Results

During the evaluation, each peer could successfully add multiple patients to PACE's cloud storage and retrieve private patient data from other peers. When a user logged in, their local records were automatically updated. The average time was calculated for adding sets of 10 and 50 patients, which can be seen in figure 2. Figure 2 also shows that the time taken to synchronise data is far less than the insertion time. This difference is due to the slow insertion time with cloud's datastore and the peers being on the same network during the test.

5   Related Research

The authors in [10] present a method of protecting data from certain parties while making it available to others. In their paper, the authors suggest dividing patient health records into domains, with certain information available to some domains but not others. In one of the paper's examples, health insurance companies may see important details of the patient's personal information, but other data is kept private to patient. The PACE system uses a similar domain structure but between clinics. However, PACE builds upon this idea by introducing a physical distance between the information and leaving the personal info in the hands of only those who need it.

In [4], the authors used a hybrid cloud system to share data between hospitals and 3rd party auditors. Data would be held on both a private and public cloud. The private cloud keeps information secure and within the hospital while the public cloud made certain data available to others when needed. The PACE system also uses a public cloud to make certain data available to users. However instead of trying to maintain a private cloud, the PACE system uses P2P networks which distributes storage and sharing duties which can help efficiency.

The authors of [5] present a P2P based healthcare system using JXTA. JXTA is a Peer-to-Peer development infrastructure allowing Java applications to connect as peers. Much like our PACE system, in the paper, they suggest using peer groups to store patient data that can then be shared by other peers, with peer groups organised based on the wards. However, for the PACE system we implemented a hybrid decentralised P2P topology with the cloud acting as an organising server. This allows for greater efficiency when locating information stored by the peers. Using the cloud as a central server also allows peers to share data between different peer groups.

6   Conclusions

In this paper, we introduced the PACE system, a healthcare architecture using both Cloud and P2P technologies to facilitate autonomy within clinics and users, while at the same time, creating an environment for sharing healthcare records. Healthcare workers are modelled as peers and their department or clinic is modelled as the super-peer, with the P2P overlay managed by the Cloud. Thus, we exploit cloud technology for the benefits of storage, elasticity and access to anonymised data, while the identifying data can reside on individual devices.

We collaborated with a number of dementia researchers to evaluate PACE, determine what types of queries were possible and how they were expressed, and used the PACE prototype (described in Section 4), for testing purposes.

In Ireland, it is not permissible to store healthcare data on the Cloud and thus, a hybrid application was necessary. The novelty in this system was the combined usage of cloud and P2P technologies to enable the types of sharing necessary across healthcare departments where user's devices are connected and disconnected in arbitrary fashion. Our evaluation was on a proof-of-concept basis, where we tested availability of peers, updating on-cloud data and the synchronisation process for peers. Insert and Update queries used an SQL-type language which was converted into low level PACE functions for execution.

References

1. Androutsellis-Theotokis, S., Spinellis, D.: A Survey of Peer-to-Peer Content Distribution Technologies. ACM Computing Surveys 36(4) (2005)
2. Bellahsène, Z., Roantree, M.: Querying Distributed Data in a Super-Peer Based Architecture. In: Galindo, F., Takizawa, M., Traunmüller, R. (eds.) DEXA 2004. LNCS, vol. 3180, pp. 296–305. Springer, Heidelberg (2004)
3. Comas-Herrera, A., Northey, S., Wittenburg, R., Knapp, M., Bhattacharyya, S., Burns, A.: Future costs of dementia-related long-term care: exploring future scenarios. International Psychogeriatrics 23, 20–30 (2011)
4. Chen, Y.-Y., Jan, J.-K., Lu, J.-C.: A Secure EHR System Based on Hybrid Clouds. Journal of Medical Systems 36(5) (2012)
5. Lim, B., Choi, K., Shin, D.: A JXTA-based Architecture for Efficient and Adaptive Healthcare Services. In: Kim, C. (ed.) ICOIN 2005. LNCS, vol. 3391, pp. 776–785. Springer, Heidelberg (2005)
6. Clarke, A., Steele, R.: Summarized Data to Achieve Population-Wide Anonymized Wellness Measures. In: Engineering in Medicine and Biology Society (EMBC), pp. 2158–2161. IEEE Press (2012)
7. Google App Engine, https://developers.google.com/appengine/
8. Halevy, A., Ives, Z.G., Madhavan, J., Mork, P., Suciu, D., Tatarinov, I.: The Piazza Peer Data Management System. IEEE Trans. Knowl. Data Eng. 16(7), 787–798 (2004)
9. Health Level Seven International, HL7 (1987), http://www.hl7.org/
10. Löhr, H., Sadeghi, A.-R., Winandy, M.: Securing the E-Health Cloud. In: IHI ACM International Health Informatics Symposium (2010)
11. Roantree, M., McCann, D., Moyna, N.: Integrating Sensor Streams in pHealth Networks. In: Proc. of 14th IEEE International Conference on Parallel and Distributed Systems (ICPADS), pp. 320–327. IEEE Computer Society Press (2008)
12. Roantree, M., Shi, J., Cappellari, P., O'Connor, M., Whelan, M., Moyna, M.: Data transformation and query management in personal health sensor networks. Journal of Network and Computer Applications 35(4), 1191–1202 (2012)
13. Spil, T., Klein, R.: Personal Health Records Success; Why Google Health failed and what does that mean for Microsoft HealthVault? In: Proceedings of HICSS-47 (Health Informatics Track), pp. 2818–2827. IEEE Computer Society Press (2014)
14. Yang, B., Garcia-Molina, H.: Designing a Super-Peer Network. In: Proceedings of the 19th International Conference on Data Engineering, pp. 49–60. IEEE Computer Society Press (2003)

Behave: Behavioral Cache for Web Content

Davide Frey, Mathieu Goessens, and Anne-Marie Kermarrec

INRIA-Rennes Bretagne Atlantique, Rennes, France

Abstract. We propose Behave: a novel approach for peer-to-peer cache-oriented applications such as CDNs. Behave relies on the principle of Behavioral Locality inspired from collaborative filtering. Users that have visited similar websites in the past will have local caches that provide interesting content for one another.

Behave exploits epidemic protocols to build overlapping communities of peers with similar interests. Peers in the same one-hop community federate their cache indexes in a Behavioral cache. Extensive simulations on a real data trace show that Behave can provide zero-hop lookup latency for about 50% of the content available in a DHT-based CDN.

1 Introduction

Publishing content on the Internet has become a daily task for a large number of users. People publish content on social networks, blogs, or on their own websites on a daily basis. The increasing availability of broadband connectivity has even prompted users to start hosting their websites themselves on small servers that are always on in their homes. Small inexpensive plug computers like the Raspberry Pi [1] allow users to set up a personal web server for as little as $30. Software solutions like FreedomBox [2] allow even inexperienced users to deploy their own websites on their plug computers within minutes.

Traffic demands for most of these self-hosted websites may appear negligible. But experience has shown that even small websites can experience instant surges of traffic due to the accidental discovery of interesting content [3]. This phenomenon, known as flash-crowd, often results from traffic redirection from social media or other popular websites. Yet, even with a very limited number of visitors, websites hosting relatively heavy content like high-definition pictures or videos can easily saturate the upload capacity available to residential users.

Commercial websites address traffic surges by relying on the elastic capabilities of Content Delivery Networks (CDN), which delegate content distribution to servers located as close as possible to users. By specializing on content delivery, CDNs platforms such as Akamai [4] allow client websites to respond to sudden traffic demands in real time without maintaining costly infrastructures.

Unfortunately, while affordable and definitely convenient for large corporate websites, CDNs remain too expensive for personal websites or even for those of small- and medium-sized businesses. Researchers have tried to address this disparity by exploiting the bandwidth and storage capabilities of users that visit

K. Magoutis and P. Pietzuch (Eds.): DAIS 2014, LNCS 8460, pp. 89–103, 2014.

a website to provide the same content to other users. This results in peer-to-peer [5–7], or peer-assisted [8] solutions that aim to provide a cheaper and thus widely accessible alternative to CDNs. However, their success is limited by the latency they introduce in the lookup of content.

Most peer-to-peer or peer-assisted CDNs rely on Distributed Hash Tables (DHTs). This provides a simple abstraction that allows nodes to retrieve the content they are looking for in a logarithmic number of hops. However, even a logarithmic number of hops may be too long, particularly in the presence of congestion, or churn. DHTs may suffer from long lookup delays in the order of minutes [9, 10] in the presence of churn. But even in a static network, typical DHT lookup times easily exceed the download times required by most content. Some authors have proposed to improve on this latency with new DHT solutions [9, 11]. Here we adopt a complementary approach and reduce lookup time to zero by maximizing the amount of content that nodes can index locally.

Our key contribution consists of *Behave*, a novel decentralized caching architecture relying on *behavioral locality*. A traditional CDN essentially consists of a large decentralized cache memory, relying on temporal locality. If a user accesses a web object, there is a relatively strong probability that she will access it again in the near future. Behave's *behavioral locality* extends this observation by exploiting similarities between the browsing behaviors of users. Unlike DHT-based solutions [6, 5], which seek to maximize the amount of web objects accessible through the peer-to-peer substrate, Behave focuses on maximizing the number of objects accessible without any lookup delay.

To achieve this, Behave builds a collaborative *behavioral cache* by relying on user-based collaborative filtering [12], a well-known technology in the context of recommender systems. Collaborative filtering relies on a simple observation: users that have exhibited similar tastes in the past will probably exhibit similar tastes in the future. In our context, this observation suggests that if two users have common items in their web caches, then they will probably exhibit commonalities in the websites they visit in the future.

We adopt a decentralized version of user-based collaborative filtering following the example of [13]. Behave nodes adopt an epidemic protocol to form an interest-based topology based on commonalities between their browsing histories. This provides each node with a set of overlay neighbors whose browsing histories most closely resemble its own. Behave's *behavioral cache* emerges from this topology as the federation of the local caches of a node's neighbors.

Behave provides the greatest benefit for applications for which lookup time using a DHT may exceed the time needed to effectively fetch the content itself. The web provides a good example of such applications, together with applications such as decentralized Domain Name Services [14]. While web pages do contain large objects, most of their content consists of a large number of relatively small files. For example, in a sample of $300,000$ web requests from the top $1,000,000$ websites crawled by the HTTP Archive initiative [15], we recorded an average web-page size of 1.62MB consisting of an average of 94 files per page, with an average size of 18KB each. The average lookup time on a DHT may significantly exceed the time required to download most of these files. Our extensive simulations on real data traces show instead that Behave can provide zero-hop lookup latency on 50% of the content indexed by an entire DHT. Moreover, mimicking the performance of a single Behave overlay with existing solutions such as FlowerCDN requires each node to participate in more than 10 gossip overlays.

2   The Behave Model

Behave maximizes the amount of cached information reachable without recurring to on-demand routing operations. To this end, it combines the notion of temporal locality at the basis of standard web-caches with a novel idea: behavioral locality. Two users that visited the same websites in the past will likely exhibit more common interests in the future.

From a practical perspective, Behave extends the caching behavior commonly implemented in web browsers by integrating a decentralized user-based collaborative filtering protocol [12, 16, 17]. Each node identifies the set of nodes that are most similar to it in terms of browsing history: its neighbors. The aggregation of the cache indexes of a node's neighbors constitutes a *behavioral cache index*. If a node visits a website not indexed by its local cache, the site will likely be in the node's behavioral cache index. If this is the case, the node will download the content directly from the corresponding neighbor with no lookup latency.

Like most peer-to-peer solutions for web-content delivery, Behave relies on signatures to ensure the integrity of content retrieved from other nodes [18, 19]. Yet, for the sake of simplicity, we ignore privacy-preserving solutions for Behave-like systems such as those in [13, 20]. Integrating them in Behave constitutes part of our future work.

Implementation. We implemented a preliminary Behave prototype in the form of a local proxy server consisting of 4000 lines of Java code. We developed a web proxy using Apache HTTP Components (http://hc.apache.org), and implemented a cache conforming to the HTTP/1.1 caching policies. We manage the cache using Ehcache (http://ehcache.org), and profiles with a small-footprint SQL Java database (http://www.h2database.com). Users can access Behave with any browser simply by configuring it to use *localhost:8080* as a proxy server. This allows our implementation to handle all requests and serve them either using the behavioral cache, or by directly contacting the target server.

We are also working on a Firefox-based implementation that leverages WebRTC, as well as the browser's internal API (Mozilla's XPCOM). Despite being in an early design stage, our code is already available at https://github.com/mgoessen/behave/. In the remainder of this section, we detail the concepts underlying the Behave architecture.

2.1   From Local Cache to Interest Profile

Like any web caching solution, Behave relies on the notion of a *local cache* based on the principle of temporal locality. If a user visits a website, there is a non-negligible probability that she will visit it again in the future. In this paper, we complement this basic idea with *behavioral locality*. For the sake of simplicity, we consider an LRU-based local cache that associates each URL visited by the local user with the corresponding web object. We use the term *local cache* to refer to the stored URLs and the associated web objects. We write instead *local-cache index* to refer to the list of URLs without the web objects.

Compact Representation of Cache Indexes. The local cache allows each node to retrieve copies of the websites it visited in the past. Behave makes these copies also available to other nodes that have similar browsing histories. To achieve this, nodes share the content of their cache indexes with other similar nodes. This poses an evident problem. Even if the local cache index does not contain the actual web objects, its size may still be very large. Considering the average length of a URL—we measured an average URL length of 99 characters over a set of 300,000 web pages—the index of a cache index containing 2000 URLs takes about 20KB. This grows even larger when we append HTTP content-negotiation headers [21]. Blindly exchanging cache indexes without any form of compression would therefore result in prohibitive network overhead.

To counter this problem, Behave uses a compact representation of local cache indexes in the form of bloom filters [22]. A bloom filter represents a set as an array of m bits by exploiting k hash functions. Each such function returns a number from 0 to $m-1$ when applied to an item (a URL in our case). Adding an element (URL) to the set is achieved by hashing it with all the k hash functions and by setting to 1 all the bits corresponding to the values returned by each of the functions. Checking if an element is in a set relies on an analogous process: hashing the element with the k functions and verifying if all the resulting k bit positions are set. If they are, the element is deemed to be in the set, otherwise it is not. It is easy to see that a Bloom filter can return false positives, but can never return false negatives.

Behave determines the size of bloom filters dynamically. Periodically, a Behave node recomputes its own bloom filter with a size of $b \cdot N$ where N is the cardinality of its profile or cache index. Such a periodic recomputation not only achieves similar size efficiency as scalable bloom filters [23], but it also allows a bloom filter to ignore the items that have been evicted from the corresponding node's local cache. When sharing its bloom filter, a Behave node appends the corresponding size so that receiving nodes can parameterize the hash functions accordingly [24]. We evaluate the impact of b in Section 4.5.

Interest Profile. The compressed form of a local-cache index allows a node to inform another node of its browsing interests. However, not all the items accessed through a web browser appear in the corresponding local cache and thus in the local-cache index. The *HTTP* specification allows [21] web designers to identify objects as *cachable* (with a specified TTL and refresh policy, allowing even dynamic content to be cached) or *non cachable*. Web browser caches only store cachable objects and Behave's local cache does the same. Not respecting this specification would clearly result in the undesirable use and propagation of stale copies of documents.

To improve the accuracy of their browsing histories while still respecting the specification, Behave nodes therefore complement the information contained in their local cache indexes. Specifically, each node maintains a separate *interest profile* consisting of a list of visited URLs. All the items in the local cache and local-cache index have a corresponding entry in the interest profile, but non-cachable items appear in the interest profile without being present in the local cache. This allows nodes to gather more information about the browsing histories of potential neighbors than would be available in their local cache indexes.

Like for the local cache index, we use a compact representation of the interest profile of a node in the form of a bloom filter, which is periodically recomputed with an appropriate size. However, we must point out an important difference between the two. Nodes use interest profiles to identify similarities between their browsing behavior and that of other nodes, but they use cache indexes to verify if a given web object is really stored locally or in the cache of a neighbor. Thus, profiles can tolerate much higher rates of false positives. A false positive in a node's profile will probably appear as a (false) positive in the profile of a neighboring node. A false positive in a cache index will instead lead to a cache miss possibly resulting in a waste of time and network resources. We will return to this important distinction in the context of our evaluation in Section 4.5.

2.2   Clustering Similar Interests

To cluster nodes according to interests, Behave adopts the approach in [13] consisting of two layered gossip protocols: random peer sampling, and clustering. The former provides each node with a continuously changing random view of the network. The latter starts from this random view, and incrementally identifies the best neighbors for each node according to a given similarity metric.

The two protocols follow similar structures. Each node maintains a *view*—a list of identifiers (for example IP address and port) of n_{view} other nodes, each associated with the corresponding interest profile, and with a timestamp indicating when the information in the entry was generated. Periodically, each node selects the entry in its view with the oldest timestamp and starts a gossip exchange with the corresponding node. Consider a node p starting such an exchange with another node q. Node p extracts a new view-like data structure G from its view: a random subset of $n_{view}/2$ entries for the RPS, and a copy of its view for the clustering protocol—in both cases node p excludes q from the extracted set. After preparing G, node p sends it to q thereby initiating the gossip interaction. The two protocols differ in the way q reacts to G.

Random Peer Sampling. In the case of the RPS, q selects $n_{view}/2$ entries from its own view and replaces them with those in G. It then takes the entries it removed from its view and packs them into a response message G', and sends them to p. Upon receiving G', node p replaces the entries it sent to q with those it received, thus completing the gossip interaction.

Clustering Protocol. In the case of the clustering protocol, q computes the union of its own cluster view, its own RPS view, and the view in G (which is p's cluster view). Then q selects the nodes in the resulting view whose profiles are most similar to its own. Several similarity metrics exist for this purpose. Here we use the one proposed in [13]. It extends the cosine-similarity metric by providing ratings for groups of nodes as opposed to individual ones. This allows q to identify the nodes that collectively best cover the interests in its own profile. After selecting the nodes to keep in its view, node q prepares a reply G' with the content of its own view before the update and sends it to p, which reacts by updating its view in an analogous manner.

Nodes open connections to other nodes using state-of-the-art mechanisms such as IPv6, ICE [25], or UPNP/PCT [26], and maintain these connections stable with the nodes in their clustering views. This speeds up the download of content as nodes do not need to wait for connection initialization. Moreover, it allows them to detect and quickly respond to other nodes' disconnections.

2.3 Collaborative Cache Index

Identifying neighbors with similar interest profiles allows Behave nodes to build collaborative *behavioral cache indexes* that federate the local cache indexes of their neighbors. In practical terms, the *behavioral cache index* of a node simply consists of a data structure that associates each of the node's neighbors with the corresponding local cache index in its bloom-filtered form. The use of bloom filters prevents nodes from organizing their collaborative cache indexes in a more efficient structure. Yet, the small number of neighbors makes the search for matching bloom filters sufficiently fast.

2.4 Speeding Up Convergence

To maximize the efficiency of behavioral cache indexes, nodes must maintain them up to date. Moreover, they must base their clustering decisions on up-to-date versions of other nodes' profiles. The gossip exchanges described above periodically refresh the information about other nodes' profiles. But they only do so to a limited extent. At each gossip cycle, the RPS exchanges information with a randomly selected node and thus cannot provide significant help in maintaining the information about one's neighbors current. The clustering protocol instead exchanges information exactly with one of the node's neighbors. Receiving updated information about n_{view} nodes therefore requires on average n_{view} gossip cycles. This is too long to provide satisfactory performance.

To maintain their behavioral cache up-to-date, nodes therefore complement their gossip exchanges by explicitly pulling profile information. At each gossip cycle, a node sends an explicit *profile request* message to each of its current neighbors from its cluster view. Nodes reply to such *profile requests* by sending copies of their interest profiles and local cache indexes.

To limit the cost of such profile updates, nodes do not reply systematically, but they use a profile-change threshold, t, expressed as a percentage of the size of their interest profile. When a node q replies to a node n, it records a snapshot of the profile it sends to n. When q receives a subsequent request from n, it first checks if its current profile contains at least t new elements with respect to the one it sent the last time it replied to a request from n. If so, q replies by sending its new profile and its updated cache index, otherwise it ignores the request.

It is worth observing that this threshold-based approach integrates particularly well with bloom filters. Alternatives like differential updates would be inapplicable due to the difficulty of removing items from a bloom filter. Moreover, differential updates with lists of full URLs would often be larger than non-differential bloom filters.

Finally, we observe that using profile requests is not equivalent to increasing the frequency of gossip interactions. In gossip interactions, a node exchanges profile information about n_{view} other nodes, while each profile request results in the exchange of at most one profile.

3 Evaluation Setting

We evaluated Behave on two real-world traces provided by the Ircache-DITL[1] initiative—a web proxy farm with servers deployed at various US universities and research institutes. The first trace refers to January 9, 2007, the second to January 10 of the same year. Each records 24 hours of logs for approximately 1000 clients. After removing NAT endpoints, the traces contain, respectively, $4.2M$ and $3.8M$ requests from 982 and 1000 unique clients for about $2M$ and $1.7M$ web objects with average sizes of $24.3KB$ and $23.7KB$. Ircache also provides more recent datasets, but these only contain data for 150–200 clients. Due to the absence of caching information in the dataset, we assume that 46% the content is cachable, consistently with the data published by the HTTP Archive initiative [15]. Similarly, we assume that all clients negotiate content in the same language. Even if the dataset does not contain such information, this is probably close to reality as the dataset records web accesses from US Universities. Finally, we assume that every client remains online during the entire experiment.

Default Parameters. Due to the large size of the datasets, we implemented a simulated version of Behave, which we configured as follows. We set the sizes of the RPS and clustering views respectively to $v_{RPS} = 12$ and $v_{CLUSTER} = 25$. We used a gossip period $p_g = 10min$ for both protocols and a profile-update period $p_u = 1min$ with a threshold of $t = 5\%$. Finally, we set the profile size to 5000 elements and the cache size to 2300 with bloom filters that use respectively 20 and 12 bits per element. We provide details about the choice of these default parameters in sections 4.3 through 4.5.

Comparison with a DHT. We compare Behave with a Squirrel-like DHT configured to use a base $b = 4$, a leaf-set size $l = 16$, a cache size of 2300 elements like

---

[1] http://ircache.net National Science Foundation (grants NCR-9616602 and NCR-9521745), and the National Laboratory for Applied Network Research.

for Behave, and an average insertion latency of 5s. To manage the CDN data, we use the *home-store-node* strategy described in [6]: the node associated with a key in the DHT stores a pointer to the node that records the actual content.

Comparison with FlowerCDN. We also compare our solution with FlowerCDN [5]. FlowerCDN reduces the lookup latency for already-visited websites by employing per-site clusters. A node joins a cluster after it visits a website for the first time, and maintains a partial view for each of the clusters it is part of. The authors of [5] do not specify how many clusters a peer can join, so we experimented with different maximum numbers of clusters with a simple LRU policy.

If a node visits a website associated with one of its clusters, it can lookup the peer hosting the content within zero hops if the content is indexed in its partial view, or within one hop if the content is in the cluster but not in its partial view. For simplicity, we ignore localities which would decrease the cluster hit-rate, and assume that joining a cluster takes 1s. We also ignore the delay for the propagation of caches indexes within a clusters: content is immediately available after the 1s joining delay. As above, we set the local cache size to 2300 entries.

4   Evaluation Results

We start by comparing the performance of Behave with that of Squirrel and FlowerCDN. Then we analyze Behave by varying its main parameters one by one. When not otherwise specified, we use the default parameters indicated in Section 3. We also point out that our results showed no significant differences between the two traces we considered. Thus, we only present those for January 9, 2007. Figure 1a gives a pictorial view of this trace by showing the total number of visited objects per minute during the course of the day.

4.1   Comparison with Squirrel and FlowerCDN

Behave aims to provide zero-hop lookup latency on as large a fraction of the content as possible. DHT-based solutions, on the other hand, focus on indexing all the content available at all peers even if this would result in a long lookup latency. In spite of this significant difference, Behave manages to achieve zero-hop lookup latency for up to 50% of the content indexed by the DHT.

Figures 1b shows how the hit rate progresses during the course of the experiment. The plot (and the plots that follow) shows, for each instant, the relative hit rate with respect to a solution that uses only the local cache. Both Behave and its competitors leverage the local cache. Thus, a hit rate of 110% means that the solution offers 10% more content than the local cache alone. Each point represents the hit rate in the previous hour of simulated time. Clearly, the DHT-based solution (indicated as Squirrel) constantly achieves a higher hit rate, but Behave still manages to offer a large fraction of the content available through the DHT. Moreover, its Behavioral cache index provides this content with zero lookup latency. Squirrel, on the other hand, serves a pointer to the content, or notifies of its absence, with a significantly higher lookup delay.

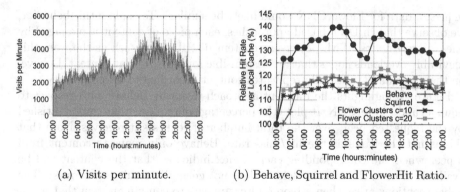

(a) Visits per minute.   (b) Behave, Squirrel and FlowerHit Ratio.

Fig. 1. Behave, Squirrel and FlowerCDN Hit Ratio and Visits Pattern

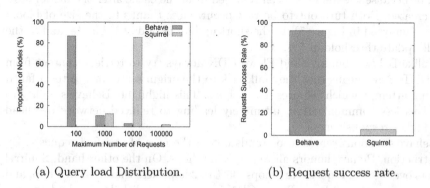

(a) Query load Distribution.   (b) Request success rate.

Fig. 2. Query load as the number of requests received by nodes (a), and request success rate

The plot also shows the hit-rate obtained by the gossip-based overlay in Flow-erCDN (labeled as Flower-clusters) for different maximum numbers of clusters. The data shows that Behave's hit-rate is between that achieved by FlowerCDN's gossip overlays with a maximum of 10 and 20 clusters. However, the cost associated with Behave's gossip exchanges roughly equals that of FlowerCDN with four clusters (Behave nodes exchange profiles and cache indexes both in the clustering and RPS protocols). This shows that a behavioral cache like Behave can be effective both as a complement and as an alternative to DHT-based solutions.

4.2 Query Load

Figure 2a presents another interesting aspect of our comparison with Squirrel by plotting the distribution of nodes according to the number of requests for content they receive (query load). The plot shows that most Behave nodes receive less than 100 requests with only a few nodes receiving more. The distribution of Squirrel nodes on the other hand is a lot more spread out. A large number of nodes receive thousands of requests: more than 80% receive more than 10000 requests (data for FlowerCDN would likely be similar). To explain this behavior, we observe that in DHT-based approaches, each piece of content is managed by one or a few nodes. With power-law content distributions such as the web, this inevitably overloads nodes that are responsible for very popular content. Behave, on the other hand, naturally replicates content according to its popularity.

Figure 2b highlights the different approach taken by Behave with respect to Squirrel and FlowerCDN. It plots the percentage of requests that can be satisfied by the requested peer, over the total number of requests it receives. Note that this is not the same as the hit/miss rate. Behave only requests content from a peer when the corresponding cache index indicates that the content will be available. So a cache miss in Behave does not generally result in a request. The only exceptions arise when a bloom filter appears to contain an item that is not in the corresponding cache. This may happen because of the filter's false positive rate, or because the item has been removed from the cache after the bloom filter was created. Both turn out to be rare occurrences thanks to the size of bloom filters (analyzed in Figure 5), to the short update period of 1 minute, and to the small update threshold of 5%.

Unlike Behave, Squirrel and FlowerCDN always try to retrieve content from the DHT. This means that they fall back to the origin server only after a failed routing attempt which requires $log(n)$ hops. This highlights Behave's ability to avoid useless communication, ultimately leading to reduced network overhead and higher responsiveness.

Behave's responsiveness also stands out in the case of satisfied requests. By construction, Behave honors all requests in 0 hops. On the other hand, Squirrel honors over 50% of requests in 3 hops, 35% in 2 hops, less than 10% in 1 hop, and a few in more than 3 hops. FlowerCDN improves this distribution by honoring 70% of requests in 1 or 0 hops, and only 15% in 3 hops.

4.3   Impact of the View Size

We start dissecting the performance of Behave by analyzing hit rate and bandwidth consumption for different values of its view size. The results, depicted in Figure 3a show that Behave offers a significant gain over the local cache even with a very limited view size of 5 peers. The hit rate increases with larger view sizes of up to 25 peers (recall that the total number of peers is about 1000), but bandwidth consumption (shown in Figure 3b) also increases.

By analyzing the two plots, we can conclude that increasing the view size beyond 25 provides almost no benefit for a significant increase in bandwidth consumption. On the other hand, a view size of 25 appears to provide the best compromise between the two metrics.

Figure 3b also highlights Behave's effectiveness in adapting bandwidth consumption to the activity of users. Figure 1a shows that the number of visits per minute has a peak around 8am, then increases until 6pm, and finally decreases after 8pm: bandwidth consumption closely follows this pattern. Our profile-change threshold causes the frequency of gossip exchanges to follow the rate of changes in nodes' profiles, which is in turn proportional to the activity of users.

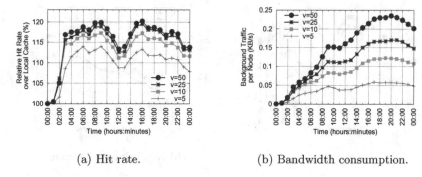

(a) Hit rate.

(b) Bandwidth consumption.

Fig. 3. Impact of the view size in Behave

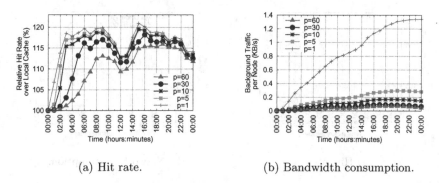

(a) Hit rate.

(b) Bandwidth consumption.

Fig. 4. Impact of the gossip period in Behave

4.4   Importance of the Gossip Period

Next, we consider the impact of Behave's gossip period, p_g. Figure 4 confirms the expectations. Faster gossiping leads to better hit rates but also to higher bandwidth consumption. The impact affects not only the maximum hit rate but also the time Behave takes to converge, starting from an empty network. After convergence, gossip updates remain important because the behavior of users never reaches a steady state. New nodes start their activity and existing nodes visit new sites. Overall, the plots justify our default choice of a gossip period $p_g = 10$min. The corresponding bandwidth consumption remains below 0.2kB/s.

4.5   Bloom-Filter Behavior

Bloom filters play an important role in the performance of Behave. Figure 5 studies the impact of the number of bits per element, b, used by the interest-profile bloom filter. Results show that very small filters ($b = 4, 8$) provide unsatisfactory performance. However, the hit ratio does not change significantly when b grows beyond 12, while bandwidth consumption continues to grow. This justifies our choice of a default value of $b = 12$ for the interest-profile bloom filter corresponding to a false-positive probability of about $P = 0.003$. For the cache bloom-filter,

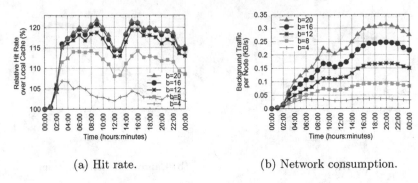

(a) Hit rate.   (b) Network consumption.

Fig. 5. Impact of bloom filter size in Behave

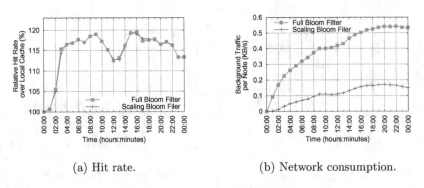

(a) Hit rate.   (b) Network consumption.

Fig. 6. Impact of scaling bloom filters in Behave

we stick to a value of $b = 20$ (false-positive rate $P = 6.7 \cdot 10^{-5}$) because false positives in the cache have a direct impact on the latency perceived by users: they cause an increase in cache misses as a result of failed requests.

Figure 6 highlights the advantage of periodically recomputing and resizing bloom filters. This prevents Behave from sending large bloom filters when profiles or caches contain only a few elements. The plot shows that scaling the size of bloom filters significantly reduces bandwidth consumption without affecting the hit rate. The increase in false positives with small bloom filters is in fact very limited. For example, with 12 bits per element, $p(\text{false positive}) = 3.14 \cdot 10^{-3}$ with 5000, while $p(\text{false positive}) = 3.29 \cdot 10^{-3}$ with only 5.

5   Related Work

Recent research has proposed a variety of solutions for peer-to-peer-oriented content-delivery networks. Squirrel [6] and Backslash [3] propose decentralized web caches that index content with a DHT. Their authors propose two strategies: replicate web objects within the DHT, or use DHT nodes as pointers to the stored data. We compared our approach with the latter strategy in Section 4.1.

CoralCDN [27, 28] uses instead peer-to-peer technology to organize a collection of servers without offloading tasks to user machines. Its authors acknowledge the limitations of standard DHTs and propose a modified DHT to implement their CDN. In a later paper [18], some of the authors propose a new completely decentralized-architecture that exploits signatures to guarantee content integrity. We adopt a similar signature-based approach in Behave.

FlowerCDN [5] combines a DHT with gossip-based communities of nodes that focus on specific content. Unlike our approach, they form these communities on a per-site and per-location basis. This means that the communities associated with two websites remain uncorrelated even if they may contain common nodes. This prevents FlowerCDN from exploiting semantic links between websites.

Maygh [7] takes advantage of the recent WebRTC and RTMP technologies to build a decentralized CDN without installing new software on clients. However, its approach requires intervention from website owners who must modify their websites in order to employ Maygh's technology. Moreover Maygh's architecture relies on coordinator nodes that must be deployed by each participating website.

SocialCDN [29] builds a collaborative cache that exploits explicit social acquaintances to aggregate peers for content distribution. This makes its approach limited to the case of distributed Online Social Networks. Behave, on the other hand offers a solution for a more general use case, even though it would be interesting to evaluate its performance in the case of online social networks.

Overall, only a few authors have focused on reducing lookup latency in the context of peer-to-peer CDNs or caches. The major example, Beehive [14], uses replication to achieve $O(1)$ lookup times in a DHT. Yet, its proactive approach focuses only on the most popular content. This makes Beehive unsuitable for optimizing the delivery of niche content. Behave, on the other hand, can perform particularly well on niche content thanks to the personalized approach provided by the Gossple similarity metric [13].

6 Conclusions

We proposed Behave, a peer-to-peer solution for building a content-delivery network based on the principle of Behavioral Locality. By adapting the concept of collaborative-filtering to decentralized caches, Behave provides zero lookup latency on about 50% of the content available through a DHT. This allows Behave to operate as a stand-alone solution, coupled with existing local caches, or in combination with a DHT.

The promising results we obtained by simulation encourage us to finalize the development of our Java and WebRTC prototypes and to explore novel research directions. First, we plan to integrate Behave with privacy and trust-based mechanisms. This would allow us to expand the applicability of Behave. Second, we envision combining our CDN architecture with non-web-oriented recommendations. This could provide benefits in both directions: more effective content delivery, and more precise recommendations. Finally we plan to study how our Behavioral cache can be integrated into existing CDN solutions.

Acknowledgments. This work was partially funded by the ERC SG GOSSPLE project (204742) (http://gossple.fr), the EIT/ICT-Labs AllYours project (CLD 13 021), and by the French National Research Agency (ANR) project SocioPlug (ANR-13-INFR-0003) (http://socioplug.univ-nantes.fr).

We would like to thank the Ircache project (National Science Foundation grants NCR-9616602 and NCR-9521745), and the National Laboratory for Applied Network Research for providing traces used in our evaluation. Finally, we are grateful to Mohammed Alaggan, Stephane Bortzmeyer, Arnaud Jegou, Julien Stainer and the Firefox "Necko" networking team, for useful comments and discussions.

References

1. Raspberry Pi, http://www.raspberrypi.org
2. FreedomBox, https://freedomboxfoundation.org
3. Stading, T., Maniatis, P., Baker, M.: Peer-to-peer caching schemes to address flash crowds. In: Druschel, P., Kaashoek, M.F., Rowstron, A. (eds.) IPTPS 2002. LNCS, vol. 2429, pp. 203–213. Springer, Heidelberg (2002)
4. Akamai, http://www.akamai.com
5. El Dick, M., Pacitti, E., Kemme, B.: Flower-cdn: a hybrid p2p overlay for efficient query processing in cdn. In: 12th International Conference on Extending Database Technology: Advances in Database Technology, pp. 427–438. ACM (2009)
6. Iyer, S., Rowstron, A., Druschel, P.: Squirrel: A decentralized peer-to-peer web cache. In: Proceedings of the Twenty-First Annual Symposium on Principles of Distributed Computing, pp. 213–222. ACM (2002)
7. Zhang, L., Zhou, F., Mislove, A., Sundaram, R.: Maygh: Building a cdn from client web browsers. Image 70(40.3), 85–87 (2013)
8. Michiardi, P., Carra, D., Albanese, F., Bestavros, A.: Peer-assisted Content Distribution on a Budget. Computer Networks (February 2012)
9. Falkner, J., Piatek, M., John, J., Krishnamurthy, A., Anderson, T.: Profiling a million user dht. In: Proceedings of the 7th ACM SIGCOMM Conference on Internet Measurement, pp. 129–134. ACM (2007)
10. Crosby, S.A., Wallach, D.S.: An analysis of bittorrent's two kademlia-based dhts. Technical Report TR07-04, Rice University (2007)
11. Jimenez, R., Osmani, F., Knutsson, B.: Sub-second lookups on a large-scale kademlia-based overlay. In: 2011 IEEE International Conference on Peer-to-Peer Computing (P2P), pp. 82–91. IEEE (2011)
12. Ekstrand, M., Riedl, J., Konstan, J.: Collaborative Filtering Recommender Systems. Now Publishers (2011)
13. Bertier, M., Frey, D., Guerraoui, R., Kermarrec, A.-M., Leroy, V.: The gossple anonymous social network. In: Gupta, I., Mascolo, C. (eds.) Middleware 2010. LNCS, vol. 6452, pp. 191–211. Springer, Heidelberg (2010)
14. Ramasubramanian, V., Sirer, E.G.: Beehive: O(1) lookup performance for power-law query distributions in peer-to-peer overlays. In: Networked Systems Design and Implementation (NSDI 2004), San Francisco, USA, pp. 99–112 (2004)
15. HTTP Archive, http://httparchive.org
16. Kermarrec, A.M., Leroy, V., Moin, A., Thraves, C.: Application of Random Walks to Decentralized Recommender Systems. In: 14th International Conference on Principles of Distributed Systems, Tozeur, Tunisie (2010)

17. Boutet, A., Frey, D., Guerraoui, R., Jégou, A., Kermarrec, A.M.: WhatsUp Decentralized Instant News Recommender. In: IPDPS 2013, Boston, USA (May 2013)
18. Terrace, J., Laidlaw, H., Liu, H., Stern, S., Freedman, M.: Bringing p2p to the web: Security and privacy in the firecoral network. In: Proceedings of the 8th International Conference on Peer-to-Peer Systems, p. 7. USENIX Association (2009)
19. Jacobson, V., Smetters, D.K., Thornton, J.D., Plass, M.F., Briggs, N.H., Braynard, R.L.: Networking named content. In: 5th International Conference on Emerging Networking Experiments and Technologies, pp. 1–12. ACM (2009)
20. Boutet, A., Frey, D., Jégou, A., Kermarrec, A.-M., Ribeiro, H.B.: FreeRec: an Anonymous and Distributed Personalization Architecture. In: Gramoli, V., Guerraoui, R. (eds.) NETYS 2013. LNCS, vol. 7853, pp. 58–73. Springer, Heidelberg (2013)
21. Fielding, R., Gettys, J., Mogul, J., Frystyk, H., Masinter, L., Leach, P., Berners-Lee, T.: Hypertext Transfer Protocol – HTTP/1.1. RFC 2616 (Draft Standard) (June 1999) Updated by RFCs 2817, 5785, 6266, 6585
22. Bloom, B.H.: Space/time trade-offs in hash coding with allowable errors. Communication of the ACM 13(7), 422–426 (1970)
23. Almeida, P.S., Baquero, C., Preguiça, N., Hutchison, D.: Scalable bloom filters. Information Processing Letters 101(6), 255–261 (2007)
24. Kirsch, A., Mitzenmacher, M.: Less hashing, same performance: Building a better bloom filter. In: Azar, Y., Erlebach, T. (eds.) ESA 2006. LNCS, vol. 4168, pp. 456–467. Springer, Heidelberg (2006)
25. Rosenberg, J.: Interactive Connectivity Establishment (ICE): A Protocol for Network Address Translator (NAT) Traversal for Offer/Answer Protocols. RFC 5245 (Proposed Standard) (April 2010) Updated by RFC 6336
26. Boucadair, M., Penno, R., Wing, D.: Universal Plug and Play (UPnP) Internet Gateway Device - Port Control Protocol Interworking Function (IGD-PCP IWF). RFC 6970 (Proposed Standard) (July 2013)
27. Freedman, M.: Experiences with coralcdn: A five-year operational view. In: Proceedings of the 7th USENIX Conference on Networked Systems Design and Implementation, p. 7. USENIX Association (2010)
28. Freedman, M., Freudenthal, E., Mazieres, D.: Democratizing content publication with coral. In: Proceedings of the 1st Conference on Symposium on Networked Systems Design and Implementation, p. 18. USENIX Association (2004)
29. Han, L., Punceva, M., Nath, B., Muthukrishnan, S., Iftode, L.: Socialcdn: Caching techniques for distributed social networks. In: 2012 IEEE 12th International Conference on Peer-to-Peer Computing (P2P), pp. 191–202 (2012)

Implementing the WebSocket Protocol Based on Formal Modelling and Automated Code Generation

Kent Inge Fagerland Simonsen[1,2] and Lars Michael Kristensen[1]

[1] Department of Computing, Bergen University College, Bergen, Norway
{lmkr,kifs}@hib.no
[2] DTU Compute, Technical University of Denmark, Lyngby, Denmark
{kisi}@dtu.dk

Abstract. Model-based software engineering offers several attractive benefits for the implementation of protocols, including automated code generation for different platforms from design-level models. In earlier work, we have proposed a template-based approach using Coloured Petri Net formal models with pragmatic annotations for automated code generation of protocol software. The contribution of this paper is an application of the approach as implemented in the PetriCode tool to obtain protocol software implementing the IETF WebSocket protocol. This demonstrates the scalability of our approach to real protocols. Furthermore, we perform formal verification of the CPN model prior to code generation, and test the implementation for interoperability against the Autobahn WebSocket test-suite resulting in 97% and 99% success rate for the client and server implementation, respectively. The tests show that the cause of test failures were mostly due to local and trivial errors in newly written code-generation templates, and not related to the overall logical operation of the protocol as specified by the CPN model.

1 Introduction

The vast majority of software systems today can be characterised as concurrent and distributed systems as their operation inherently relies on protocols executed between independently scheduled software components and applications. The engineering of correct protocols can be a challenging task due to their complex behaviour which may result in subtle errors if not carefully designed. Furthermore, ensuring interoperability between independently made implementations is also challenging due to ambiguous protocol specifications. The use of formal modelling in combination with verification and model checking provides a prominent approach to the development of reliable protocol implementations.

Coloured Petri Nets (CPNs) [8] is formal language combining Petri Nets with a programming language to obtain a modelling language that scales to large systems. In CPNs, Petri Nets provide the primitives for modelling concurrency and synchronisation while the Standard ML programming language provides the primitives for modelling data and data manipulation. CPNs have been successfully applied for the modelling and verification of many protocols, including

K. Magoutis and P. Pietzuch (Eds.): DAIS 2014, LNCS 8460, pp. 104–118, 2014.

Internet protocols such as the TCP, DCCP, and DYMO protocols [2,11]. Formal modelling and verification have been useful in gaining insight into the operation of the protocols considered and have resulted in improved protocol specifications. However, earlier work has not fully leveraged the investment in modelling by also taking the step to automated code generation as a way to obtain an implementation of the protocol under consideration.

In earlier work [15], we have proposed the PetriCode approach and developed a supporting software tool [17] for automatically generating protocol implementations based on CPN models. The basic idea of the approach is to enforce particular modelling patterns and annotate the CPN models with code generation *pragmatics*. The pragmatics are bound to code generation templates and used to direct the model-to-text transformation that generates the protocol implementation. As part of earlier work, we have demonstrated the use of the PetriCode approach on small protocols. In addition, we have shown that our approach supports code generation for multiple platforms, and that it leads to code that is readable and also upwards and downwards compatible with other software [16].

The main contribution of this paper is to demonstrate that our approach and tool scale to support an industrial-sized protocol by automatically generating code for the WebSocket [5] protocol for the Groovy [7] platform. The WebSocket protocol is a relatively new protocol currently under development by the IETF. The WebSocket protocol makes it possible to upgrade an HTTP connection to an efficient message-based full-duplex connection. The WebSocket protocol address the performance problems of the HTTP protocol caused by the request-response interaction model and verbose headers. This is done by allowing HTTP to upgrade to a WebSocket connection in which a session is kept alive and messages may be transmitted in both directions freely with much lower overhead than with HTTP. WebSocket has already become a popular protocol for several web-based applications where bi-directional communication with low latency is needed such as games and media streaming services. The contributions of this paper include showing how we have been able to model the WebSocket protocol following the PetriCode modelling conventions, and to verify the model through state space exploration. Furthermore, we demonstrate in this paper that the generated code is interoperable with other WebSocket implementations, and we test the our implementation using the Autobahn WebSocket test-suite [18].

Outline. Section 2 presents the CPN model of the WebSocket protocol. In Sect. 3 we show how state space exploration was used to verify the operation of the model focusing on the proper establishment and termination of WebSocket connections. Section 4 describes the procedure to generate an implementation of the WebSocket protocol from the CPN model using the PetriCode tool. In Sect. 5, we present the results from testing the generated code by showing that it is interoperable with other WebSocket implementations and by employing the Autobahn WebSocket test-suite. Finally, in Sect. 6 we provide a discussion of related work, and sum up the conclusions and directions for future work. Due to space limitations, we refer to [8] for a detailed introduction to CPN concepts.

2   The CPN WebSocket Code Generation Model

The CPN model of the WebSocket protocol follows the structure imposed by our code generation approach, and consists of a set of modules hierarchically organised into three levels: the protocol systems level, the principal level, and the service level. In the following, we present representative parts of the CPN model which was constructed using CPN Tools [4].

Figure 1 shows the top-level module of the CPN model constituting the protocol system level. The protocol system consists of a Client and a Server principal as modelled by the two accordingly named *substitution transitions* drawn as rectangles with a double-lined border. These two substitution transitions are annotated with the ⟨⟨principal⟩⟩ code generation pragmatic to denote that they represent protocol principals. The Channel substitution transition annotated with the ⟨⟨channel⟩⟩ pragmatic represents the channel connecting the two principals. The two substitution transitions are connected by *places* (drawn as ellipses) modelling send and receive buffers for the client and server. The rectangular tags attached to the substitution transitions specify the name of the *submodule* which refines the compound behaviour represented by the substitution transition.

The Client principal level module is depicted in Fig. 2. It is the submodule associated with the Client substitution transition in Fig. 1. The principal level makes explicit the *services* offered by the principal by means of the ⟨⟨service⟩⟩ and ⟨⟨internal⟩⟩ pragmatics attached to substitution transitions. The ⟨⟨service⟩⟩ pragmatic is used to denote substitution transitions where the attached submodule represents a service that is intended to be used by the application employing the protocol. Substitution transitions annotated with ⟨⟨internal⟩⟩ represent services that are used internally in the protocol principal. It can be seen that the client has six external and two internal services. A principal level module also models the *internal state* of the principal via places annotated with the ⟨⟨state⟩⟩ pragmatic, and captures the life-cycle of the principal via places annotated with the ⟨⟨LCV⟩⟩ pragmatic. The life-cycle determines the possible orders in which the services can be invoked. Initially, the only ⟨⟨LCV⟩⟩-annotated place that contains a token is the READY place (top) which enables the OpenConnection service. After the OpenConnection service has completed, there will be a token on the OPEN place, and all the external services (except OpenConnection) will be enabled allowing the employing application to send and receive messages, send

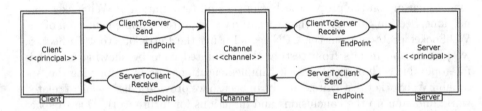

Fig. 1. The top level of the WebSocket protocol model

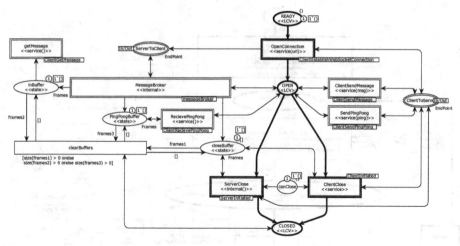

Fig. 2. The Client principal module

and receive ping and pong messages, and close the connection. The exchange of ping and pong messages provides a keep-alive mechanism in the protocol.

The MessageBroker module which is the submodule of the MessageBroker substitution transition is shown in Fig. 3. The MessageBroker is an example of an internal service. It is responsible for dispatching the incoming messages into the appropriate buffer represented in the module by places annotated with the ⟨⟨state⟩⟩ pragmatics. There is one such buffer for each of the message types: the inBuffer keeps text and binary messages, the pingpongBuffer keeps ping and pong messages, the closeBuffer keeps the closing messages while the fragments place keeps frames of messages that have not yet been completely received. The messages are dispatched by inspecting the type of the messages. The Message-Broker internal service is enabled when the WebSocket connection is in an OPEN state and the module captures the control flow in dispatching received messages as indicated by the places annotated with an ⟨⟨Id⟩⟩ pragmatic. The execution of the service starts at the transition ReceiveDataFrame. Then it enters a loop starting at place wait receive. At the transition receive a new frame is received. This is modelled as a single operation to keep the model at a high level of abstraction. This means that the details of actually receiving a message must be encoded in the code generation template associated with the ⟨⟨receive⟩⟩ pragmatic. If the frame is the last frame of a fragmented message, the entire message is reconstructed. Next, there is a branch in the model based on the Fin and Op-Code fields in the frame. The message is dispatched to either the inBuffer (data), PingPongBuffer, closeBuffer, or nonFinal. After the message or frame has been dispatched, the branches merge before the next iteration.

The getMessage service shown in Fig. 4 returns the next message in the buffer. This service will be used to illustrate code generation in Sect. 4.

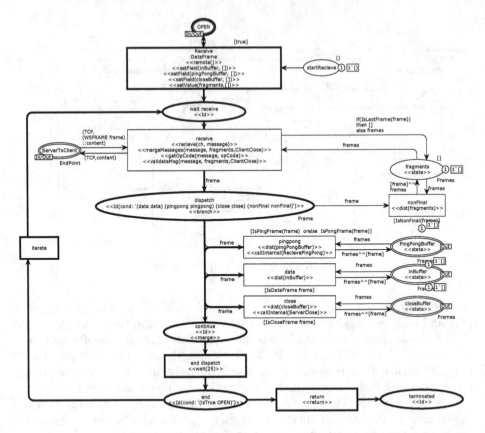

Fig. 3. The MessageBroker internal service

This is an example of a service with only a single transition. The transition is annotated with the ⟨⟨service⟩⟩, ⟨⟨getMessage⟩⟩ and ⟨⟨return⟩⟩ pragmatics. This models that the service is first entered, then the ⟨⟨getMessage⟩⟩ operation is performed, and the service terminates. The transition getMessage is only enabled when there is at least one message in the message buffer as modelled by the place inBuffer.

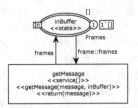

Fig. 4. The getMessage service

The complete CPN model consists of 19 modules. Each of the two principals have eight sub-modules which all correspond to the external and internal services in the protocol. In total, the model consists of 136 places and 84 transitions. This reflects the complexity of the protocol, but also the high-level nature of the model which has been important in keeping the number of elements manageable.

3   CPN WebSocket Model Verification

CPNs have a formal semantics which makes it possible to conduct model simulation and model checking (verification) prior to code generation. This is a major advantage of an approach based on a formal modelling language as this can be used to eliminate design errors prior to code generation and testing of the generated protocol implementation. CPN Tools used for construction of the WebSocket CPN model supports model checking of behavioural properties by means of *state space exploration*. The basic idea of state space exploration is to explore all the reachable states of the model to determine whether a model satisfies a given property or not. This means that state space exploration will exhaustively explore (test) all the possible executions of the CPN model. As the CPN model specifies the behaviour of both the client and the server, the state space exploration exercises the client against all the possible behaviours of the server and visa versa.

Our aim has been to apply state space exploration of the CPN model as a first test to eliminate possible errors in the logical specification of the WebSocket protocol. For this, we adopted a lightweight approach where we consider the following behavioural properties **P0**, **P1** and **P2** of the CPN model:

P0 From the initial state it is possible to reach states in which the WebSocket connection has been opened (i.e., both the client and the server are in the *open* state). In the model this means that the places names OPEN in the Client and the Server modules each have one token and none of the other places other places modelling the life-cycle of the principals have a token. It should be noted that we cannot establish that the WebSocket connection will eventually be opened since the server side may initiate a close before the client side is in the *open* state.

P1 All terminal states (i.e., states without enabled transitions) correspond to states in which the WebSocket connection has been properly closed (i.e., both the client and the server are in the *closed* state). In the model this means that the places named CLOSED in the Client and Server modules each have one token and that none of the other places modelling the life-cycle of the principals have a token.

P2 From any reachable state, it is always possible to reach a state in which the WebSocket connection has been properly closed. This means that independently of how messages are exchanged, it is always possible to properly close the WebSocket connection.

In order to check that in all terminal states both the client and the server are in the *closed* state, we wrote a simple query in the Standard ML language using functions that are built into CPN Tools. The query can be seen in Listing 1.1.

The functions `server_open` and `client_open` are predicates for the client and server that take a state as argument and return true if and only if the principal is in an open state, i.e., the place OPEN has one token, and all the other LCV places have no tokens. The functions `server_close` and `client_close`

Listing 1.1. The queries used to verify properties P0-P2

```
fun client_open (n) = (State.Client'CLOSED 1 n) = [] andalso
  (State.Client'OPEN 1 n) = [()] andalso (State.Client'READY 1 n) = [];

fun server_open (n) =
  (State.Server'CLOSED 1 n) = [] andalso (State.Server'OPEN 1 n) = [()] andalso
  (State.Server'Idle 1 n) = []    andalso (State.Server'READY 1 n) = [];

fun client_closed (n) = (State.Client'CLOSED 1 n) = [()]
  andalso (State.Client'OPEN 1 n) = [] andalso (State.Client'READY 1 n) = [];

fun server_pred (n) =
  (State.Server'CLOSED 1 n) = [()] andalso (State.Server'OPEN 1 n) = [] andalso
  (State.Server'Idle 1 n) = []     andalso (State.Server'READY 1 n) = [];

fun IsProperOpen(n) = server_open(n) andalso client_open(n);
fun IsProperClosed(n) = server_closed(n) andalso client_closed(n);

PredAllNodes(IsProperOpen) <> []              (* property P0 *)
List.all IsProperClosed (ListTerminalStates()); (* property P1 *)
HomeSpace(ListTerminalStates());               (* property P2 *)
```

Table 1. Results of verification of the WebSocket CPN model

Client Messages	Server messages	Nodes	Arcs	Time (secs)	Terminal states
yes	no	2747	9,544	1	2
no	yes	2867	9,956	2	2
yes	yes	39189	177,238	246	4

are similar for the case of closed. The predicates are used to obtain the predicates isProperOpen and isProperClosed that characterises properly open and closed states, respectively. The property P0 is checked using the query function PredAllNodes which returns all states satisfying a given predicate (in this case IsProperOpen). It is then checked whether the resulting list of states is non-empty. For establishing P1, we check that all terminal states in the state space which are returned by the built-in query function ListTerminalStates satisfies the IsProperClosed predicate. Finally, P2 is checked using the query function HomeSpace which checks if the list of nodes provided constitute a *home space*, i.e, constitute a set of states where at least one of the states can always be reached.

Table 1 summarises the results from the verification. We have considered three possible configurations of the model. One where the client sends data to the server; one where the server sends data to the client; and one where both the client and the server sends data. The table lists the number of Nodes and Arcs in the state space, the amount of Time used to generate the state space, and the number of Terminal States. For all configurations, we were able to establish the properties P0, P1 and P2 which provides confidence in the correctness of the model. During the verification process, several minor modelling errors were identified and fixed. For example, this lead to the inclusion of the clearBuffers transition (see Fig. 2) which was added to properly clean up message buffers and reduce the number of terminal states.

The major drawback with state space exploration techniques is the state explosion problem which means that the state space in many cases grows too large to be handled with the available computing power. It is interesting to observe that the size of the state space for the model described in Sect. 2 is relatively small for the configurations considered. This shows how our modelling approach makes it possible to construct models at a high-level of abstraction so that it is feasible to fully verify even industrial-sized protocols.

4   Automated Code Generation

In this section we describe the code generation process for the WebSocket protocol targeting the Groovy platform and illustrate it with examples of code generation templates and code snippets. Groovy is also the implementation language of the PetriCode tool [17] and has been chosen because it has several features that makes it easy to implement and debug templates including dynamic typing, closures and iterators.

The automatic code generation process, as implemented in the PetriCode tool, starts with a CPN model annotated with pragmatics. The model is first transformed into an intermediary representation in the form of an *abstract template tree* (ATT). The ATT reflects the hierarchical structure of the CPN model down to the service level. On the service level, the ATT contains *blocks* that are derived from the control flow path specified by the $\langle\langle \mathsf{Id} \rangle\rangle$ pragmatics of the service level modules. The next step in the code generation process is to traverse the ATT and emit code for each node by applying code generation templates bound to the pragmatics of a node. Pragmatics are bound to templates using *template bindings* which are defined in a domain specific language (DSL). When this is done, the code is stitched together using special markers in the generated code. The details are described in [15,17]. Our approach makes it possible to produce code for several platforms and programming languages. This is achieved by using different sets of code generating templates and binding them as appropriate to code generation pragmatics through the use of the DSL.

When the code generator, on its traversal through the ATT, encounters a node annotated with a $\langle\langle \mathsf{principal} \rangle\rangle$ pragmatic it executes the associated templates which, in the Groovy platform, defines a class. Then the traversal continues to the child nodes of the principal. When the generation traverses child nodes of a principal and encounters a node containing a $\langle\langle \mathsf{service} \rangle\rangle$ or $\langle\langle \mathsf{internal} \rangle\rangle$ pragmatic it executes the service template. The code generation for the principal is completed by replacing a special tag, %%yield%% with the result for the service template for all underlying services. The generated code of the client with declaration and method bodies omitted is shown in Listing 1.2. As can be seen when comparing with Fig 2, there is one method defined for each external and internal service. This comprises the API for the WebSocket client implementation with all the callable methods and their signature.

The template for the $\langle\langle \mathsf{service} \rangle\rangle$ pragmatic is shown in Listing 1.3. Lines 1-2 define a new method and its signature. The lines 3-12 set up preconditions (if applicable) based on the manipulation of places at the service level that are annotated

Listing 1.2. The generated code for the services in the client

```
1   class Client {
2   ...
3   def MessageBroker(){ ... }
4   def ServerClose(){ ... }
5   def OpenConnection(uri){ ... }
6   def ClientSendMessage(msg){ ... }
7   def ReceivePingPong(){ ... }
8   def SendPingPong(ping){ ... }
9   def ClientClose(){ ... }
10  def getMessage(){ ... }
11  }
```

Listing 1.3. The template bound to the $\langle\langle$service$\rangle\rangle$ pragmatic

```
1   def ${name}(${binding.getVariables()
2                   .containsKey("params") ? params.join(", ") : ""}){
3   <%
4     if(binding.variables.containsKey('pre_conds')){
5       for(pre_cond in pre_conds){
6         %>if(!$pre_cond) throw
7           new Exception('unfulfilled precondition: $pre_cond')
8         <%
9         if(!pre_sets.contains("$pre_cond")){%>$pre_cond = false<%}
10        }
11      }
12    %>
13      %%yield_declarations%%
14      %%yield%%
15      <%if(binding.variables.containsKey('post_sets')){
16        for(post_set in post_sets){
17          %>$post_set = true<%
18        }
19      }%>
20   }
```

with the $\langle\langle$LCV$\rangle\rangle$ pragmatic. The next two lines are place-holder tags that show where declarations and the method body will be inserted respectively. Finally, post-conditions are set and the method body ends in line 20.

Listing 1.4 shows the template for the $\langle\langle$getMessage$\rangle\rangle$ pragmatic used on the transition in Fig. 4. The template takes two parameters. The name of variable to set the next message to, and the name of the buffer to retrieve the next message from. First, the template checks to see if the buffer is not empty. If it is not empty, the first message is retrieved from the buffer. Then the payload is translated into a String or a byte array depending on the message type and the variable given in the first parameter to the pragmatic is set to the payload of the message. If the buffer is empty the variable given in the first parameter to the pragmatic is set to *null*.

The generated code for the getMessage service is shown in 1.5. Lines 1-4 and 21 are generated by the service template. The rest of the code, except from the return line, follows the template for $\langle\langle$getMessage$\rangle\rangle$ where the first and second parameters have been replaced with inBuffer and message respectively since those are the two parameters given to the pragmatic in Fig. 4.

Listing 1.4. The template for the ⟨⟨getMessage⟩⟩ pragmatic

```
1   if(${params[1]} != null && ${params[1]}.size() > 0){
2     ${params[0]} = ${params[1]}.remove(0)
3     byte[] bArr = new byte[${params[0]}.payLoad.size()]
4     for(int i = 0; i < bArr.length; i++){
5       bArr[i] = ${params[0]}.payLoad.get(i)
6     }
7     if(${params[0]}.opCode == 1){
8       ${params[0]} = new String(bArr)
9     }else if(${params[0]}.opCode == 2) {
10      ${params[0]} = bArr
11    }
12  }else{
13    ${params[0]} = null
14  }
15  %%VARS: ${params[0]}, ${params[1]}%%
```

Listing 1.5. The generated code for the getMessage service in the client

```
1   def getMessage(){
2     /*vars: [__TOKEN__:, message:]*/
3     def __TOKEN__
4     def message
5     //getMessage
6     if(inBuffer != null && inBuffer.size() > 0){
7       message = inBuffer.remove(0)
8       byte[] bArr = new byte[message.payLoad.size()]
9       for(int i = 0; i < bArr.length; i++){
10        bArr[i] = message.payLoad.get(i)
11      }
12      if(message.opCode == 1){
13        message = new String(bArr)
14      }else if(message.opCode == 2) {
15        message = bArr
16      }
17    }else{
18      message = null
19    }
20    return message
21  }
```

In order to generate code for the WebSocket protocol, we reused 10 templates from the library of templates provided by PetriCode. In addition, 22 new templates were needed, including two templates that override existing templates. New templates were needed because the WebSocket protocol has many features we have not encountered with earlier examples, such as receiving and interpreting binary messages, and validating handshakes and frames.

5   Testing the Generated WebSocket Implementation

We validated the operation and interoperability of the generated code in two ways. First, we created test drivers for the generated WebSocket implementation to connect to the example chat server and client [1] that comes with the GlassFish Application Server [14]. Secondly, we submitted the generated implementation to the Autobahn Testsuite [18] version 0.5.5[1].

---

[1] The test results can be seen at http://t.k1s.org/wsreport

Listing 1.6. The code for the client runner

```
1   def client = new Client()
2   client.OpenConnection(new URI("ws://localhost:31337/chat/websocket"))
3   def t = Thread.start {
4     while(true){
5       def msg =  client.getMessage()
6       if(msg) println "RECEIVED: $msg"
7       Thread.sleep(1000)
8   }}
9   client.ClientSendMessage("${args[0]} joined")
10  BufferedReader br = new BufferedReader(new InputStreamReader(System.in))
11  while(true){
12    print "#: "
13    def msg = br.readLine()
14    if(msg == "#quit"){
15      client.ClientClose()
16      try{ Thread.wait(1000) }
17      catch(Exception ex){  }
18      System.exit(0)
19    } else if(msg == "#close"){
20      client.ClientClose()
21    }else{
22      client.ClientSendMessage("${args[0]}: $msg")
23    }
24  }
```

Chat Application. The code for the chat client using the generated API (cf. Listing 1.2) is shown in Listing 1.6. The chat client uses the generated WebSocket protocol as an API given the signatures of the principal level. The client begins by creating a `Client` object from the generated code and opens a WebSocket connection to the server. Then, a thread is started to receive messages which polls the client object for new messages and prints any received messages to the console. After the message receiving thread is started, the client sends a message notifying the server that the client has joined the chat. Finally, the client enters an infinite loop that listens to the console for messages and sends any messages to the server. The server is implemented in a similar way using the generated `Server` class as the server-side WebSocket API.

Listing 1.6 demonstrates that our approach is upwards compatible, i.e., that the services of the generated code can easily be used by third party software. A key feature that provides this is that we include the API in the model as the services at the principal level of the CPN model.

Figure 5 shows the chat client (upper right) and server (lower right) running together with the web-based chat client from [1]. The web-based client has only been modified to connect to the server using the generated API by changing a hard-coded server address. We also tested that the chat client is able to connect and communicate with a chat-server from [1].

Autobahn Test-suite. The Autobahn WebSocket test-suite provides comprehensive validation of server and client implementations of the WebSocket protocol. The test-suite has been used by several high-profile projects to develop and validate WebSocket implementations including the Firefox and Jetty projects. When running the Autobahn test-suite several problems with the implementation were

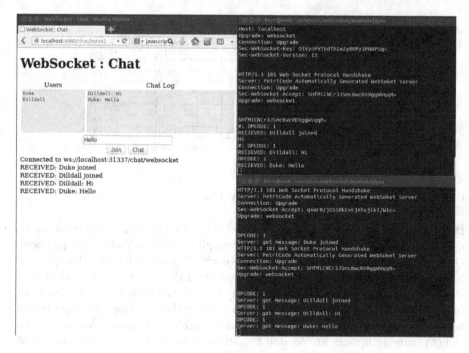

Fig. 5. Chat server and client using the generated API (right) and a web-based chat client connected to the same server (left)

discovered. Most of the problems were simple oversights in the code generation templates that were easily fixed once they were identified. An example of the trivial problems that were not evident when running the chat application was that the HTTP header lines were terminated with LF instead of the mandated CRLF. However, one change to the CPN model was necessary. This was related to fragmented messages where we added a buffer for temporarily storing frames of unfinished messages and a transition to distributing non-final frames. This was necessary because a WebSocket endpoint should be able to handle control messages intermingled with fragmented messages. The new elements, which can be seen in Fig. 3, are the place fragments, the transition nonFinal, and the arcs connected to those two elements.

A summary of the result for the final Autobahn tests can be seen in Table 2. The Autobahn test suite contains 301 tests cases for the client and server. For the client, 10 test cases fail and for the server, 4 test cases fail. The extra test cases that fail on the client concern performance with large messages. The test cases that fail for both the server and client are UTF-8 parser errors. This is because the Java implementation of UTF-8 parsers is more lenient than the Autobahn test-suite expects. Therefore, we had to create our UTF-8 validator which fails to identify some UTF-8 errors.

Table 2. Results for the Autobahn tests

Tests	Server Passed	Client Passed
1. Framing (text and binary messages)	16/16	16/16
2. Pings/Pongs	11/11	11/11
3. Reserved bits	7/7	7/7
4. Opcodes	10/10	10/10
5. Fragmentation	20/20	20/20
6. UTF-8 handling	137/141	137/141
7. Close handling	38/38	38/38
9. Limits/Performance	54/54	48/54
10. Auto-Fragmentation	1/1	1/1

6   Conclusions and Related Work

In this paper we have shown that the PetriCode code generation approach can be applied to industrial sized protocols as exemplified by the WebSocket protocol. Obtaining the implementation was achieved with limited effort even though quite a few new templates were created. We have found that the template provides an effective way to force the code to be modular. This means that the templates can be developed in a certain degree of isolation, giving the developer the opportunity to concentrate on getting a single template right at a time. Therefore, even though many templates are created for only a single protocol, this is an efficient way to prototype protocols based on a CPN model.

Compared to previous examples, the WebSocket model had many more services. This makes the principal level somewhat harder to read and suggests that some kind of mechanism of grouping the services in several layers might be advantageous. At the service level, the models are approximately the same size as in previous examples. The readability of the service level modules can also be controlled by offloading behaviour to pragmatics such as we do for the ⟨⟨receive⟩⟩ pragmatic in the message broker. All in all, the WebSocket model shows that we can make code generation models for real protocols without necessarily losing descriptiveness.

We have also showed that the code generation model can be verified by state space exploration. This highlights a major advantage of using CPN models which are directly executable. This allows us to perform analysis on high-level models and thereby keep the state spaces small. Although the verification presented only considers basic connection establishment and termination properties, other more elaborate properties including liveness properties can be checked using similar techniques. We are also working on using the sweep-line method, and advanced state space exploration method, to alleviate the state space explosion problem.

Finally, we have validated the automatically generated WebSocket implementation both by applying it to a well-known example in the form of the example chat application which is distributed with the GlassFish Application server and also by using the Autobahn test-suite which thoroughly tests most aspects of WebSocket protocol implementations.

To the best of our knowledge there does not exist any examples of using model-based techniques for generating an implementation of the WebSocket protocol in the literature. However, there exists a few examples for other industrial sized protocols. In [12] PP-CPNs, another class of Petri Nets, was used to generate code for the DYMO routing protocol for the Erlang platform. In our approach, we have a more flexible code generation approach through pragmatics that allows us to create new custom templates for new situations. Another approach to code generation is exemplified by the RENEW tool [13]. RENEW uses a simulation based approach where the implementation is a simulation of the underlying Petri Net. The direct use of simulation code makes it harder to meaningfully inspect the generated programs.

Other formalisms such the Specification and Description Language (SDL) has also been used as a starting point for code generation. For example, an early warning system for earthquake was developed using SDL in combination with UML [6,3]. Both simulation and prototype code were generated using C++ as the target language. Our approach differs from the above mentioned approaches by the flexibility in abstraction level because of our pragmatics, by being platform independent by simply substituting templates and by the fact that we model the API explicitly at the service level and thereby easy interoperability with third-party software. Our approach also allows us to model the service interface, which is not available to the same degree in PP-CPNs and Renew. Another approach to generating software for reactive systems from UML models is the SPACE method [10] and its tool Arctis. This approach employs collaborations to compose services. The collaborations are then transformed into state machines that are executed together with Java snippets which are bound to actions of the collaborations. This approach relies on the state machines to either be translated to code or executed directly by some other tool. This is in contrast to our approach where we generate code directly instead of going through other formalisms and tools. MACE [9] is a textual state-transition language that is used to create distributes systems. It uses a compiler to compile the textual state-transition language into C++ code. This means that MACE is not as platform independent as our template-based approach is. In MetaEdit+ [19], models are mapped to some underlying formalism on which analysis is then performed. This tends to produce larger state space sizes compared with our approaches where the model is executable and allows verification at a high level of abstraction.

In the future we will apply more advanced state-space techniques, such as the sweep-line method, in order to do a more through verification of the model with larger and more complex configurations. Furthermore, we will investigate how errors in code generated by PetriCode can be traced back to the relevant pragmatics and model elements.

References

1. Gupta, A.: Chat Sever using WebSocket in GlassFish 4,
   https://blogs.oracle.com/arungupta/entry/chat_sever_using_
   websocket_totd
2. Billington, J., Gallasch, G.E., Han, B.: A Coloured Petri Net Approach to Protocol Verification. In: Desel, J., Reisig, W., Rozenberg, G. (eds.) ACPN 2003. LNCS, vol. 3098, pp. 210–290. Springer, Heidelberg (2004)

3. Brumbulli, M., Fischer, J.: SDL Code Generation for Network Simulators. In: Kraemer, F.A., Herrmann, P. (eds.) SAM 2010. LNCS, vol. 6598, pp. 144–155. Springer, Heidelberg (2011)
4. CPN Tools. Home Page, http://cpntools.org/
5. Fette, I., Melnikov, A.: The websocket protocol (2011), http://tools.ietf.org/html/rfc6455
6. Fischer, J., Kühnlenz, F., Ahrens, K., Eveslage, I.: Model-based Development of Self-organizing Earthquake Early Warning Systems. In: Proceedings of MATHMOD (2009)
7. Groovy. Project Web Site, http://groovy.codehaus.org
8. Jensen, K., Kristensen, L.M., Wells, L.: Coloured Petri Nets and CPN Tools for modelling and validation of concurrent systems. International Journal on Software Tools for Technology Transfer 9(3-4), 213–254 (2007)
9. Killian, C.E., Anderson, J.W., Braud, R., Jhala, R., Vahdat, A.M.: Mace: language support for building distributed systems. ACM SIGPLAN Notices 42, 179–188 (2007)
10. Kraemer, F.A., Bræk, R., Herrmann, P.: Compositional Service Engineering with Arctis. Telektronikk 105(2009.1) (2009)
11. Kristensen, L.M., Simonsen, K.I.F.: Applications of Coloured Petri Nets for Functional Validation of Protocol Designs. In: Jensen, K., van der Aalst, W.M.P., Balbo, G., Koutny, M., Wolf, K. (eds.) Transactions on Petri Nets and Other Models of Concurrency VII. LNCS, vol. 7480, pp. 56–115. Springer, Heidelberg (2013)
12. Kristensen, L.M., Westergaard, M.: Automatic Structure-Based Code Generation from Coloured Petri Nets: A Proof of Concept. In: Kowalewski, S., Roveri, M. (eds.) FMICS 2010. LNCS, vol. 6371, pp. 215–230. Springer, Heidelberg (2010)
13. Kummer, O., Wienberg, F., Duvigneau, M., Schumacher, J., Köhler, M., Moldt, D., Rölke, H., Valk, R.: An Extensible Editor and Simulation Engine for Petri Nets: Renew. In: Cortadella, J., Reisig, W. (eds.) ICATPN 2004. LNCS, vol. 3099, pp. 484–493. Springer, Heidelberg (2004)
14. Oracle Corporation. GlassFish Application Server, https://glassfish.java.net/
15. Simonsen, K.I.F., Kristensen, L.M., Kindler, E.: Generating Protocol Software from CPN Models Annotated with Pragmatics. In: Iyoda, J., de Moura, L. (eds.) SBMF 2013. LNCS, vol. 8195, pp. 227–242. Springer, Heidelberg (2013)
16. Simonsen, K.I.F.: An Evaluation of Automated Code Generation with the PetriCode Approach. Submitted to: PNSE 2014 (2014)
17. Simonsen, K.I.F.: PetriCode: A Tool for Template-Based Code Generation from CPN Models. In: Counsell, S., Núñez, M. (eds.) SEFM 2013. LNCS, vol. 8368, pp. 151–163. Springer, Heidelberg (2014)
18. Tavendo GmbH. Autobahn|Testsuite, http://autobahn.ws/testsuite/
19. Tolvanen, J.-P.: Metaedit+: domain-specific modeling for full code generation demonstrated. In: Proc. of OOPSLA 2004, pp. 39–40. ACM (2004)

GreenBrowsing: Towards Energy Efficiency in Browsing Experience

Gonçalo Avelar and Luís Veiga

Instituto Superior Técnico - ULisboa
INESC-ID Lisboa, Portugal
luis.veiga@inesc-id.pt,
goncalo.avelar@ist.utl.pt

Abstract. Web 2.0 allowed for the enhancement and revamp of web pages' aesthetics and interaction mechanics. Moreover, current web browsers function almost as a *de facto* operating system: they run "apps", along with other background plug-ins. All of which have an increasing energy impact, proportional to the rate of appearance of more sophisticated browser mechanisms and web content. We present the architecture of GreenBrowsing. A system that proposes the provision of (i) a Google Chrome extension to monitor, rationalize and reduce the energy consumption of the browsing experience and (ii) a Certification Scheme for dynamic web pages, based on web-page performance counter statistics and analysis, performed on the cloud.

Keywords: web browser, web page certification, green IT, energy efficiency, power consumption.

1 Introduction

The creation of more capable technologies (HTML5, CSS, JavaScript) improved connectivity and content delivery in the last few years. Now, website contents that are sent to web browsers require substantial resource usage, while being processed, in order to perform reasonably and match user expectations. This ultimately leads to increased power consumption, being reasonable to assume that power consumption is increased with resource usage. Users should be aware of the power cost induced by visiting each web page, locally and remotely, relative to the power cost of other web pages, allowing them to choose between two or more functionally equivalent set of web pages the least power hungry.

Hence, we consider web browsers as suitable candidates for the deployment of a power management solution, and present GreenBrowsing: a system that aims at extending Google Chrome [1], in its *Desktop* and *Laptop* versions, in order to decrease the energy costs of browsing, by managing idle tabs regarding resource usage and adapting the content of selected tabs, to perform energy-related optimizations. GreenBrowsing also aims at certification of web pages, to ensure that users become aware of which web domains are the less green and

K. Magoutis and P. Pietzuch (Eds.): DAIS 2014, LNCS 8460, pp. 119–125, 2014.
© IFIP International Federation for Information Processing 2014

which pages are more resource hungry. We assume many devices where Chrome will be running are Wi-Fi enabled.

The main challenge of this work is to provide mechanisms that effectively reduce the energy cost when browsing the web, without sacrificing much of the responsiveness and performance that is expected, and (at the same time) to provide means to certify web pages energetically-wise, in order to inform users of the energetic inefficiencies related to different web page visualizations.

2   Related Work

In this section, we address Dynamic Power Management (DPM), since its rationale is very similar to part of what we want to achieve with GreenBrowsing – to reduce the resource usage of idle tabs (unselected, not visualized at some moment). We will also address some of the work done in terms of energy-related certification.

Dynamic Power Management. Dynamic Power Management (DPM) techniques try to achieve power dissipation reductions by employing policies that reduce the performance of system components (typically by inducing them into some sort of sleep state) when they are idle, while under performance constraints [4]. Therefore the greatest challenge in DPM is to know when and what components should be put to sleep, to the end of achieving the minimum power dissipation possible, given the performance constraints imposed. In that case, the policy is said to be optimal.

One pioneering example of DPM is the work by Qiu et al. [8] that follows a stochastic approach. The authors describe a continuous-time Markov Decision Process (MDP) as the system's power model. Markov Decision Processes can be thought of as state machines whose state transitions depend on actions performed and are done with a certain probability. Each state transition has a score assigned to it, consisting of the product of the probability of that transition occurring, the energy cost of that transition and a certain weight. The idea is to minimize the sum of all scores over time, by iteratively adjusting the weights. After a certain number of iterations, an optimal policy is guaranteed to be found.

Shen et al. propose an approach [10] to dynamic power management using Reinforced Learning, specifically the *Q-Learning* algorithm, in order to learn an optimal Markov Decision Process, after a certain set-up time, as the power manager executes. Each state-action pair of the MDP has a quality value associated with it, that is computed considering the expected average power and request delay caused by the action taken at each state. In this way, the policy can be consistently adjusted, in order to consider states that minimize the delay cost at each state and expected average power wasted, given the decisions taken.

Energy-Related Certification. In terms of Energy-related Certification, there is some work targeting different kinds of computational systems, both mobile devices [11] and software [3]. However, to our knowledge, there is no substantial volume of work regarding certification of web pages. Camps et al. proposed a solution to do so [5], still, certification is done accounting only for the downloadable content of pages, disregarding other system metrics (e.g. CPU).

3   Architecture

There are two major sub-systems that comprise the GreenBrowsing architecture (Fig. 1): a Google Chrome Extension, and a Web Page Certification Back End.

Chrome Extension Sub-system. The main roles of the Chrome Extension are *to reduce the resource consumption of tabs*, and *to send to the Back End resource-related data*, that can be used to certify web pages in terms of their energy consumption while being accessed.

Chrome Extension modules. The **Observer-Controller-Adapter (OCA)** provides interfaces for gathering performance counters of each running tab and the process(es) it is associated with. It also provides interfaces for issuing commands to tabs and the operating system itself. Moreover, it will be possible to adapt web pages through this module. The **Certification Front End** consists in the necessary code to communicate with the Certification Back End, to the end of sending performance counters. The **Certification Renderer** has the functionality needed to render an energy-related rating of each web page, based on its certification. It serves visualization purposes mostly.

The **Policy Enforcer** includes all the power reduction logic and can use the OCA interface, to gather performance counters and to issue content adaptation and power reduction related commands. In particular, it includes the *Tab management Policy*, which is responsible for choosing when to reduce performance and resource consumption of tabs.

The **Web Page Certifier** fetches performance counters, through the Observer-Controller-Adapter. It also interfaces with the Certification Front End to send the counters gathered to the Back End (for energy-related certification of web pages). Communications with the Certification Renderer are done to visually associate an energetic certification stamp to each domain and page, on each tab.

The **Profile Manager** displays graphical interface the user might use to further tune GreenBrowsing to his/her preferences. Interfacing with the Policy Enforcer is done to communicate user preferences.

Resource Usage & Tab Management. We distinguish *Selected Tabs* (at each time, only one tab is selected in Chrome and therefore only one tab is visualized) from *Idle Tabs* (every tab that is available and open, but that is not selected).

Selected Tabs can have the resources they use reduced by employing adaptation techniques defined by the user. Examples are the removal of images or sound.

Regarding Idle Tabs, they are said to be *Suspended* when they are target of any power management action (other than adaptation), in order to reduce their

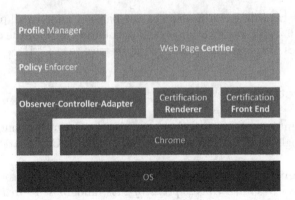

Fig. 1. Layered View of The Chrome Extension

resource usage. In this way, we make only two assumptions regarding general browsing behavior, that will be considered when managing tabs:

- **Last Time Usage.** Tabs that were accessed more recently are more likely to be accessed again and therefore are less likely to be suspended.
- **Distance to other Tabs.** We also assume that tabs closer to the selected tab are more likely to be accessed, and therefore they are also less likely to be suspended.

We can infer power consumption from resource usage. In particular, the CPU intensiveness (in terms of load and number of cycles), and the bandwidth in terms of bits-per-second, all of which on average and over fixed periods of time.

Moreover, we intend to leverage recent work in our research group, addressing resource management and elastic scheduling in cloud infrastructures. It takes into account relative efficiency of scheduled resources usage, with application progress monitoring, factoring in perceived utility depreciation by users when resources are sub-allocated [14,13,12]. We address similar constraints in this work, as the best possible performance is only achievable with high resource usage, and we want users to obtain experiences that combine adequate performance within the intended energy consumption profile.

Analytics and Certification Back End Sub-system. The Certification Back End Sub-System (Fig. 2) is moved to a separate remote sub-system, intended to be deployed in the cloud, as a way to reduce the computational intensiveness that would be required by the extension, in the certification process. The Back End has the objective of *providing a clear and meaningful notion of how much energy web pages consume*, certifying also the domain of each web page, to give an overall notion of how *green* that domain's pages are.

Certification Back End Components.

- A **Network Communication task** that receives energy-related web page certification requests and forwards these requests to specialized workers;
- **Analytics Certifier tasks** that do the work of certifying a given page, according to a specific certification model.
- A **Certification Modeler task** that adjusts the certification model, taking into account all the resource data sent from the extension subsystem. For performance purposes, this design sub-intends the usage of specified **Worker Tasks** to whom parts of the analytical calculations are *mapped* to. The results of processing data at workers are assembled back to the Modeler Task, as soon as they are ready.
- An **Analytics Data Store** that stores the models used in the certification of pages and tuples with information relative to the performance counters of each page;

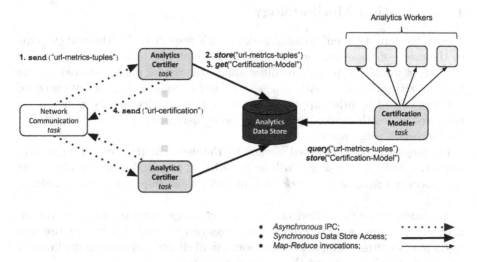

Fig. 2. The Communicating tasks of the Back End

The Certification Process. The power consumption induced by web pages can be indirectly determined by some of the performance counters gathered on the Chrome Extension. For each page, the metrics considered are: (i) the CPU clock cycles, or percentage, because of their relation to power consumption [9] and (ii) the network bandwidth in terms of bit-rate, because wireless communications are one of the major causes for power consumption on Wi-Fi enabled devices [7].

The information sent from the Chrome Extension to the Certification Back End is a 4-tuple $<domain, page\text{-}url, number\text{-}of\text{-}cycles, bits/sec>$.

In order to divide different resource consumption patterns in different ranks, we can employ the clustering algorithm *Expectation-Maximization* (EM) [6] in order to find no fewer than 4 categories of certification (clusters), in a 2-dimensional space that comprehends one dimension for the CPU clock cycles and another for the network bandwidth bit-rate. If we consider that each dimension has 2 possible qualitative scores (good or bad) depending on the actual value of the measurement obtained for a certain dimension, there are 2^2 possible score combinations. Hence, 4 possible categories or clusters. More scores per dimension can be considered for increased detail.

Each one of the clusters is associated with a vector called the centroid. We assume that given two categories whose clusters C_i and C_j have centroid c_i and c_j, respectively, if $||c_i|| > ||c_j||$ (where $||c_i||$ denotes the norm of c_i), then the vectors that are members of the cluster C_i are more power consuming than the ones of C_j. In this way and by assessing which cluster an incoming observation is more likely belonging to (given the clusters obtained with previous observations), we are able to classify, and therefore certify, pages regarding power consumption.

To certify domains, the arithmetic mean and the geometric mean of the page classifications (obtained with the method explained previously) are computed.

4   Evaluation Methodology

The evaluation of GreenBrowsing is done with respect to (1) the energy gains by the usage of the extension and (2) perceived latency by the user.

Since it would be difficult to differentiate the actual energy wasted by the browser with idle pages, with and without our extension, from noisy energetic patterns caused by other applications and system activity, energy gains can be measured indirectly through other more direct metrics: (i) *CPU load per tab* and (ii) *bandwidth usage per tab*.

For measuring the perceived latency by the user, the (i) *overall time to load pages* (i.e. fully render pages) will be considered. It will also be considered the (ii) *processing time at the Back End*, in order to account for late certification stamps.

To conduct the evaluation of the resource usage optimization that Green-Browsing provides, a set of typical web pages can be used. These comprise web pages of news sites, social networks, sports, mail clients and multimedia in order to provide a rich and varied Web page suite to test.

To extract the measurements intended for each metric, we use the Performance Profiling Capabilities along with the Timeline monitor [2], from the Chrome DevTools suite.

5   Conclusions

We observe that in spite of the modern (and resource hungry) web technology, the processing of web pages/applications done by web browsers leads to considerable power consumption, on end-users devices. This hinted us that browsers should be tailored to power management extensions. To that end, we presented the architecture of GreenBrowsing, comprised of a Chrome Extension to manage the power consumption of tabs and a web page energy-related Certification Back End, to be deployed on the cloud. The implementation of GreenBrowsing is ongoing for further evaluation according to the methodology proposed.

References

1. Chrome browser, https://www.google.com/intl/en/chrome/browser/
2. Chrome devtools, https://developers.google.com/chrome-developer-tools/
3. Amsel, N., Tomlinson, B.: Green Tacker: A Tool for Estimating the Energy Consumption of Software. In: CHI 2010 Extended Abstracts on Human Factors in Computing Systems, CHI EA 2010. ACM, New York (2010)
4. Benini, L., Bogliolo, A., Cavallucci, S., Riccó, B.: Monitoring System Activity for OS-directed Dynamic Power Management. In: Proceedings of the 1998 International Symposium on Low Power Electronics and Design. ACM, New York (1998)
5. Camps, F.: Web browser energy consumption (2010)
6. Dempster, A.P., Laird, N.M., Rubin, D.B.: Maximum likelihood from incomplete data via the EM algorithm. Journal of The Royal Statistical Society, Series B 39(1), 1–38 (1977)
7. Perrucci, G.P., Fitzek, F.H.P., Widmer, J.: Survey on Energy Consumption Entities on the Smartphone Platform. In: VTC Spring, pp. 1–6. IEEE (2011)
8. Qiu, Q., Pedram, M.: Dynamic Power Management Based on Continuous-time Markov Decision Processes. In: Proceedings of the 36th Annual ACM/IEEE Design Automation Conference, DAC 1999. ACM, New York (1999)
9. Rodrigues, R., Koren, I.K.S.: A Study on the Use of Performance Counters to Estimate Power in Microprocessors. IEEE Transactions on Circuits and Systems II: Express Briefs (2013)
10. Shen, H., Tan, Y., Lu, J., Wu, Q., Qiu, Q.: Achieving Autonomous Power Management Using Reinforcement Learning. ACM Trans. Des. Autom. Electron. Syst. 18(2) (2013)
11. de Siebra, C., Costa, P., Marques, R., Santos, A.L.M., da Silva, F.Q.B.: Towards a Green Mobile Development and Certification. IEEE (2011)
12. Silva, J.N., Veiga, L., Ferreira, P.: A2HA - Automatic and Adaptive Host Allocation in Utility Computing for Bag-of-Tasks. Journal of Internet Services and Applications (JISA) 2(2), 171–185 (2011)
13. Simão, J., Veiga, L.: QoE-JVM: An Adaptive and Resource-Aware Java Runtime for Cloud Computing. In: Meersman, R., et al. (eds.) OTM 2012, Part II. LNCS, vol. 7566, pp. 566–583. Springer, Heidelberg (2012)
14. Simão, J., Veiga, L.: Flexible SLAs in the Cloud with Partial Utility-driven Scheduling. In: IEEE 5th International Conference on Cloud Computing Technology and Science (CloudCom 2013) - Best-Paper Award Runner-up. IEEE (December 2013)

Making Operation-Based CRDTs Operation-Based

Carlos Baquero, Paulo Sérgio Almeida, and Ali Shoker

HASLab/INESC TEC and Universidade do Minho, Portugal

Abstract. Conflict-free Replicated Datatypes (CRDT) are usually classified as either state-based or operation-based. However, the standard definition of op-based CRDTs is very encompassing, allowing even sending the full-state, blurring the distinction. We introduce *pure* op-based CRDTs, that can only send operations to other replicas, drawing a clear distinction from state-based ones. Datatypes with commutative operations can be trivially implemented as pure op-based CRDTs using standard reliable causal delivery. We propose an extended API – *tagged reliable causal broadcast* – that provides causality information upon delivery, and show how it can be used to also implement other datatypes having non-commutative operations, through the use of a *PO-Log* – a partially ordered log of operations – inside the datatype. A semantically-based PO-Log compaction framework, using both causality and what we denote by *causal stability*, allows obtaining very compact replica state for pure op-based CRDTs, while also benefiting from small message sizes.

1 Introduction

Eventual consistency [1] is a relaxed consistency model that is often adopted by large-scale distributed systems [2–5] where losing availability is normally not an option, whereas delayed consistency is acceptable. In eventually consistent systems, data replicas are allowed to temporarily diverge, provided that they can eventually be reconciled into a common consistent state. Reconciliation (or merging) used to be error-prone, being application-dependent, until new datatype-dependent models like the Conflict-free Replicated DataTypes (CRDTs) [6, 7] were recently introduced. CRDTs allow both researchers and practitioners to design correct replicated datatypes that are always available, and are guaranteed to eventually converge once all operations are known to all replicas. Though CRDTs have been successfully deployed in practice [2], a lot of work is still required to improve their designs and performance.

CRDTs support two complementary designs: operation-based (or simply, op-based) and state-based. In principle, op-based designs are supposed to disseminate operations, while state-based designs disseminate object states. In op-based designs [8, 7], the execution of an operation is done in two phases: *prepare* and *effect*. The former is performed only on the local replica and looks at the operation and current state to produce a message that aims to represent the operation, which is then shipped to all replicas. Once received, the representation of the

K. Magoutis and P. Pietzuch (Eds.): DAIS 2014, LNCS 8460, pp. 126–140, 2014.

operation is applied remotely using *effect*. Different replicas are guaranteed to converge as long as messages are disseminated through a reliable causal broadcast messaging middleware, and *effect* is designed to be commutative for concurrent operations. On the other hand, in a state-based design [9, 7], an operation is only executed on the local replica state. A replica propagates its local changes to other replicas through shipping its entire state. A received state is incorporated with the local state via a *merge* function that, deterministically, reconciles the *merged* states. To maintain convergence, *merge* is defined as a join: a least upper bound over a join-semilattice [9, 7].

Typically, state-based CRDTs support ad hoc dissemination of states and can handle duplicate and out-of-order delivery of messages without breaking causal consistency; however, they impose complex state designs and store extra meta-data. On the other hand, in the systems where the message dissemination layer guarantees reliable causal broadcast, operation-based CRDTs have more advantages as they can allow for simpler implementations, concise replica state, and smaller messages.

In standard op-based CRDTs the designer is given much freedom in defining *prepare*, namely using the state in an arbitrary way. This is needed to have the *effect*s of concurrently invoked data-type operations commute, and thus provide replica convergence despite the absence of causality information in current causal delivery APIs. This forces current op-based designs to include causality information in the state to be used in *prepare*, sent in messages, and subsequently used in *effect*. The designer ends up intervening in many components (the state, *prepare*, *effect*, and *query* functions) in an ad hoc way. This can result in large complex state structures and also large messages.

Currently, a *prepare* not only builds messages that duplicate the information already present in the middleware (even if it is not currently made available), but causality meta-data is often incorporated in the object state, hence, reusing design choices similar to those used in state-based approaches. Such designs, made to work assuming little messaging guarantees, impose larger state size and do not fully exploit causal delivery guarantees. This freedom in current op-based designs is against the spirit of 'sending operations', and leads to confusion with the state-based approach. Indeed, in the current op-based framework, a *prepare* can return the full state, and an *effect* can do a full state-merge (which mimics a state-based CRDT) [9, 7].

We believe that the above weaknesses can be avoided if the causality meta-data can be provided by the messaging middleware. Causal broadcast implementations already posses that information internally, but it is not exposed to clients. In this paper we propose and exploit such an extended API to achieve both simplicity and efficiency in defining op-based CRDTs.

We introduce a *Pure* Op-Based CRDT framework, in which *prepare* cannot inspect the state, being limited to returning the operation (including potential parameters). The entire logic of executing the operation in each replica is delegated to *effect*, which is also made generic (i.e., not datatype dependent). For pure op-based CRDTs, we propose that the object state is a *partially ordered log of operations – a PO-Log* . Causality information is provided by an extended messaging API: *tagged reliable causal broadcast* (TRCB). We use this information to preserve convergence and also design compact and efficient CRDTs through a *semantically based PO-Log compaction* framework, which makes use of a datatype-specific *obsolescence* relation, defined over timestamp-operation pairs.

Furthermore, we propose an extension that improves the design and implementation of op-based CRDTs through decomposing the state into two components: a PO-Log (as before), and a causality-stripped-component which, in many cases, will be simply a standard sequential datatype. The idea is that operations are kept only transiently in the PO-Log, but once they become *causally stable*, causality meta-data is stripped, and the operations are stored in the sequential datatype. This reduces the storage overhead to a level that was never achieved before in CRDTs, neither state-based nor op-based.

2   System Model and Notations

2.1   System and Fault Models

The system is composed of a fixed set of nodes, each with a globally unique identifier in a set I. Nodes execute operations at different speeds and communicate using asynchronous message passing, abstracted by reliable causal broadcast (or gossip in the brief discussion about state-based CRDTs). Messages can be lost, reordered or duplicated, and the system can experience arbitrary, but transient, partitions. A node can fail by crashing and can recover later on; upon recovery, the last durable state of a node is assumed to be intact (not destroyed). We do not consider Byzantine faults. A fixed membership is assumed for causal broadcast: messages towards a node that is temporarily crashed or partitioned are buffered until it becomes reachable.

For presentation purposes, and without loss of generality, we consider a single object that is replicated at each node; each replica initially starts with the same state. Once a datatype operation is locally applied on a replica, the latter can diverge from the other replicas, but it may eventually convergence as new operations arrive. A local operation is applied atomically on a given replica.

2.2   Definitions and Notations

Σ denotes the type of the state. $\mathcal{P}(V)$ denotes a *power set* (the set of all subsets of V). The initial state of a replica i is denoted by $\sigma_i^0 \in \Sigma$. Operations are taken from a set O and can include arguments (in which case they are surrounded by brackets, e.g., inc and $[\mathsf{add}, v]$). We use total functions $K \to V$ and maps (partial functions) $K \hookrightarrow V$ from keys to values, both represented as sets of pairs (k, v). Given a function m, the notation $m\{k \mapsto v\}$ maps k to v, and behaves like m on other keys, e.g., Fig. 1a.

$$\Sigma = I \to \mathbb{N} \quad \sigma_i^0 = \{(r,0) \mid r \in I\}$$
$$\mathsf{apply}_i(\mathsf{inc}, m) = m\{i \mapsto m(i) + 1\}$$
$$\mathsf{eval}_i(\mathsf{rd}, m) = \sum_{r \in I} m(r)$$
$$\mathsf{merge}_i(m, m') = \{(r, \max(m(r), m'(r))) \mid r \in I\}$$

$$\Sigma = \mathbb{N} \quad \sigma_i^0 = 0$$
$$\mathsf{prepare}_i(\mathsf{inc}, n) = \mathsf{inc}$$
$$\mathsf{effect}_i(\mathsf{inc}, n) = n + 1$$
$$\mathsf{eval}_i(\mathsf{rd}, n) = n$$

(a) State-based counter (b) Op-based counter

Fig. 1. Counter CRDT in both state-based and op-based approaches

2.3 Conflict-Free Replicated Data Types Approaches

State-Based CRDTs. These CRDTs maintain a *state* representation of an object, which evolves according to a well defined partial order. A state evolves via executing datatype operations or through applying a *join* operation, which merges any two states, thus resolving conflicting states. State-based replicas of an object converge by always shipping the entire local state, and applying the join operation on received states. State-based CRDTs are costly as the entire replica state must be shipped, but they demand less guarantees from the network because joins are designed to be commutative, idempotent, and associative. Figure 1a represents a state-based increment-only counter. In this paper we do not address state-based CRDTs.

Operation-Based CRDTs. In op-based CRDTs, representations of operations issued at each node are reliably broadcast to all replicas. Once all replicas receive all issued operations (on all nodes), they eventually converge to a single state, if: (a) operations are broadcast via a reliable causal broadcast, and (b) 'applying' representations of concurrently issued operations is commutative. Op-based CRDTs can often have a simple and compact state since they can rely on the exactly-once delivery properties of the broadcast service, and thus do not have to explicitly handle non-idempotent operations. Figure 1b represents an op-based increment-only counter. The state contains a simple integer counter that is incremented for each inc operation that is delivered.

The API of the underlying middleware at each node i provides an interface method $\mathsf{cbcast}_i(m)$ that sends a message m using causal broadcast. When applying an operation o at some node i with state σ, function $\mathsf{prepare}_i(o, \sigma)$ is called returning a message m. This message is then broadcast by calling $\mathsf{cbcast}_i(m)$. Once m is delivered to each destination node j, $\mathsf{effect}_j(m, \sigma)$ is called, returning the new replica state σ'. For each node that broadcasts a given operation, the broadcast, the corresponding local delivery, and the *effect* on the local state are executed atomically. When a query operation q is performed, $\mathsf{eval}_i(q, \sigma)$ is invoked. eval takes the query and the state as input and may return a result (leaving the state unchanged).

$$\Sigma = \mathbb{N} \times \mathcal{P}(I \times \mathbb{N} \times V) \quad \sigma_i^0 = (0, \{\})$$

$$\mathsf{prepare}_i([\mathsf{add}, v], (n, s)) = [\mathsf{add}, v, i, n+1]$$

$$\mathsf{effect}_i([\mathsf{add}, v, i', n'], (n, s)) = (n' \text{ if } i = i' \textbf{ otherwise } n, s \cup \{(v, i', n')\})$$

$$\mathsf{prepare}_i[\mathsf{rmv}, v], (n, s)) = [\mathsf{rmv}, \{(v', i', n') \in s \mid v' = v\}]$$

$$\mathsf{effect}_i([\mathsf{rmv}, r], (n, s)) = (n, s \setminus r)$$

$$\mathsf{eval}(\mathsf{rd}, (n, s)) = \{v \mid (v, i', n') \in s\}$$

Fig. 2. Standard op-based observed-remove add-wins set

3 Pure Op-Based CRDTs

In this section we introduce *pure op-based CRDTs* and discuss what datatypes can be implemented as pure using standard causal broadcast.

Definition 1 (Pure op-based CRDT). *An op-based CRDT is pure if messages contain only the operation (including arguments, if any). Given operation o and state σ,* prepare *is always defined as:*

$$\mathsf{prepare}(o, \sigma) = o.$$

This means that prepare cannot build an arbitrary message depending on the current state; in fact, in pure op-based CRDTs the operation can be immediately broadcast without even reading the replica state. As an example, the counter in Fig. 1b is pure op-based, while the observed-remove set implementation (from [6]) in Fig. 2 is not, because in a remove operation prepare builds a set of triples present in the current state, to be removed from the state at each replica when performing effect.

3.1 Pure Implementations of Commutative Datatypes

As we discuss now, the pure model of op-based CRDTs can be directly applied, using standard reliable causal broadcast [10], to implement datatypes whose operations are commutative.

Definition 2 (Commutative datatype). *A concurrent datatype is commutative if (a) for any operations f and g, their (sequential) invocation commutes: $f(g(\sigma)) = g(f(\sigma))$, and (b) concurrent invocations are defined as equivalent to some linearization.*

Commutative datatypes reflect a *principle of permutation equivalence* [11] stating that "If all sequential permutations of updates lead to equivalent states, then it should also hold that concurrent executions of the updates lead to equivalent states".

As the extension to concurrent scenarios follows directly from their sequential definition, with no room for design choices, commutative datatypes can have a

$$\Sigma = \mathbb{N} \quad \sigma_i^0 = 0$$
$$\mathsf{prepare}_i(o, \sigma) = o$$
$$\mathsf{effect}_i(\mathsf{inc}, n) = n + 1$$
$$\mathsf{effect}_i(\mathsf{dec}, n) = n - 1$$
$$\mathsf{eval}_i(\mathsf{rd}, n) = n$$

$$\Sigma = \mathcal{P}(V) \quad \sigma_i^0 = \{\}$$
$$\mathsf{prepare}_i(o, \sigma) = o$$
$$\mathsf{effect}_i([\mathsf{add}, v], s) = s \cup \{v\}$$
$$\mathsf{eval}_i(\mathsf{rd}, s) = s$$

(a) Pure PN-counter

(b) Pure grow-only set

Fig. 3. Pure op-based CRDTs for commutative datatypes

standard sequential specification and implementation. As such, a pure op-based CRDT implementation is trivial: as when using the standard causal broadcast, the message returned from **prepare**, containing the operation, will arrive exactly once at each replica, it is enough to make **effect** consist simply in applying the received operation to the state, over a standard sequential datatype, i.e., defining for any datatype operation o:

$$\mathsf{effect}_i(o, \sigma) = o(\sigma).$$

Two examples of commutative datatypes, presented in Fig. 3, are: a PN-counter with **inc** and **dec** operations; a grow-only set (G-set) with **add** operation. Both cases use a standard sequential datatype for the replica state, and applying **effect** is just invoking the corresponding operation in the sequential datatype. Both these examples explore commutativity and rely on the exactly-once delivery, leading to a trivial pure implementation.

3.2   Non-commutative Datatypes

In the case where datatype operations are not commutative, such as a set with **add** and **rmv** operations, where $\mathsf{add}(v, \mathsf{rmv}(v, s)) \neq \mathsf{rmv}(v, \mathsf{add}(v, s))$, we have two reasons that prevent **effect** from being simply applying the operation over a sequential datatype.

One reason is that, even when the semantics of concurrent invocations can be defined as equivalent to some linearization of those operations, the messages corresponding to concurrent operations will be, in general, delivered in different orders in different replicas. Therefore, as the operations do not commute, simply applying them in different orders in different replicas makes replicas diverge. Under the assumption of causal delivery and the aim of convergence, **effect** must always be commutative, and therefore, cannot be defined directly as operations that are not commutative themselves. It must be defined in some other way.

The other reason is that it is useful to specify concurrent datatypes in which the outcomes of concurrent executions are not equivalent to some linearization. The best example is the multi-value register, where two concurrent writes make a read in their causal future return a set with both values written. This outcome could not arise under a sequential specification.

state:
$\quad \sigma_i \in \Sigma$
on operation$_i(o)$:
$\quad$ tcbcast$_i$(prepare(o, σ_i))
on tcdeliver$_i(m, t)$:
$\quad \sigma_i := $ effect(m, t, σ_i)
on tcstable$_i(t)$:
$\quad \sigma_i := $ stable(t, σ_i)

Algorithm 1. Distributed algorithm for node i using tagged causal broadcast

In general, a concurrent datatype will have a specification depending on the partial order of operations over the datatype. Given that such information about that partial order is already present in metadata in causal delivery middleware, we propose an approach for pure op-based CRDTs for general non-commutative datatypes that leverages this metadata, now exposed by an extended causal delivery API, what we call *tagged reliable causal broadcast*.

4 Tagged Reliable Causal Broadcast (TRCB)

A common implementation strategy for a reliable causal broadcast service [12] is to assign a vector clock to each message broadcast and use the causality information in the vector clock to decide at each destination when a message can be delivered. If a message arrives at a given destination before causally preceding messages have been delivered, the service delays delivery of that message until those messages arrive and are delivered. Unlike totally ordered broadcast, which requires a global consensus on the delivery order, causal broadcast can progress with local decisions. For general datatypes, causal consistency is likely the strongest consistency criteria compatible with an always-available system that eventually converges [13].

By leveraging this information, we can specify a reliable causal broadcast service with an extended API, and refer to its broadcast operation at each replica i as tcbcast$_i(m)$. Algorithm 1, running on each node i, shows how the events triggered by the tagged causal delivery service are used to invoke the generic functions for pure op-based CRDTs: prepare, effect and stable; these functions, in different variants, will be discussed in the following sections. This extended service provides nodes with information about two aspects.

4.1 Partial Order

The first salient difference is that message delivery on each node i, given by the event tcdeliver$_i(m, t)$, provides not only the message m itself, but also the vector clock timestamp t corresponding to m. When implementing pure op-based CRDTs, in which only the operations are sent in messages, we can use the timestamp supplied by the service upon delivery in the definition of effect;

i.e., we can have $\mathsf{effect}(o, t, s)$ as a function of the operation, the timestamp and the current state.

As we will see in the next section, this information about the partial order can be embedded in the state in a general way so that effect is commutative and reference implementations of general possibly non-commutative datatypes can be obtained, following their specification. Moreover, in Sect. 6 we will see how realistic efficient pure CRDTs can be obtained, in which the use of this causality information, together with the semantics of the datatype operations is essential.

4.2   Causal Stability

Definition 3 (Causal Stability). *A clock t, and corresponding message, is causally stable at node i when all messages subsequently delivered at i will have timestamp $t' \geq t$;*

This implies that no message with a timestamp t' concurrent with t can be delivered at i when t is causally stable at i. This notion differs from classic message stability [10] in which a message is stable if it has been received by all nodes. Here we not only need this to happen but also that no further concurrent messages may be delivered. Therefore, causal stability is a stronger notion, implying classic message stability.

The extended API will provide an event $\mathsf{tcstable}_i(t)$ which will be triggered when it is determined that t is stable at i. The middleware at node i can check if timestamp t is causally stable at i by checking if a message with timestamp $t' \geq t$ has already been delivered at i from every other other node j, i.e.:

$$\mathsf{tcstable}_i(t) \text{ when } \forall j \in I \setminus \{i\} \cdot \exists t' \in \mathsf{delivered}_i() \cdot \mathsf{origin}(t') = j \wedge t \leq t',$$

where $\mathsf{delivered}_i()$ returns the set of messages that have been delivered at node i, while $\mathsf{origin}(t)$ denotes the node from where the message corresponding to t has been sent. To evaluate this clause efficiently, the middleware only needs to keep the most recently delivered timestamp from each origin [14].

We will see in Sect. 6 how causal stability can be used to reduce CRDT state size, by stripping causality information from causally stable operations.

5   Pure CRDTs Based on a Partially Ordered Log

Having a tagged causal broadcast service, it is now possible to obtain a universal mechanism for obtaining pure reference implementations for any (possibly non-commutative) concurrent datatype in which semantics are defined over the partial order of operations.

The reference mechanism, presented in Fig. 4, uses a uniform notion of state for a replica: a *partially ordered log of operations*, what we call a PO-Log. This uses the ordering information offered by the messaging middleware to keep information about concurrent operations, not trying to impose a local total-order over them, contrary to a classic sequential log.

$$\Sigma = T \hookrightarrow O \quad \sigma_i^0 = \{\}$$

$\mathsf{prepare}(o, s) = o$

$\mathsf{effect}(o, t, s) = s \cup \{(t, o)\}$

$\qquad \mathsf{eval}(q, s) = [\text{datatype-specific query function over partial order}]$

Fig. 4. PO-Log based reference implementation for pure op-based CRDTs

$$\Sigma = T \hookrightarrow O \quad \sigma_i^0 = \{\}$$

$\mathsf{prepare}(o, s) = o \qquad\qquad\qquad (\text{with } o \text{ either } [\mathsf{add}, v] \text{ or } [\mathsf{rmv}, v])$

$\mathsf{effect}(o, t, s) = s \cup \{(t, o)\}$

$\qquad \mathsf{eval}(\mathsf{rd}, s) = \{v \mid (t, [\mathsf{add}, v]) \in s \wedge \nexists(t', [\mathsf{rmv}, v]) \in s \cdot t < t'\}$

Fig. 5. PO-Log based observed-remove add-wins set

The PO-Log can be defined as a map (a partial function) $T \hookrightarrow O$ from messagesage timestamps (as given by the tagged causal broadcast service) to the corresponding operation. Here we have a universal datatype-independent definition of effect as:

$$\mathsf{effect}(o, t, s) = s \cup \{(t, o)\},$$

which is trivially commutative, as needed. Only the query functions will need datatype-specific definitions according to desired semantics. Their definition over the PO-Log will typically be a direct transposition of their specification.

Figure 5 shows a pure PO-Log based implementation of an *add-wins* observed-remove set over the new tcbcast service. The *add-wins* semantic is defined in the rd query function: the set of values reported to be in the set are those values that have been added with no rmv causally in the future of the add. Another example, shown in Fig. 6, is a multi-value register. Here a read reports the set of all concurrently written values that have not been subsequently overwritten.

These reference implementations are not realistic to be actually used, namely because state size in each replica is linear with the number of operations. They are a starting point from which actual efficient implementations can be derived, by semantically based PO-Log compaction, as we show in the next section. But they are relevant, as they provide a clear description of the concurrent semantics of the replicated datatype. This is possible since we are capturing the partial ordered set of all operations delivered to each replica. (A similar approach to express the semantics is found in [15] when relating to the *visibility* relation.)

6   Semantically Based PO-Log Compaction

We now show how PO-Log based CRDTs can be made efficient by performing PO-Log compaction. There are two ingredients that we explore. The first one is to prune the PO-Log after each operation is delivered in the effect, so as to keep

$$\Sigma = T \hookrightarrow O \quad \sigma_i^0 = \{\}$$

$$\mathsf{prepare}([\mathsf{wr}, v], s) = [\mathsf{wr}, v]$$

$$\mathsf{effect}([\mathsf{wr}, v], t, s) = s \cup \{(t, [\mathsf{wr}, v])\}$$

$$\mathsf{eval}(\mathsf{rd}, s) = \{v \mid (t, [\mathsf{wr}, v]) \in s \land \nexists (t', [\mathsf{wr}, v']) \in s \cdot t < t'\}$$

Fig. 6. PO-Log based multi-value register

$$\Sigma = T \hookrightarrow O \quad \sigma_i^0 = \{\}$$

$$\mathsf{prepare}(o, s) = o$$

$$\mathsf{effect}(o, t, s) = \{x \in s \mid \neg\, \mathsf{obsolete}(x, (t, o))\} \cup \{(t, o) \mid x \in s \Rightarrow \neg\, \mathsf{obsolete}((t, o), x)\}$$

$$\mathsf{obsolete}() = [\text{datatype-specific relation to identify obsolete operations}]$$

$$\mathsf{eval}(q, s) = [\text{datatype-specific query function over partial order}]$$

Fig. 7. Reference implementation for PO-Log compaction

the minimum number of operations such that all queries return the same result as when the full PO-Log is present. The second one is to explore causal stability information, to discard timestamp information for elements once they become stable, possibly merging some elements.

6.1 Exploring Causality Information

As the possibility of discarding operations while preserving semantics is datatype dependent, we propose a unified framework which includes the PO-Log, prepare, and a more sophisticated effect which makes use of a datatype-specific relation to discard operations made irrelevant by newer arrivals, according to both operation content and corresponding timestamp, as shown in Fig. 7.

This relation between pairs timestamp-operation – $\mathsf{obsolete}((t, o), (t', o'))$ – is used by effect in the following way: when a new pair (t, o) is delivered to a replica, effect discards from the PO-Log all elements x such that $\mathsf{obsolete}(x, (t, o))$ holds; also, the delivered pair (t, o) is only inserted into the PO-Log if it is not redundant itself, according to the current elements, i.e., if for any current x in the PO-Log $\mathsf{obsolete}((t, o), x)$ is false. This relation is not restricted to be a partial-order, but can be a more general relation, allowing, e.g., a newly arrived operation to discard others in the PO-Log without necessarily being itself added.

It is easy to see by simple induction that this execution mechanism provides the invariant that for any two different pairs p_1 and p_2 in the PO-Log, $\mathsf{obsolete}(p_1, p_2)$ is false. This invariant allows reasoning about the datatype, namely to be able to write simplified query functions that give the same result over the compact PO-Log as the original query functions over the full PO-Log.

An observed-remove add-wins set using the PO-Log compaction framework can be seen in Fig. 8 (which presents only the datatype-specific functions). Here it can be clearly seen that obsolete was defined directly according to the essence

$$\text{obsolete}((t, [\text{add}, v]), (t', [\text{add}, v'])) = t < t' \land v = v'$$
$$\text{obsolete}((t, [\text{add}, v]), (t', [\text{rmv}, v'])) = t < t' \land v = v'$$
$$\text{obsolete}((t, [\text{rmv}, v]), x) = \text{true}$$
$$\text{eval}(\text{rd}, s) = \{v \mid (t, [\text{add}, v]) \in s\}$$

Fig. 8. Observed-remove add-wins set with PO-Log compaction

$$\text{obsolete}((t, [\text{wr}, v]), (t', [\text{wr}, v'])) = t < t'$$
$$\text{eval}(\text{rd}, s) = \{v \mid (t, [\text{wr}, v]) \in s\}$$

Fig. 9. Multi-value register with PO-Log compaction

of the datatype: a subsequent add obsoletes a previous add of the same value; a rmv obsoletes an add of the same value. The more interesting rule is that any rmv is made obsolete by any other timestamp-operation pair; this implies that a rmv can only exist as the single element of a PO-Log (if it was inserted into an empty PO-Log), being discarded once other operation arrives (including another rmv), and never being inserted into a non-empty PO-Log. This reflects the *add-wins* nature, in which the role of a rmv is basically to discard same-value additions in its causal past. Under the now compacted PO-Log, the query function rd can be defined in a simple way, and clearly seen to give the same result as the original one over the full PO-Log (in Fig. 5).

Another example where PO-Log compaction leads to an efficient datatype is the multi-value register, in Fig. 9, where it is obvious the effect of a write in making all writes in its causal past obsolete, regardless of value written. The set of concurrent writes that have not been made obsolete will be returned in a read, which is equivalent to the original definition in Fig. 6 over the full PO-Log.

6.2   Exploring Causal Stability Information

The second component of PO-Log compaction involves using causal stability to strip logical clocks from the PO-Log. From the definition of causal stability, if some pair (t, o) is in the PO-Log, with t causally stable, all future deliveries (t', o') used in effect will be causally in the future, i.e., $t' > t$.

Because effect only compares, through obsolete, new arrivals and PO-Log elements – but never PO-Log elements among themselves – and for a stable t, all future deliveries will be causally in its future, the value of t is no longer needed, and it can be replaced by any timestamp that is less than all other timestamps: the bottom ($\bot$) of the timestamp domain; e.g., a null map $\{\}$ for a vector-clock timestamp.

In practice this means that, instead of having timestamps that are maps or vectors with size linear on the number of replicas, we can have a special marker denoting bottom (e.g. a null pointer). This greatly diminishes the size of a replica state for two reasons. For some CRDTs where size may be a problem,

$$\Sigma = \mathcal{P}(O) \times (T \hookrightarrow O) \quad \sigma_i^0 = (\{\}, \{\})$$

$$\mathsf{prepare}(o, (s, p)) = o$$

$$\mathsf{effect}(o, t, (s, p)) = (s', p'), \text{ where}$$

$$s' = \{x \in s \mid \neg\mathsf{obsolete}((\bot, x), (t, o))\}$$

$$p' = \{x \in p \mid \neg\mathsf{obsolete}(x, (t, o))\}$$

$$\cup \{(t, o) \mid x \in p \Rightarrow \neg\mathsf{obsolete}((t, o), x)\}$$

$$\mathsf{stable}(t, (s, p)) = (s \cup p(t), p \setminus \{(t, p(t))\})$$

$$\mathsf{obsolete}() = [\text{datatype-specific relation to identify obsolete operations}]$$

$$\mathsf{eval}(q, (s, p)) = [\text{datatype-specific query function over PO-Log}]$$

Fig. 10. Full PO-Log compaction framework exploring causal stability

like sets of integers, values may take considerably less space than timestamps, which constitute the great percentage of state size; stripping a timestamp from an element can be a huge improvement per element. The second reason is that, again in such scenarios with large states, the percentage of elements in the PO-Log that are not yet causally stable will be quite small, with most already stable. This means that this optimization, which gives good results per element, will be applied to most elements, leading to a large overall improvement.

Instead of being a map $T \hookrightarrow O$, the PO-Log is split in $\mathcal{P}(O) \times (T \hookrightarrow O)$, detaching into a plain set all operations that have stable timestamps (i.e., making the $\bot$ timestamp implicit). A new framework using the split PO-Log is presented in Fig. 10. In effect a new delivery possibly discards elements both from the set of operations and the partially ordered set of operations; elements from the latter are used to decide on the addition of the new delivery, as before. (The possibility of a stable operation obsoleting a new arrival, in its causal future, is not considered, but this can easily be changed if some example shows its usefulness.) In stable, the operation corresponding to a stable timestamp is fetched, to be added to the set and the corresponding entry removed from the map.

The PO-Log split allows implementations tailored to specific datatypes to achieve further improvements. As an example, an or-set will have only $(t, [\mathsf{add}, v])$ entries in its PO-Log (except for the singleton $\{(t, [\mathsf{rmv}, v]\}$) which can be prevented by a special rule); when elements become causally stable, only the value v needs to be migrated and not the operation name. The set component of the split PO-Log becomes a plain set of values, allowing traditional implementations of sets to be used; e.g., a bitmap if the datatype is for a dense set of integers.

By exploiting both causality and causal stability information, made available by the proposed tagged causal delivery API, we have paved the way for these optimizations that allow pure op-based CRDTs that are much more suitable for large datatypes than current designs.

7   Related Work

Weakly Consistent Replication. The design of replicated systems that are always available and eventually converge can be traced back to historical designs in [14, 16, 17], among others. Lazy Replication [18] allows enforcing causal consistency, but may apply concurrent operations in different orders in different replicas, possibly leading to divergence if operations are not commutative; TSAE [19] also either applies concurrent operations in possibly different orders, or allows enforcing a total order compatible with causality, at the cost of delaying message delivery. Both these systems use a message log, the former with complete causality information, but the log is *pre-delivery*, unseen by the application: operations are applied sequentially to the current state and queries use only the state. In our framework the PO-Log is *post-delivery*, being part of the datatype state, maintains causality information and is used in query operations.

Conflict-Free Replicated Data Types. The formalization of the commutativity requirements for concurrent operations in replicated datatypes was introduced in [8, 20], and that of the state based semi-lattices was presented in [9]. Afterwards, the integration of the two models with many extensions was presented in Conflict-free Replicated Datatypes [6, 7]. Currently, CRDTs have made their way into the industry through designing highly available scalable systems in cloud databases like RIAK [2], and mobile gaming industry such as Rovio [21].

Message Stability. The notion of message stability was defined in [10] to represent a message that has been received by all recipients; each replica can discard any message it knows to be stable after delivering it. Similar notions are used in Lazy Replication [18] and TSAE [19]. In all these cases the aim is message garbage collection. Our definition of *causal stability* is the stronger notion that *no more concurrent messages will be delivered*; we use it inside the datatype to discard causality information while keeping the operation. Causal stability is close to what is used in the mechanics of Replicated Growable Arrays (RGA) [20], although no definition is presented there.

Message Obsolescence. Semantically reliable multicast [22] uses the concept of *message obsolescence* to avoid delivering messages made redundant by some newly arrived message, where obsolescence is a strict partial order that is a subset of causality, possibly relating messages from the same sender or totally ordered messsages from different senders. Our obsolescence relation is more general, being defined on clock-operation pairs, and can relate concurrent messages. Also, it is defined per-datatype, being used inside each datatype, post-delivery.

8   Conclusions

In this paper we improved the CRDT model by introducing the stricter notion of *pure* op-based, and establishing a clear frontier with state-based models.

We have shown which pure datatypes are possible over off-the-shelf causal delivery middleware and then introduce an extended API, *tagged* reliable broadcast, that supports the remaining datatypes, those non-commutative in their sequential specifications. Supported by this API, that conveys causal information present in the middleware, we were able to define a partially ordered log, named PO-Log, that supports a clear semantic description and abstract implementation of each concurrent datatype.

To obtain efficient implementations we developed a framework for semantic compaction of a PO-Log and, in a final step, resorted to a notion of *causal stability* to determine when it is safe to strip PO-Log entries of their causal order metadata. This final step allows eventually moving all data to a standard sequential datatype, or a local database, and harvest the efficiency gains of re-using existing optimized data structures and database engines.

Having exemplified the framework with relevant non-trivial datatypes (replicated sets and registers) we expect that future research, and the existing developer community, can apply these techniques to other derived datatypes, such a maps, graphs, and sequences.

Acknowledgments. We thank Marek Zawirski, Ricardo Gonçalves and anonymous reviewers for comments that helped improve this work. Project Norte-01-0124-FEDER-000058 is co-financed by the North Portugal Regional Operational Programme (ON.2 O Novo Norte), under the National Strategic Reference Framework (NSRF), through the European Regional Development Fund (ERDF). Project FCOMP-01-0124-FEDER-037281 financed by National Funds by FCT, and by ERDF. Funding from the European Union Seventh Framework Programme (FP7/2007-2013) under grant agreement 609551, SyncFree project.

References

1. Vogels, W.: Eventually consistent. ACM Queue 6(6), 14–19 (2008)
2. Cribbs, S., Brown, R.: Data structures in Riak. In: Riak Conference (RICON), San Francisco, CA, USA (October 2012)
3. Bailis, P., Ghodsi, A.: Eventual consistency today: Limitations, extensions, and beyond. Queue 11(3), 20:20–20:32 (2013)
4. Terry, D.B., Theimer, M.M., Petersen, K., Demers, A.J., Spreitzer, M.J., Hauser, C.H.: Managing update conflicts in Bayou, a weakly connected replicated storage system. In: Symp. on Op. Sys. Principles (SOSP), Copper Mountain, CO, USA, pp. 172–182. ACM SIGOPS, ACM Press (1995)
5. DeCandia, G., Hastorun, D., Jampani, M., Kakulapati, G., Lakshman, A., Pilchin, A., Sivasubramanian, S., Vosshall, P., Vogels, W.: Dynamo: Amazon's highly available key-value store. In: Symp. on Op. Sys. Principles (SOSP), Stevenson, Washington, USA. Operating Systems Review, vol. 41, pp. 205–220. Assoc. for Computing Machinery (October 2007)

6. Shapiro, M., Preguiça, N., Baquero, C., Zawirski, M.: A comprehensive study of Convergent and Commutative Replicated Data Types. Rapp. Rech. 7506, Institut National de la Recherche en Informatique et Automatique (INRIA), Rocquencourt, France (January 2011)

7. Shapiro, M., Preguiça, N., Baquero, C., Zawirski, M.: Conflict-free replicated data types. In: Défago, X., Petit, F., Villain, V. (eds.) SSS 2011. LNCS, vol. 6976, pp. 386–400. Springer, Heidelberg (2011)

8. Letia, M., Preguiça, N., Shapiro, M.: CRDTs: Consistency without concurrency control. Rapp. Rech. RR-6956, Institut National de la Recherche en Informatique et Automatique (INRIA), Rocquencourt, France (June 2009)

9. Baquero, C., Moura, F.: Using structural characteristics for autonomous operation. Operating Systems Review 33(4), 90–96 (1999)

10. Birman, K., Schiper, A., Stephenson, P.: Lightweight causal and atomic group multicast. ACM Trans. Comput. Syst. 9(3), 272–314 (1991)

11. Bieniusa, A., Zawirski, M., Preguiça, N., Shapiro, M., Baquero, C., Balegas, V., Duarte, S.: Brief announcement: Semantics of eventually consistent replicated sets. In: Aguilera, M.K. (ed.) DISC 2012. LNCS, vol. 7611, pp. 441–442. Springer, Heidelberg (2012)

12. Schmuck, F.B.: The use of efficient broadcast protocols in asynchronous distributed systems. Technical Report TR 88-928, Cornell University (1988)

13. Mahajan, P., Alvisi, L., Dahlin, M.: Consistency, availability, and convergence. Technical Report UTCS TR-11-22, Dept. of Comp. Sc., The U. of Texas at Austin, Austin, TX, USA (2011)

14. Wuu, G.T.J., Bernstein, A.J.: Efficient solutions to the replicated log and dictionary problems. In: Symp. on Principles of Dist. Comp (PODC), Vancouver, BC, Canada, pp. 233–242 (August 1984)

15. Burckhardt, S., Gotsman, A., Yang, H., Zawirski, M.: Replicated data types: specification, verification, optimality. In: Jagannathan, S., Sewell, P. (eds.) POPL, pp. 271–284. ACM (2014)

16. Johnson, P.R., Thomas, R.H.: The maintenance of duplicate databases. Internet Request for Comments RFC 677, Information Sciences Institute (January 1976)

17. Quarterman, J.S., Hoskins, J.C.: Notable computer networks. Commun. ACM 29(10), 932–971 (1986)

18. Ladin, R., Liskov, B., Shrira, L., Ghemawat, S.: Providing high availability using lazy replication. ACM Trans. Comput. Syst. 10(4), 360–391 (1992)

19. Golding, R.A.: Weak-consistency group communication and membership. PhD thesis, University of California Santa Cruz, Santa Cruz, CA, USA (December 1992) Tech. Report no. UCSC-CRL-92-52

20. Roh, H.G., Jeon, M., Kim, J.S., Lee, J.: Replicated Abstract Data Types: Building blocks for collaborative applications. Journal of Parallel and Dist. Comp. 71(3), 354–368 (2011)

21. Rovio Entertainment Ltd.: Rovio gaming (2013), http://www.rovio.com/en

22. Pereira, J., Rodrigues, L., Oliveira, R.: Semantically reliable multicast: Definition, implementation, and performance evaluation. IEEE Trans. Comput. 52(2), 150–165 (2003)

Autonomous Multi-dimensional Slicing for Large-Scale Distributed Systems

Mathieu Pasquet[1,*], Francisco Maia[2], Etienne Rivière[3], and Valerio Schiavoni[3]

[1] École Normale Supérieure Rennes, France
mathieu.pasquet@ens-rennes.fr
[2] High-Assurance Software Laboratory, INESC TEC & University of Minho, Portugal
fmaia@di.uminho.pt
[3] Université de Neuchâtel, Switzerland
first.last@unine.ch

Abstract. Slicing is a distributed systems primitive that allows to autonomously partition a large set of nodes based on node-local attributes. Slicing is decisive for automatically provisioning system resources for different services, based on their requirements or importance. One of the main limitations of existing slicing protocols is that only single dimension attributes are considered for partitioning. In practical settings, it is often necessary to consider best compromises for an ensemble of metrics.

In this paper we propose an extension of the slicing primitive that allows multi-attribute distributed systems slicing . Our protocol employs a gossip-based approach that does not require centralized knowledge and allows self-organization. It leverages the notion of domination between nodes, forming a partial order between multi-dimensional points, in a similar way to SkyLine queries for databases. We evaluate and demonstrate the interest of our approach using large-scale simulations.

Keywords: Slicing, Self-organization, Skyline, Gossip-based protocols.

1   Introduction

Very large-scale heterogeneous distributed systems will be commonplace with the advent of connected objects, the internet-of-things and in general with the massive increase in the number of machines connected through multiple networks. Such very large systems can no longer be operated using the system services and support mechanisms that were designed and implemented for moderate to small scale distributed systems. In particular, system-level primitives and services, that were once supported by centralized entities or by the close collaboration of a few synchronized nodes, may not be adequate or even possible to use in these scenarios. The characteristics of large-scale heterogeneous systems call instead for fully decentralized and autonomous protocols. Such protocols can provide system-wide fundamental system services but do not require centralized components or complex synchronization between nodes. Self-organization is another key requirement. It denotes the ability of a system or service to seamlessly

---

* Work done while interning at Université de Neuchâtel.

K. Magoutis and P. Pietzuch (Eds.): DAIS 2014, LNCS 8460, pp. 141–155, 2014.
© IFIP International Federation for Information Processing 2014

adapt to dynamic conditions, such as nodes heterogeneity, dynamic membership, or faults. It allows always ending up in a regular operating state, regardless of the starting conditions or perturbations imposed to the system.

Self-organizing, autonomous distributed protocols and services are typically implemented using the *gossip-based* paradigm. Gossip-based protocols rely on periodic exchange of information between pairs of peers and appropriate node-local decisions. They allow implementing a variety of system services based on overlay networks, such as membership management [16], dissemination [7,19], structure and overlays management [15,24], or key-based routing [18,20].

An important class of services for large-scale heterogeneous distributed systems is *resource provisioning*. A system might need to support multiple services and applications, each with different requirements in terms of computational capabilities, network requirements, or criticality (i.e., the need for the service to be dependable and available). Resource provisioning allows determining, for each service or application, which resources should be used. In particular, when services are implemented through distributed protocols running on a subset of all the nodes of the system, provisioning can be generalized to the action of splitting the entire set of nodes in subsets, one for each of the service or application.

For instance, in a system that supports indexing and dependable storage atop highly volatile nodes [18], a small set of nodes –typically the most stable ones– can be dedicated to the routing service that implements the indexing layer while the remaining ones handle best effort replication of data items. The selection of the most stable nodes can be based on their uptime. As demonstrated in [4] based on measurements on a real large peer-to-peer system, uptime is correlated with stability. Nodes with large uptimes tend to stay online for a longer time than nodes with a small uptime, regardless of their other characteristics. Another example is that of a system that supports a BitTorrent-like dissemination and download service. The subset of the most stable node could be used for supporting a self-organizing distributed hash table (DHT) [15,20,24], nodes with the largest available bandwidth could be used as helpers for others to download faster [9], while the remaining ones only act as clients.

1.1   Distributed Slicing

The prominent implementation of resource provisioning for very large scale systems is *distributed slicing* [8,11,13,17]. It allows splitting a large set of nodes, based on discrete representations of their characteristics, in the form of node-local *attributes*. Slicing allows forming groups of nodes with increasing attribute values. A *slicing schema*, known by all nodes, indicate the relative size of each of the slices with respect to the total size of the system. It is important to note that the actual total size of the system does not need to be known by the nodes themselves. As an example, say that the considered characteristic of nodes is their available disk space, as exemplified on the top of Figure 1. Nodes all know the slicing schema $S = \{50\%, 30\%, 20\%\}$. A slicing protocol must create three slices of size 50%, 30% and 20% of the total size of the system, e.g., 5,000, 3,000 and 2,000 nodes for a network of 10,000 nodes, and 7, 4 and 3 nodes for the small

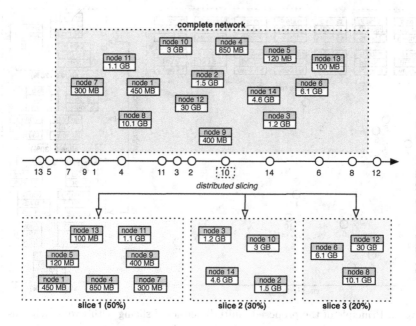

Fig. 1. Basic principle of slicing with attributes of a single dimension (available disk)

network of Figure 1. Slices correspond to group of nodes of increasing attribute values. Nodes in the first slice all have attributes that are lower than those of the second and third slices, and similarly between the second and the third slice.

Slicing neither requires a centralized view of the system, nor it requires assumptions about the distribution of attribute values. Each node must estimate the position its attribute would have in the sorted list of all attributes, if such a list was materialized. This position is typically obtained by estimating the proportion of nodes in the system that have lower values for the attribute and the proportion of nodes that, instead, have higher values for the attribute. When this information is available, it is then straightforward for a node, based on the slicing schema, to determine the slice it belongs to. For instance, node 10 is able to determine that it belongs to the second slice of the schema knowing that there are 9 nodes with lower values, and 4 nodes with higher values. Several variants of protocols allow to implement this basic principle. We give further details of one of these protocols, *sort ranking*, in Section 2.

1.2   Problem Definition

The major drawback of slicing for node provisioning in large-scale network is that it intrinsically only supports a single dimension for attributes. It is possible to form slices based on the available disk space, or the network connectivity, or CPU power, but considering a single of these characteristics at a time only. It is often desirable to be able to provision nodes based on a combination of metrics,

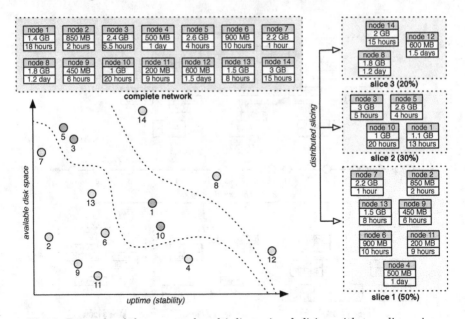

Fig. 2. Principle of the proposed multi-dimensional slicing with two dimensions

in order to form slices that represent classes of lower to better *compromises* for a set of characteristics. This would allow for instance to provision a large-scale network with a set of super-nodes with the best compromise in terms of available bandwidth and processing capacity, for serving as storage nodes or for participating to a backbone indexing overlay, and use nodes with less interesting characteristics for less demanding tasks, such as dissemination [7] or monitoring [14]. Other examples of compromises involve the node stability as measured by their uptime and processing capacity, in order to form a support overlay composed only of the peers that have both a good capacity, and whose stability ensures good resilience of the structure.

We propose and evaluate in this paper a novel approach to support slicing based on multiple attributes. Our main objective is to form slices that group nodes in classes of quality of the compromises between their different characteristics. This should not require knowing the range of definition for any of the dimensions, which can be practically unbounded. Multi-dimensional slicing should also be independent of the distribution of values for each dimension. Figure 2 illustrates the principle of the considered problem from a high-level perspective. It presents a set of nodes with attributes along two dimensions, the available disk space and the uptime. The latter links to expected stability [4]. Nodes form three slices under the same schema as for Figure 1 over a single dimension, $S = \{50\%, 30\%, 20\%\}$. These slices should represent classes of increasingly better compromises.

We see for instance that node 8 presents both a high uptime and a large amount of available disk space. It is thus expected to be stable, and has enough capacity. On the other hand, node 12 has moderate available disk space but is the most ancient node, so supposedly the stablest. Taking into account this heterogeneity, the first slice will include nodes such as node 8 or 12 that exhibit the best attribute compromises. Alongside, nodes in the second slice shall represent intermediate compromises among the set of available nodes, while nodes with either small storage space for their stability or small stability for their storage space, are left to the first slice.

Our contribution is based on the determination of *domination relations* between nodes. This notion has been applied to data points in the context of databases for the definition of the SkyLine query [12]. The domination relation between nodes allow comparing compromises between nodes characteristics, and allows nodes to estimate their position in a global domination partial order that would contain all nodes if materialized. This position is used, as for the uni-dimensional slicing, to determine the slice a node belongs to.

The remaining of this paper is organized as follows. In Section 2, we present the principle of a representative slicing algorithm for single-dimension attributes, which serves as the basis for the multi-dimensional slicing presented in Section 3. We present an evaluation of our contribution in Section 4. Related work is surveyed in Section 5. Section 6 concludes the paper.

2 Background

We present in this Section the principles of gossip-based protocols and the algorithm for single-dimension slicing that we extend for supporting multi-dimensional slicing. This algorithm, which we name *sort slicing* is based on a self-organizing gossip-based distributed sort and was initially presented in [13].

Gossip-based distributed systems allow implementing autonomous and self-organizing protocols. An early gossip-based protocol was proposed for the reconciliation of database replicas in the 1980s [6]. Gossip came back into fashion in the 2000s as the complexity of using centralized or rigid management became clear with the increase of systems scales. A typical use of gossip is reliable application-level broadcast [7]. Another class deal with overlay management [15,16,20,21,24]. Slicing protocols [8,11,13,17] are a subset of it.

In an overlay management gossip-based protocol, each node maintains a small set of links to other nodes. This small set of nodes is called the node's *view*. It is often of fixed size. Each node features an active and a passive thread. The active thread periodically initiates a gossip interaction between the node and another node from the system. The period between two consecutive interactions is defined as a *cycle*. The passive thread is in charge of replying to incoming interaction requests. The interaction typically involves the exchange of information between the two nodes. It results in the two nodes potentially changing their state, or taking some action based on that exchanged information. Gossip-based protocols solely rely on this simple interaction/exchange pattern and do not require further synchronization between nodes. The nature of the information exchanged and the action taken define the nature and goal of a gossip-based protocol.

The partner node for the interaction is either randomly picked from the view, or obtained from a Peer Sampling Service (PSS) [16, 23]. The PSS is a

---

Algorithm 1. Simplified Sorting-Slicing Algorithm on node p [13]

```
1  variables
2  |   a_p ← ...                                         // local attribute
3  |   e_p ← rand(0,1)                                   // local position estimation
4  |   S ← ...                // slice schema, array [1..N]: ∑_{i=1}^N S[i] = 1

5  every Δ time units do                                 // active thread
6  |   select partner q randomly from view ∪ PSS.getView()
7  |   e_p ← q.receive(a_p, e_p)                          // initiate exchange

8  function receive(a_q, e_q)                             // passive thread
9  |   if (a_p < a_q ∧ e_p > e_q) ∨ (a_p > a_q ∧ e_p < e_q) then   // order violation?
10 |   |   t ← e_p                                        // save current position estimation
11 |   |   e_p ← e_q                                      // exchange current position estimation
12 |   |   return t
13 |   else                                              // no order violation, no exchange
14 |   |   return e_q

15 function getSlice()
16 |   t ← 0, r ← 1
17 |   while t < e_p do                                   // calculate slice estimation
18 |   |   t ← t + S[r], r ← r + 1
19 |   return r
```

---

fundamental service for other gossip-based protocols. It is also itself using a gossip-based implementation. It manages nodes' membership to the system and maintains connectivity. It provides other gossip protocols with a constantly updated stream of random peers drawn from the entire system, forming an overlay that has similar properties to a random graph. It inserts new nodes in the stream of other nodes and ensures that removed nodes do not appear in other nodes' streams after some bounded time. The use of a PSS is mandatory for all gossip-based overlay management protocols to provide convergence and associated self-organizing guarantees [24]: this also applies to gossip-based slicing protocols.

All gossip-based slicing algorithms share the following characteristics. Each node possesses an attribute value a, over a single dimension, that represents one of its characteristics (e.g., the available disk space in Figure 1). The domain of a is unknown and unbounded. It also knows the slicing schema S, a system-wide parameter. Finally, each node's goal is to obtain a position estimation e, that indicates its estimated position in the sorted list of all attribute values, if such a list was materialized. The value of e lies in the bounded domain $[0, 1]$. Knowing S and e, it is straightforward to determine which slice the node belongs to. For instance, with $e = 0.55$ and $S = \{50\%, 30\%, 20\%\}$, node 10 in Figure 1 can determine it belongs to the second slice.

The gossip-based *sort slicing* [13] algorithm determines e based on the following method, detailed in Algorithm 1 for a given node p. The view is composed of nodes that had numerically close values of e to the current node, at the last time an interaction took place. Interaction partners are selected randomly from nodes in the union of the view and the current stream of nodes exposed by the PSS. The use of the view is only meant to speed-up the convergence, while the use of the PSS is required for that convergence to happen [24]. Each node is boot-strapped with a *random* value for e in $[0, 1]$. The goal of the gossip interactions is to match the ordering of e values on all nodes, to the ordering of a values on all nodes. It implements a distributed swap-sort for this. At each gossip inter-action, the two interacting nodes p and q compare the ordering of their values of e and the ordering of their values of a. If the two orders are the same (i.e., if $(a_p < a_q \wedge e_p < e_q) \vee (a_p > a_q \wedge e_p > e_q)$), no action is taken. Otherwise, there is an order violation that needs to be corrected. Nodes proceed to this correction by simply exchanging their position estimations e_p and e_q. The authors of [13] show that this simple method yields an exponential reduction of the disorder metric (the sum of the squared distances of position estimation from their final value) with the number of cycles. This translates in a rapid convergence towards the correct slice attribution at each node.

3   Multi-dimensional Slicing

We present in this Section our contributions towards autonomous slicing for large-scale distributed systems based on attributes over multiple dimensions. We start by noting that using a utility function does not fit the requirements we have set for multi-dimensional slicing. A utility function maps multiple dimensions onto a single one by applying a linear combination of the values over these dimensions. This requires knowing or estimating the boundaries for each dimension. It also requires assigning weights to metrics (the values over each dimension) that are not comparable. It finally requires making assumptions on the distribution of values over each dimension, as skewed distributions for the value of one attribute would result in the order for other attributes dominating the selection process. We thus dismiss this naive option and consider instead solutions that preserve the multi-dimensional aspect of the workload. First, we report on a negative result on our initial use of space-filling curves. Then, we present our approach using domination relations between multi-dimensional nodes' attributes, the resulting partial order and order violation resolutions, and the resulting multi-dimensional slicing.

Using Space Filling Curves? Our first attempt to provide multi-dimensional slicing was to map attributes of multiple dimensions onto a single dimension using space filling curves (SFC). A SFC is a curve that covers the entire unit square. It can be generalized to a d-dimensional space. Each d-dimensional point in the space is associated with a single point on the curve. The distance on the curve of the representations of two d-dimensional points can be used to estimate the distance between the two original d-dimensional points in the space. SFC are typically defined by a recursive definition, as a special case of fractal construction.

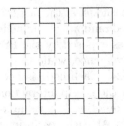

Fig. 3. 2-D Hilbert SFC

There exists many SFCs but we chose to use the Hilbert SFC (illustrated for 2 dimensions on Figure 3). This curve has the property that it tends to preserve ordering for a large number, but not all, possible couple of points mapped on the curve with respect to the ordering of their corresponding vector to the origin in the space. This initial approach proved unsatisfactory for the following two reasons. First, a major issue with SFC is that they require knowing in advance –or estimating– the boundaries of the domain space. This condition is not met by typical workloads for resource provisioning in large-scale systems. Second, while the use of a SFC allows forming a total order between multi-dimensional points, the ordering inconsistencies (e.g., between [2:1], [3:3] and [2,2] on Figure 3) prevent the algorithm from converging towards stable position estimations. As a result, we discarded the SFC approach and looked into a solution that intrinsically does not feature these two limitations, and does not require mapping multiple dimensions into a single one.

3.1 Domination Relations

Our approach for multi-dimensional slicing is based on the intuitive notion of quality of compromises that we presented in our problem definition. It does not require knowing the range of definition of any of the dimensions. It is based on a domination relation $\lhd$. We say that a node n_a dominates another node n_b when n_a is strictly a better compromise than n_b according to the value of their attributes over all dimensions. The definition of $\lhd$ is as follows, where n_a^i denotes the value of the attribute of n_a for dimension i and where d is the number of dimensions: $n_a \lhd n_b$ if $\forall\, i \mid 1 \leq i \leq d, n_a^i \leq n_b^i$. This relation is transitive: $n_a \lhd n_b \wedge n_b \lhd n_c \Rightarrow n_a \lhd n_c$ and its inverse is $\rhd$: $n_a \lhd n_b \Leftrightarrow n_b \rhd n_a$.

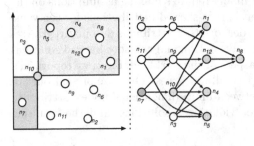

Fig. 4. Domination relations and partial order

Figure 4 (left) gives an example of domination relations between a node n_{10} and a set of other nodes, over a 2-dimensional space. Relations that can be determined based on transitivity are not shown. In particular, we have $n_{10} \lhd \{n_1, n_4, n_5, n_8, n_{12}\}$ and $n_{10} \rhd \{n_7\}$. The $\lhd$ relations define a partial order $\mathcal{O}_\lhd$ between nodes. The partial order for nodes $n_1, \ldots, n_{12}$ is shown on the right side of Figure 4: we note that some pairs of nodes have no defined ordering according to $\lhd$ and $\rhd$. For instance, n_{11} and n_7 have no established $\lhd$ or $\rhd$ relation.

We note that our notion of domination between nodes is similar to the notion of domination between data points that is used in the context of databases, and in particular for the definition of SkyLine queries [12]. A SkyLine query allows collecting the best-compromise points from a structured multi-dimensional

Algorithm 2. Multi-dimensional domination-based slicing algorithm on node p (*getSlice()* is unchanged from Algorithm 1)

```
1  variables                                          // in addition to the ones in Algorithm 1
2     a_p = {a_p^1, ..., a_p^d} ← ...                 // local multi-dimensional attribute
3     ◁-view ← ∅                                       // view, close dominated nodes
4     ▷-view ← ∅                                       // view, close dominating nodes

5  every Δ time units do                              // active thread
6     select partner q randomly from ◁-view ∪ ▷-view ∪ PSS.getView()
7     e_p ← q.receive(a_p, e_p, p)                     // initiate exchange

8  function receive(a_q, e_q, q)                       // passive thread
9     if a_p ◁ a_q then
10       ◁-view ← ◁-view ∪ q                           // maintain close dominated nodes view
11       foreach n ∈ ◁-view do
12          if ∃ n' ∈ ◁-view | n ≠ n' ∧ a_{n'} ◁ a_n  then
13             ◁-view ← ◁-view \ n
14       if e_q < e_p then return exchange(e_q)         // order violation?
15    else if a_p ▷ a_q then
16       ▷-view ← ▷-view ∪ q                           // maintain close dominating nodes view
17       foreach n ∈ ▷-view do
18          if ∃ n' ∈ ▷-view | n ≠ n' ∧ a_{n'} ▷ a_n  then
19             ▷-view ← ▷-view \ n
20       if e_q > e_p then return exchange(e_q)         // order violation?
21    return(e_q)                                       // no order violation, no exchange

22 function exchange(e_q)
23    t ← e_p, e_p ← e_q, return t
```

database: the SkyLine points are the points that are not dominated by any other point, under the same definition as above. The SkyLine of Figure 4 would be $\{n_7, n_{11}, n_2\}$. The SkyLine operator has been extended towards the SkyBand operator [22]. A k-SkyBand is a set of points that are not dominated by more than k points. The 2-SkyBand of Figure 4 would be $\{n_7, n_{11}, n_2, n_6, n_9, n_{10}, n_3\}$. The slicing problem is however different than the k-SkyBand in several ways. First, there is no omniscient view of the data set as in a database. Nodes only know a small amount of other nodes in their view and have no global knowledge of the boundaries of the space, the number of nodes, or the distribution of values for each dimension. Second, the slices are not defined in terms of the number of dominating nodes but in terms of a size relative to the totality of the system. We detail below how we modify the uni-dimensional slicing from Algorithm 1 to support multi-dimensional slicing based on domination relations.

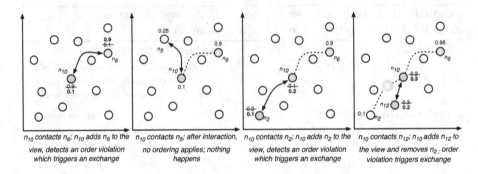

n_{10} contacts n_6; n_{10} adds n_6 to the view, detects an order violation which triggers an exchange

n_{10} contacts n_5; after interaction, no ordering applies; nothing happens

n_{10} contacts n_2; n_{10} adds n_2 to the view, detects an order violation which triggers an exchange

n_{10} contacts n_{12}; n_{10} adds n_{12} to the view and removes n_2 ; order violation triggers exchange

Fig. 5. Evolution of the view of a node according to Algorithm 2

3.2   Multi-dimensional Slicing from Domination-Based Ordering

The multi-dimensional slicing algorithm is presented by Algorithm 2. It extends the previous Algorithm 1 for slicing over one dimension. An illustration of the algorithm is provided by Figure 5. Description of the illustrated algorithm steps is directly provided below the figure itself. Similarly as before, each node p has access to a PSS and maintains a view. This view of p is split in two parts: the ◁-view and the ▷-view. The former holds the peers that are directly dominated by p and by no other node in ◁-view. The latter has the same semantics for dominating peers under the ▷ relation. Each time a gossip exchange takes place, if the domination relation ◁ holds between p and the exchange partner q, q is first added to ◁-view (line 10). The ◁-view is then pruned out of nodes that are already dominated by another one from the set (lines 11 to 13). The same principle is applied to dominating nodes and the ▷-view (lines 15 to 19). When an order violation is detected (line 14 or line 20), the position estimation e_p and e_q are exchanged, in the same way as for Algorithm 1. The slice determination itself is strictly identical as for Algorithm 1.

Algorithm 2 can be enhanced in a number of ways. First, instead of keeping the directly dominated nodes and directly dominating nodes in ◁-view and ▷-view, we can keep a set of nodes to ensure a faster resolution of "local" order violations ("global" order violations between nodes are expected to be resolved more frequently due to the interactions from the PSS, but close links help in the final steps of convergence as demonstrated in [24]). To this end, node p might keep a set of peers that is not actually the Skyline of the dominated (resp. dominating) nodes but an overset of it, nodes are removed from the ◁-view and ▷-view only when it goes over a target view size (by modifying the conditions on lines 12 and 18). Second, the interaction depicted is single-way: while both p and q participate in the exchange, only p takes advantage of it to fill its views as part of its passive thread (this is known as a push-only operation). It is straightforward for q to operate in the same manner while on its active thread (push-pull). We use these two optimizations in our implementation.

We note that several of the interactions with random nodes chosen using the PSS will lead to no action as the two values will not be comparable in the partial order $\mathcal{O}_\lhd$.[1] These random interactions are necessary however when the attributes value change over time, as expected in a dynamic provisioning scenario (e.g., the uptime, available disk space, etc. evolve over time). Unlike with uni-dimensional slicing, no total order on the nodes exists. This means that there are a multitude of possible total ordering of the position estimates e_p that are compatible with the partial ordering $\mathcal{O}_\lhd$. As we point out in our evaluation, this also means that the scheme is unsurprisingly subject to the *curse of dimensionality* [3]. When using over 8 or 10 dimensions, the partial order tends to become a very sparse graph as most nodes are not comparable against $\mathcal{O}_\lhd$ anymore. We believe however that the problem of dynamic node provisioning in large-scale systems does not require more than this limit number of dimensions to fulfill its intended role.

4   Evaluation

We now present the evaluation of our protocol. Our implementation uses Peer-Sim [1], a Java-based cycle-oriented simulation framework that is well adapted to the study of gossip-based protocols. We simulate a network of 10,000 nodes for all the presented experiments. Each node uses an attribute over 2 to 15 dimensions (when not specified, we present results for 2 dimensions). Values for each dimension are random float numbers. Each node has access to an independent PSS. We use an instantiation of the Cyclon [23] PSS in the framework of [16]. Each node maintains a $\lhd$-view and a $\rhd$-view of up to 10 entries each.

The reminder of this section is organized as follows. We start by evaluating the protocol correctness. Then, we evaluate the convergence speed with different view configurations. Finally we study the scalability in terms of number of dimensions.

Correctness. We evaluate the correctness of the protocol by its capacity to reduce the number of *order violations* as defined in Section 3.1. An order violation between two nodes p and q with position estimates e_p and e_q occurs when $((p \lhd q \wedge e_p > e_q) \vee (p \rhd q \wedge e_p < e_q))$. We count the number of such violations per node when compared in an omniscient way against all other nodes in the system. Note that we cannot use a disorder metric as in [13] as the partial order between nodes is not based on an Euclidean distance but on domination relationships. Figure 6 depicts the evolution of the average and maximum number of order violations for nodes in the system, as nodes engage in cycles of gossip exchanges (during one cycle, each node initiates one gossip exchange with one partner). As expected from previous work on gossip-based overlay construction protocols [8, 11, 15–17, 20, 21, 24] and similarly to the uni-dimensional slicing in [13], the reduction in the number of violations is exponential. After only 10 cycles, the system converges to less than 0.05% violations per node on average and 3.7% as worst case. This indicates that the node provisioning quality will highly resemble the "ideal" slicing for the given attributes values set. We note

---

[1] The choice of the partner for the gossip interaction could be based on semantic information piggybacked on the PSS messages. This requires however one more round of interaction to check that the actual known attribute values are up to date (as detailed in [13]). We did not implement this optimization in our prototype.

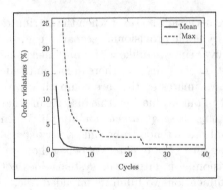
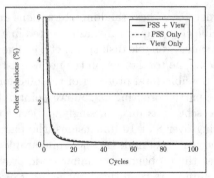

Fig. 6. Convergence speed   **Fig. 7.** Impact of the PSS

that the max converges slowly to 0: this is a result of remaining violations being slowly resolved by using random PSS links in a network where a majority of nodes have converged views. This behavior was pointed out in [24]. It does not pose a significant problem in practice as it has little influence on the slicing decision itself, which is already converged as we see in our last experiment.

Influence of the Gossip Interaction Partner Selection. Figure 7 illustrates the influence of the selection of the gossip interaction partner (line 6 in Algorithm 2) on the convergence speed and correctness. We use the same metric as before and present the mean number of violations for the three following cases. The gossip exchanges are initiated by randomly picking a node from the view only (config-ured by a static bootstrapping using random peers), using nodes obtained from the PSS only, or using a combination of both. As expected, we observe that the convergence *requires* the use of the PSS. Using only the views bootstrapped with initial random nodes but not constantly updated with new random nodes, the system ends up in a state where nodes with order violations lie in disconnected islands and never get to resolve these violations anymore, preventing the whole system from converging. We also observe that the use of the view for choosing the gossip partner has a slight, but almost negligible impact on the convergence speed. These two observations are in line with the observations made for other gossip-based overlay construction protocols [15, 20, 24].

Scalability in Number of Dimensions. Our next series of experiments evaluate the impact of the number of dimensions used for nodes' attributes on the sta-bility and observed convergence speed. Figure 8 reports the evolution of the number of order violations when using 2, 4, 6 and 15 dimensions. More dimen-sions mean less possible comparisons between nodes against ◁. The convergence speed remains good with up to 6 dimensions. As expected, when using a large number of dimensions (in general, starting from 8), an embarrassing majority of couples of nodes are not comparable with ◁. This means that the slicing opera-tion using domination-based order is no longer possible, unless one restricts the operation to a subset of representative dimensions. We believe 6 dimensions is

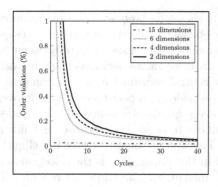

Fig. 8. Convergence vs dimension

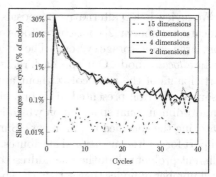

Fig. 9. Slice allocation stability

enough characteristics to consider for dynamic node provisioning in large-scale systems.

Finally, we evaluate the impact of the number of dimensions on the stability of the system, in terms of the steadiness of the slice allocation for each node. Figure 9 presents the number of slice changes per cycle (note the logarithmic scale) as the protocol converges. The cost of a slice depends on the supported application. In general, a good practice is to export the slice allocation only when it has been steady for a configurable number of cycles. With 15 dimensions, nodes are basically stuck with the slice that corresponds to their initial random value for the position estimation p, as there are almost no order violations to resolve. Along with the previous observation, this exemplifies the expected effect of the *curse of dimensionality* [3] on multi-dimensional slicing. With 1 to 6 dimensions though, we see that the system quickly converges to stable slice allocations. The protocol starts its execution after the 2nd cycle, where 40% of the nodes decide to change their slide. After about 10 cycles, only 100 slice changes per cycle happen. This concerns a mere 1% of the network. After 30 cycles, there are only 10 such changes (0.1%). In a practical deployment, one can freeze the slice allocation around these times depending on the required precision.

5 Related Work

Besides the *sort slicing* protocol that we described in Section 2, the following slicing protocols were proposed. Ranking [8] is not based on the exchange of position estimates but on counting mechanisms that estimate how many nodes have lower, resp. higher values for the single-dimension attribute. Sliver [11] improves this protocol by introducing a technique to improve slicing accuracy avoiding mistakenly considering duplicate information. Slead [17] is an extension of this idea that make use of Bloom filters to reduce the high memory consumption of these protocols and proposes a hysteresis mechanisms for the slice determination to gain more stability. All these protocols are based on the gossip-based paradigm, for which we covered related work in Section 2.

We review below alternative proposals to slicing for large-scale system resource allocation. Minerva [2] contributes tools to efficiently assign host machines to support large-scale storage systems. The assignment of the hosts is centrally executed by an *allocator* node. Our approach relies on autonomous decisions taken by each participants of the protocol, without any central coordinator. The autonomous resource selection presented in [5] organizes nodes in a peer-to-peer system over a multi-dimensional space, upon which lookup queries are issued to select nodes matching the specified requirements. Similarly to ours, this protocol has built-in support for multi-dimensional attributes. This system solves a related but slightly different problem than the one addressed in this paper, that is the selection of a fixed number of nodes that satisfy the specified queries, and does not rely on self-organizing techniques but explicit query/response mechanisms.

In [10], a notion of resource dominance is also used. It differs however from the domination between nodes we use in our work. Domination in [10] relates to the prevalence of the usage of one type of resource (CPU, memory, ...) over the other types of resources on one node. This information is used by a centralized resource allocator in order to achieve resource allocation fairness for a given workload.

6   Conclusion

Distributed slicing is a fundamental primitive for resource allocation in large-scale distributed systems. Existing distributed slicing protocols did not offer support to perform this allocation considering nodes with multidimensional attributes. In practical settings, it is often desired to choose a best compromise between various characteristics (i.e. CPU, volatile memory, uptime, etc.). We contribute a gossip-based distributed slicing protocol that fills this need. The proposed protocol exploits domination relations between nodes to define the membership of a node to a given slice. Our evaluation confirms the contributed solution as a sound approach to the problem. We support experimental reproducibility: source code and datasets are released under open-source and available at: https://github.com/mpasquet/multidimslicing_dais2014.

Acknowledgments. This work received support from the Portuguese Foundation for Science and Technology under grant SFRH/BD/71476/2010.

References

1. http://peersim.sourceforge.net/
2. Alvarez, G.A., Borowsky, E., Go, S., Romer, T.H., Becker-Szendy, R., Golding, R., Merchant, A., Spasojevic, M., Veitch, A., Wilkes, J.: Minerva: An automated resource provisioning tool for large-scale storage systems. ACM Transactions on Computer Systems (TOCS) 19(4), 483–518 (2001)
3. Bellman, R.: Curse of dimensionality. In: Adaptive Control Processes: A Guided Tour. Princeton, NJ (1961)

4. Bhagwan, R., Savage, S., Voelker, G.M.: Understanding availability. In: Kaashoek, M.F., Stoica, I. (eds.) IPTPS 2003. LNCS, vol. 2735, pp. 256–267. Springer, Heidelberg (2003)
5. Costa, P., Napper, J., Pierre, G., van Steen, M.: Autonomous resource selection for decentralized utility computing. In: ICDCS 2009 (2009)
6. Demers, A., Greene, D., Hauser, C., Irish, W., Larson, J., Shenker, S., Sturgis, H., Swinehart, D., Terry, D.: Epidemic algorithms for replicated database maintenance. In: PODC 1987 (1987)
7. Eugster, P.T., Guerraoui, R., Handurukande, S.B., Kouznetsov, P., Kermarrec, A.-M.: Lightweight probabilistic broadcast. ACM Trans. Comput. Syst. 21(4), 341–374 (2003)
8. Fernandez, A., Gramoli, V., Jimenez, E., Kermarrec, A.-M., Raynal, M.: Distributed slicing in dynamic systems. In: ICDCS 2007 (2007)
9. Garbacki, P., Iosup, A., Epema, D., van Steen, M.: 2Fast: Collaborative Downloads in P2P Networks. In: IEEE P2P 2006 (2006)
10. Ghodsi, A., Zaharia, M., Hindman, B., Konwinski, A., Shenker, S., Stoica, I.: Dominant resource fairness: Fair allocation of multiple resource types. In: USENIX NSDI 2011 (2011)
11. Gramoli, V., Vigfusson, Y., Birman, K., Kermarrec, A.-M., van Renesse, R.: Slicing distributed systems. IEEE Trans. Comput. 58(11) (November 2009)
12. Hose, K., Vlachou, A.: A survey of skyline processing in highly distributed environments. The VLDB Journal 21(3), 359–384 (2012)
13. Jelasity, M., Kermarrec, A.-M.: Ordered slicing of very large-scale overlay networks. In: IEEE P2P 2006 (2006)
14. Jelasity, M., Montresor, A., Babaoglu, O.: Gossip-based aggregation in large dynamic networks. ACM Transactions on Computer Systems 23(3) (2005)
15. Jelasity, M., Montresor, A., Babaoglu, O.: T-man: Gossip-based fast overlay topology construction. Computer Networks 53(13), 2321–2339 (2009)
16. Jelasity, M., Voulgaris, S., Guerraoui, R., Kermarrec, A.-M., Van Steen, M.: Gossip-based peer sampling. ACM Transactions on Computer Systems (TOCS) 25(3), 8 (2007)
17. Maia, F., Matos, M., Rivière, E., Oliveira, R.: Slead: Low-memory, steady distributed systems slicing. In: Göschka, K.M., Haridi, S. (eds.) DAIS 2012. LNCS, vol. 7272, pp. 1–15. Springer, Heidelberg (2012)
18. Maia, F., Matos, M., Vilaça, R., Pereira, J., Oliveira, R., Rivière, E.: Dataflasks: An epidemic dependable key-value substrate. In: DCDV (2013)
19. Matos, M., Schiavoni, V., Felber, P., Oliveira, R., Rivière, E.: Lightweight, efficient, robust epidemic dissemination. Journal of Parallel and Distributed Computing 73(7), 987–999 (2013)
20. Montresor, A., Jelasity, M., Babaoglu, O.: Chord on demand. In: IEEE P2P 2005 (2005)
21. Montresor, A., Jelasity, M., Babaoglu, O.: Decentralized ranking in large-scale overlay networks. In: SASOW 2008 (2008)
22. Vlachou, A., Doulkeridis, C., Norvag, K., Vazirgiannis, M.: Skyline-based peer-to-peer top-k query processing. In: ICDE 2008 (2008)
23. Voulgaris, S., Gavidia, D., Steen, M.V.: Cyclon: Inexpensive membership management for unstructured P2P overlays. Journal of Network and Systems Management (2005)
24. Voulgaris, S., van Steen, M.: VICINITY: A pinch of randomness brings out the structure. In: Eyers, D., Schwan, K. (eds.) Middleware 2013. LNCS, vol. 8275, pp. 21–40. Springer, Heidelberg (2013)

Bandwidth-Minimized Distribution
of Measurements
in Global Sensor Networks

Andreas Benzing, Boris Koldehofe, and Kurt Rothermel

Institute of Parallel and Distributed Systems, 70569 Stuttgart, Germany
firstname.lastname@ipvs.uni-stuttgart.de
http://www.ipvs.uni-stuttgart.de/abteilungen/vs

Abstract. Global sensor networks (GSN) allow applications to integrate huge amounts of data using real-time streams from virtually anywhere. Queries to a GSN offer many degrees of freedom, e.g. the resolution and the geographic origin of data, and scaling optimization of data streams to many applications is highly challenging. Existing solutions hence either limit the flexibility with additional constraints or ignore the characteristics of sensor streams where data points are produced synchronously.

In this paper, we present a new approach to bandwidth-minimized distribution of real-time sensor streams in a GSN. Using a distributed index structure, we partition queries for bandwidth management and quickly identify overlapping queries. Based on this information, our relay strategy determines an optimized distribution structure which minimizes traffic while being adaptive to changing conditions. Simulations show that total traffic and user perceived delay can be reduced by more than 50%.

Keywords: Data Streams, Global Sensor Networks, Optimization.

1 Introduction

The deployment of wired and wireless sensor networks is making rapid progress all around the globe. Sensors are installed in virtually all areas of everyday life and a huge amount of real-time data has become available. For example, the CeNSE project by HP [12] envisions one trillion sensors to enervate the entire Earth. To globally enable scalable access to this data, broker networks providing high bandwidth data streams need to be established and managed using appropriate middleware solutions. Previous approaches focused on extending methods from local to global sensor networks [2,13]. By utilizing in-network aggregation or lossy compression, a significant reduction of sensor data can be achieved. However, the gain of these methods comes at the cost of reduced precision to which many critical applications are highly sensitive. For example, the simulations for the dispersion of pollutants require precise wind data. Numerical errors due to compression artifacts can lead to highly disturbed results.

K. Magoutis and P. Pietzuch (Eds.): DAIS 2014, LNCS 8460, pp. 156–170, 2014.

A promising alternative to reducing precision is to avoid sending information multiple times over a physical network link. The main problem then is to find an optimized and dynamically adapting dissemination structure for a large number of requests in the complex Internet. Group communication middleware such as application layer multicast [24] or publish/subscribe [9] tackle the complexity of the problem by reducing the number of requests which need to be served by a broker. In multicast, communication is limited to a fixed number of channels, prohibitively restricting the expressiveness of queries. Publish/subscribe offers high expressiveness for queries and scalability is achieved by merging similar subscriptions from different subscribers to avoid redundant transmissions. However, since the bandwidth requirements of an individual subscription are unknown, this solution misses optimization potential for high-bandwidth sensor streams.

Contrary, for global sensor streams, measurements are generated for every point at discrete time steps. Knowledge on the spatial and temporal resolution – as specified, for example, in scientific simulations – allows for exact determination of the data to expect from any given query. This poses a great so far unused potential to minimize bandwidth usage of a global sensing system.

Towards this end, we present the Global Sensor Grid Middleware (GSGM). The GSGM provides a new method to precisely query and scalably deliver real-time sensor data streams. The query interface allows for a flexible specification of geographic regions and resolutions of data of interest. Our main contribution is a new underlay-adaptive stream management algorithm to minimize traffic by exploiting the predictable network load of each query. Redundant parts of queries are quickly identified using a distributed index structure. Identical portions of data streams are merged and sent to dynamically established relay points where the data is distributed towards client nodes based on local knowledge.

The paper is structured as follows: Section 2 introduces the system model followed by a problem formalization in Section 3. The detailed description of our approach is provided in Section 4. Evaluation results are presented in Section 5. Related work is provided in Section 6 and Section 7 concludes the paper.

2   System Model

System Components. The GSG is built up of *brokers*, which gather data from sensor networks, and *clients*. The sensor networks expose coordinates of their nodes and send raw sensor measurements to brokers where they are pre-processed and distributed to interested clients as shown in Figure 1. In doing so clients can pose a query to a broker, identifying the type of sensor, the spatial region, and spatial as well as temporal resolution. The brokers in turn identify the relevant data and establish a continuous sensor stream to the clients. In order to access the sensor data provided by a sensor network, we assume the sensor networks provide specific interfaces to the GSGM. These interfaces allow querying sensor data at varying temporal dimensions as well as coordinates in a global coordinate system. Note, however, that the GSGM is not concerned with managing the internals of the sensor network and how the sensor network is established.

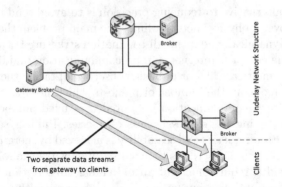

Fig. 1. Naive operation of the GSG with a separate data stream per client

To uniformly manage the sensors and sensor networks connected to the brokers, the GSGM manages a global coordinate system which comprises the world of all possible sensor coordinates. This world is partitioned into disjoint geographic regions, each managed by a single broker denoted the *gateway* of said region. This way each sensor is associated with exactly one region. However, a broker may serve as gateway for multiple regions. The gateways perform preprocessing of the raw sensor data to integrate sensor data into the global coordinate system and being able to offer sensor data at full resolution (cf. [3]).

Additional brokers in the GSG support the distribution of sensor streams. We refer to brokers that forward sensor data on behalf of gateways as *relays*. Note that also gateways may serve as relays on behalf of other gateways. Gateways or relays, which send data to a client, form the end of a data stream inside the GSG and hence called *target brokers* of that client. The number of brokers as well as the assignment of gateways to regions is manually fixed by the operator of the Global Sensor Grid. This choice determines the number of queries as well as the performance characteristics that can be supported by the GSGM. However, the brokers will autonomously optimize the network resources used depending on the client requests for sensor data.

Query Model. Building on our previous work [4] we introduce the query model for the GSGM. A query to the GSGM is bound to one data type and includes the region of the data requested. Optionally, clients can specify the time of the beginning and duration of the data stream. Each query q is therefore given by a tuple $q = (R_q, t_q, d_q)$ where R_q specifies the geographical extent and resolution of the query. t_q and d_q denote the optional start time and duration of the query. If the latter two are not specified, the resulting data stream will start as soon as possible and run until the client fails or cancels the query.

Besides the geographical area of interest, the query region contains the requested resolution. This way, clients can directly query a grid of data points as required for the simulation at hand. The region of query q is represented by

$$R_q = (x_{min}, x_{max}, y_{min}, y_{max}, res_x, res_y, res_t),$$

where x_{min} and x_{max} describe the lower and upper bound of the latitude. y_{min} and y_{max} limit the longitude correspondingly. Note that the system is not limited to geographic coordinates but can process any 2D coordinates. The last three values res_x, res_y, and res_t specify the spatial and temporal resolution of the query as a fraction of the maximum available data. A value of $res_x = 0.3$ therefore returns 3 out of 10 data points equally distributed over the corresponding axis. Similarly, only a subset of updates is transmitted for each data point if $res_y < 1$ or $res_t < 1$.

Cost Model. The primary goal of the GSGM is to minimize the bandwidth used for distributing data. The bandwidth used by each data stream is proportional to the amount of data per update and the update frequency. On the one hand, the amount of data is given by the geographical extent of the area and the spatial resolution. On the other hand, the frequency depends on the temporal resolution. For a data stream serving a query q the corresponding total size $|q|$ is therefore given by:

$$|q| = (x_{max} - x_{min}) \times (y_{max} - y_{min}) \times res_x \times res_y \times res_t$$

While the size of a query determines the bandwidth required to send the data from a broker, the load on the network depends on how data is distributed in the network. To serve a query q, the corresponding data stream s_q uses a set L_{s_q} of underlay links, which depends on the chosen path in the network. The number of underlay links for this path is consequently denoted by $|L_{s_q}|$. The overall cost $c(s_q)$ can now be calculated as the product of the number of links and the bandwidth which is identical for each link: $|L_{s_q}| \times |q|$. Note that the delay of a link is not taken into account as it does not affect the load.

3 Sensor Stream Distribution Problem

Recall that the bandwidth usage of the GSGM is driven by the overall number of underlay hops over which a given sensor datum is forwarded. To achieve minimal bandwidth usage it is therefore important to i) exploit the overlap between distinct sensor streams to reduce the amount of sensor data which is forwarded, ii) carefully choose the brokers which contribute in relaying to ensure short underlay paths. These goals conflict in general since longer underlay paths are required to share an underlay link between multiple streams.

We focus on two interconnected sub-problems to find a distribution structure with minimized bandwidth usage. The first sub-problem is to efficiently identify *intersections* between distinct queries. For each intersection, the data covered by the overlapping region must be sent to multiple clients. Solving the problem allows us to identify a set of k non-overlapping sensor streams from a single gateway to possibly multiple clients. The second task, and main problem addressed in this paper, is to reduce the bandwidth required for each stream by finding a minimal cost distribution graph. Clearly, both problems are in general hard to solve: First, the amount of possible intersections grows quickly with the number of queries in the system. Second, the path distribution problem can be reduced to the Minimal-Steiner-Tree-Problem (MST) [8] which is known to be NP-hard.

Proof. We can formulate this optimization problem similar to the MST w.r.t. each intersection. In the generic version of the problem, we are given a graph $G = (V, E)$, one source node $s \in V$, and a set $R \subseteq V$ of required nodes. The sought-after Steiner Tree is the graph which connects s to all nodes in R using nodes in $V \setminus R$ as Steiner Points, i.e. relays, with minimal sum of edge weights.

To formulate our stream distribution problem for a single intersection, let $V = \{b_i\}_{i \in \{1, \ldots, n\}}$ be the set of brokers, b_s be the source broker which provides the data, and R be the target brokers to which the clients are connected. Since a direct connection between any broker $b_i \in V$ can be established using IP-routing, The solution to this problem is the desired tree which provides the connectivity at minimal cost.

Even though multiple approaches to the MST exist, finding the exact solution to the presented problem is infeasible in a real-world GSG for multiple reasons. First of all, the MST is an NP-hard problem and has to be solved for a very large graph, i.e. the Internet with all its links. A restriction to all direct connections between brokers still involves a an extremely large graph. Second, a solution is needed for every intersection, resulting in numerous instances of the problem. Finally, the topology of the Internet is not known. This knowledge gap is broadened by the continuously changing network conditions caused by other applications using the Internet. In the remainder of this paper, we therefore present a new approach to solving the sensor stream distribution problem.

4   Sensor Stream Organization

In this section, we describe our new approach to approximate a solution to the sensor stream distribution problem and show how data streams in the GSG are organized to minimize bandwidth consumption. An example is given in Figure 2 The approach is divided into four main parts: query processing, management of network information, relay selection algorithm, and merging algorithm.

Query Processing. The query processing framework builds on our previous work [4] and provides three functions: i) find the gateway for a given query, ii) identify the overlap of distinct queries, and iii) determine which queries to serve with incoming or locally generated data. We use the GBD-Tree [16] which is able to index very large, high dimensional spatial data sets. In our case, each broker maintains a GBD-tree to store queries according to their regions as well as gateways by the regions they serve. This way, a broker can determine which parts of a query can be served locally and where to forward other parts.

Each region in the GBD-Tree is labeled by a binary string called a DZ expression as illustrated in Figure 3. The DZ expression exposes two important properties: First, the shorter a DZ expression, the larger is the extent of the

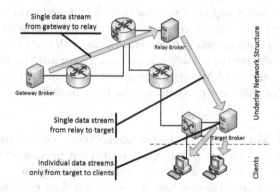

Fig. 2. Merged data streams using a relay broker in the network. A single data stream is sent over the relay to the target broker which then serves both clients.

region. In particular, the empty DZ expression ϵ corresponds to the entire coordinate space of the GSGM. Second, if the DZ expression of region r is the prefix of another region r' then r' is fully contained in r. For example, regions 010 and 011 both reside completely inside region 01. The mapping of DZ expressions to a region can be efficiently achieved by means of recursive spatial decomposition.

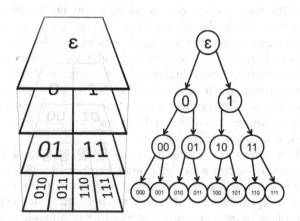

Fig. 3. Example for DZ expressions generated by spatial indexing

To determine the gateways for a query, the region of a query is converted to a set of DZ expressions according to the illustrated spatial decomposition scheme. As the tree is traversed top-down, the nodes will eventually contain information about the gateway on which the sensor data for the corresponding region is located. Similarly, for locally generated data or an incoming stream, the queries which are served by that stream can be found. By traversing the tree in a bottom-up fashion, we can aggregate information about overlapping queries as detailed in Section 2. Note that we only used two-dimensions in the example for clarity. The scheme supports various spatial and temporal dimensions. As queries are dynamically relayed to remote brokers, additional state is maintained by the GSGM. For each incoming relay stream, the path from the corresponding gateway to the local broker is stored in the index structure to prevent circular relaying. Each query is additionally annotated with the corresponding target broker to allow for efficient processing on the relay broker.

Neighborhood Maintenance. Direct connections, i.e. IP routing without any relay points in between, provide fast routing of queries and low delay in responses. However, for increasing load, multiple streams might carry redundant data over the same underlay link. These similar data streams are therefore *merged* and only a single stream will be forwarded to a selected relay point. As described in Section 3, selecting a relay point requires information about the underlying network.

Each broker maintains a local view on the network, to infer the structure of the underlying topology. This view contains a limited number of topographically close brokers, called local neighborhood and additional information about each of these brokers. Initially, all the brokers from the information about the region assignment are added to the neighborhood. The neighborhood is then continuously updated with new candidates during query routing and neighborhood maintenance itself. When a broker learns about another, from the region assignment or through an update, the remote broker is added to the neighborhood and delay measurements to the new broker are initiated. The delay is used to estimate the topological distance to each of the remote brokers which a broker uses to decide which remote brokers to keep in the neighborhood. Close brokers are kept in the neighborhood while brokers with higher delay are removed from the neighborhood and measurements to them are stopped. However, to adapt to changing network conditions, the brokers which are currently not in the neighborhood are periodically measured. No additional topology information, e.g. data from network oracles, is used by the middleware.

To assess the network location of a remote broker, the local view contains additional information. After a broker is added to the local neighborhood, the neighborhood of that new broker is requested together with the respective measurements. This way, each broker can check the network from the point of view of any of the brokers in its neighborhood, resulting in a two-hop view. Brokers in the remote neighborhood that were previously unknown are considered for the local neighborhood as previously described.

Relay Selection. In this section, we describe our approach to relay selection which serves as the basis for merging data streams. Relay selection is executed locally on each broker to determine where to send relay data streams and which clients to serve directly. In the following, we first introduce our notion of data stream similarity to provide an intuitive optimization goal. We then work towards our strategy for selecting relay candidates accordingly.

Basic Principles Merging overlapping data streams will only reduce the bandwidth consumption if they share at least part of an underlay path. Although the query index allows us to efficiently identify overlapping queries, we do not yet know whether the corresponding streams share any links in the underlay path. We approach this problem by introducing a similarity metric to provide an intuition about the problem at hand and a qualitative measure whether or not it is worth merging two streams.

For the GSGM, the similarity of two overlapping data streams is determined by the fraction of underlay links which they have in common in relation to the total path length. Formally, given two data streams s_1 and s_2 which carry the same data on paths p_1 and p_2 respectively, where $|p_i|$ denotes the length of path i and $l_{i,j}$ denotes the jth link on path i, the similarity is given by:

$$sim(p_1, p_2) = \sum_{l_{1,k}=l_{2,l}} \frac{2}{(|p_1| + |p_2|)}$$

If the paths are identical, $|p_1| = |p_2|$ links will be summed up, resulting in a similarity of one. If the paths have no links in common, the similarity is zero.

Note that calculating the exact value of similarity requires knowledge of the entire underlay network. However, as described previously, the network graph is neither known, nor can it be measured exactly. Instead of first calculating the similarity, we therefore directly approach the relay selection problem in the GSGM. Relay selection is executed locally for each known target broker since their number is small compared to the large count of intersections. A solution to the problem ensures two properties: a) the network stretch is minimized, i.e. the path including the relay is as short as possible, while b) the probability of selecting the same relay for similar streams is maximized. The path segment from the originating broker to the selected relay can then be merged, i.e. served by a single stream, to reduce the load on the network.

Analysis of Simple Relay Strategies. The simplest relay strategy is to forward data streams directly to a client's target broker. We refer to this as *direct relay* strategy. Since the target broker is chosen by location close to the client in our setup, the introduction of the relay will result in a small network stretch. At the same time the strategy allows to remove all redundant transmissions with respect to clients which have overlapping queries and the same target broker.

Clearly, selecting additional relays between a gateway and the target brokers will increase the chance of multiple overlapping streams on the same relay link. At the same time, however, additional relays increase network stretch resulting in additionally used underlay links and higher overall bandwidth usage. In general, relying on the local neighborhood allows us to limit the stretch introduced by each additional relay. Furthermore, limiting the set of relay candidates increases the chance to find a common relay point for overlapping data streams.

This basic reasoning results in a simple greedy strategy, *closest to destination*. To establish the relay path, the gateway will initially identify the relay which is topologically closest to the client. Each established relay broker, will then do the same until the target broker has been reached and the data is forwarded to the clients. While this greedy approach achieves low network stretch, its drawback is the large number of different relays chosen. As a result, the merging algorithm can only join streams which already have a very high similarity and the traffic reduction properties of this approach are sub-optimal.

To exploit lower similarity of data streams by having more relays, the *closest to source* strategy selects the relay based on the distance to the originating broker. First, the neighbors are sorted by increasing distance to the originating broker. Then, the first candidate which is closer to the target broker is chosen as relay. Note that this strategy is very fast, independent of the size of the neighborhood. As a result, the data streams are routed over a relatively large number of hops. While this provides the possibility to merge small common path segments, the network stretch grows very quickly.

Data: dst: Destination Broker, neighbors: Neighbors Sorted by Distance
Result: relay: Relay Broker
$oldDist = MAX\_DIST$;
$relay = dst$;
for $n \in$ neighbors **do**
    if getDelay$(n, dst) >$ getDelay$(this, dst)$ **then**
        | continue;
    end
    $newDist =$ getDelay$(n, dst) +$ getDelay$(this, n)$;
    if $newDist < oldDist$ **then**
        | $oldDist = newDist$;
        | $relay = n$;
    end
end

Algorithm 1. Closest to Path Relay Selection

Combined Strategy for Minimized Usage We conclude the previous analysis with the relay selection strategy used in the GSGM. Rather than selecting a position relative to the source or target of a data stream, the relay is chosen *closest to the path* between the two. The pseudo code for the strategy is given in Algorithm 1. Before the relay selection is started, the brokers in the neighborhood are sorted with increasing distance to the source broker. For each candidate we first check whether it is closer to the target broker than the direct connection to avoid detours. Then we estimate the network stretch each suitable relay candidate. The broker with the least estimated distance to the direct path is kept as the result of the relay selection. If no suitable relay broker is found in the local neighborhood, the target broker is selected as relay.

We gain in two aspects towards our goal. First, the distance to the next relay is limited not only by the neighborhood but by selecting closer brokers with higher priority. This allows for an increased number of relays compared to the greedy closest to destination strategy. Since we ensure that relays are located in the direction to the respective targets, similar streams will be merged with high probability. Second, the network stretch is limited as the relay nodes lie close to the direct path towards the target brokers. By selecting the relays with possibly low network stretch, we limit the number of underlay links used in the path. Data is therefore delivered with low delay and bandwidth usage is reduced.

Merging Algorithm. The relay selection provides a relay for each target broker and therefore for each data stream. Based on the selection, each broker has to locally select which streams to merge towards each relay. The goal of the merging operation is to find possibly large intersections for relaying to merge as many streams as possible. A basic approach for this operation is to find large queries which carry a superset of data of smaller queries. The query index provides the foundation for quickly identifying this containment of distinct queries. Our novel merging algorithm furthermore exploits the structure to split queries in order to increase the overlap and therefore increase efficiency and flexibility. A parameter thereby limits extreme fragmentation to ensure a low overhead.

The selection and adaption of regions works in two main steps. First, additional information in the index is gathered. A query q is contained in the sub-tree marked by node n if the region assigned to n covers the region of q denoted by $R_q \leq R_n$. In addition, we use the result of the relay selection to group queries by their relay candidate. For a target broker t_q of query q the relay is given by $relay(t_q) = r$. The set of queries for a node n and relay r is now given by $Q_{n,r} = \{q : R_q \leq R_n \wedge relay(t_q) = r\}$. The total size of queries per node n and relay broker r can then be described by the total size of queries in $Q_{n,r}$:

$$size(n, r) = \sum_{q \in Q_{n,r}} |q|$$

Recall that the size of queries is proportional to the bandwidth required by them. By calculating $size(n, r)$ for all nodes and relay candidates, we annotate the index with the size of queries per relay candidate in each node. Note that this operation can be computed very efficiently as query sizes can be aggregated by a bottom-up traversal of the index.

In the second step, the query index is traversed top-down for nodes containing at least one query by recursively calling `mergeStreams` as described in Algorithm 2. If a node contains more than one query which can be relayed by the same broker, a new relay is established, the corresponding region is added to R. All matching queries in the sub-tree, including any existing relay streams, are merged into that relay, i.e. added to the set Q of queries to forward. If there is only a single query for the currently considered relay and $size(n, relay) > R_n + \Delta$, the query is split and the two parts are added to the two corresponding child nodes; the process then continues on each of the two child nodes. Δ is a system parameter which controls how small queries are split to limit fragmentation.

To establish the relay data stream, all affected queries are forwarded to the relay. A copy of the queries is kept locally for future merging attempts. Once all

Data: n: Index Node, relay: Relay Broker
Result: Q: Set of Queries to Forward, R: Set of Regions to Stream to Relay
if $getQueries(n, relay) == 0 \wedge size(n, relay) > 2\Delta$ **then**
     for $child \in getChildren(n)$ **do**
         mergeStreams$(child, relay)$;
     end
end
if $getQueries(n, relay) >= 2$ **then**
     $Q = Q \cup getUnassigned(n, relay)$;
     $R = R \cup getRegion(n)$;
else
     if $size(n, relay) > R_n + \Delta$ **then**
         $pushToChildren(getQueries(n, relay))$;
         for $child \in getChildren(n)$ **do**
             mergeStreams$(child, relay)$;
         end
     end
end

Algorithm 2. Stream Merging Algorithm

queries have been sent to the relay broker, the source broker signals the relay broker the end of the relay step. The single data stream containing the requested region is then sent to the relay broker and the relay broker starts relaying queries.

5   Evaluation

The GSGM has been implemented using the OMNeT++ network simulator [23] with the inet framework for IP-traffic simulation. A realistic topology was generated using the tools of ReaSE [10]. The topology consists of seven autonomous systems, two of which are set up as transit domains. The AS themselves have a hierarchical structure, based on up to three core routers on the top level which are fully connected. The second level consists of up to three gateway routers per core which are connected to the edge routers on the third level. Client nodes are connected to the edge routers using asymmetric DSL. Brokers are placed depending on the scenario. The network setup included 577 clients and an average of 48 brokers where the brokers where directly connected to routers on different levels. Clients generated queries in uniformly distributed time intervals between 30s and 300s. Each query lasted between 60s and 250s. The total simulated time span was 20 minutes. The queried regions were distributed around a single point with exponentially decreasing probability of larger distance to simulate peak load on a region. Since the location of brokers in the networks is crucial for the performance of the overall system we varied the broker placement. For the core placement, Brokers are either placed in data centers at the core of the network and connected to gateway and core routers or placed at the edge to simulate sensor gateways executing the GSGM. The full placement comprises brokers distributed randomly among all routers. We measured the data transmitted by core and gateway routers only since the links to brokers are dedicated to the GSG and the links to clients cannot be optimized.

All evaluations include the native operation (OFF). As benchmark setups, we chose to add the simple strategies presented in Section 4, including DIRECT relay only, closest to destination (CTD), and closest to source (CTS). In the farthest from source (FFS) strategy a relay is selected farthest from the source broker. By prioritizing the distance to source, the strategies result in higher network stretch and therefore diversity in paths for load balancing. Our newly developed closest to path strategy is abbreviated CTP. The numbers attached to the label show the corresponding neighborhood size, where applicable. Overall, all relay selection strategies perform well considering the total traffic used by the system. Note that by selecting a relay closest to the path (CTP) and restricting the neighborhood, the data transmission is reduced most in all runs.

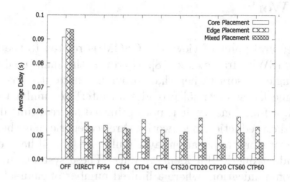

Fig. 4. Average user perceived delay for core placed brokers

The reduced bandwidth usage of our system has a positive effect on the quality of service. In a high bandwidth streaming system, the user perceived delay is significantly caused by queuing. By distributing fewer data on a single broker and leveraging more relay nodes, a larger neighborhood is beneficial for reducing the client perceived delay. However, the additional processing and propagation delay leads to increased client perceived delay for many overlay hops. For direct relaying, the many outgoing data streams on the gateway broker lead to increased queuing delay, while the prohibitively large network stretch of the farthest from source strategy increases propagation delay even for small neighborhood sizes. The trade-off can be seen in Figure 4 which also shows that closest to path (CTP) also performs best for this metric.

To investigate capacity improvement, queries were added to the system for a single gateway broker distributed over five minutes. We measured the degradation in QoS over time to show the gain in overall scalability. As Figure 5 shows, the system is able to serve all queries with stream merging enabled whereas without the delay quickly becomes prohibitively high. Note that the size of client queries is limited in all cases by the bandwidth of links to the client to avoid any effects from queuing delay and packet drops on the last mile.

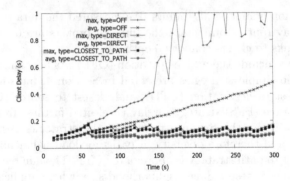

Fig. 5. Client perceived delay with increased load over time for core placed brokers

6 Related Work

From an architectural point of view, the GSGM is related to the OGC sensor web enablement (SWE) framework [18]. However, the main goal of the SWE is to contact single sensors rather than providing data streams for scientific simulations. While DataCutter [5] provides an interface similar to the GSGM and extended filter functionality, it is not optimized for real-time data.

In the field of data reduction in networks, three categories have been addressed so far: The first category, application layer multicast [15, 24] has been proposed to handle redundant queries for identical data. These systems are tailored for channel-based communication, where a limited number of channels needs to be served to a high number of clients. Consequently, they rely on the expensive detailed generation of a distribution tree. However, the content of sensor data streams is determined by individual queries rather than channels. Although extensions have been proposed to map queries to channels [7], the resulting false positives incur prohibitively high load on the network. Content-based pub/sub systems [9] as the second category aim to establish a containment relationship between the data sources and sinks, i.e. sensors and clients. They provide a flexible subscription interface which is capable of handling arbitrary queries. Pub/sub systems typically use clustering [21] or merging [6, 14] of subscriptions to reduce the processing overhead at the cost of increased bandwidth usage. Recent approaches also consider the physical structure of the network [22]. However, events occur rarely compared to sensor data which is sent out in high volume for all queried regions. Therefore, these approaches are not suitable to serve arbitrarily intersecting queries for sensor data and their resulting high bandwidth data streams. A third related category, stream processing systems [1, 11, 17, 19, 20], move processing tasks to optimize application performance and minimize network usage. Based on the underlying assumption that some of the processing tasks which can be moved reduce the bandwidth, these tasks are placed closer to the data sources. The remaining tasks are placed in a way to minimize the amount of data that is currently in transit on the network. However, the goal of these systems is to optimize latency in presence of complex interaction graphs rather than to minimize total bandwidth usage.

7 Conclusion

In this paper we presented our approach to minimize bandwidth usage for measurement distribution in a Global Sensor Grid. Using a distributed index, we partitioned queries for bandwidth management and could efficiently identify intersections between queries. Based on this knowledge, our relay strategy built an optimized distribution structure for data streams. Redundant streams are thereby joined by our new merging algorithm. The approach has been evaluated on an Internet like network topology. The results show that our optimized relay strategy yields at least 33% reduction in overall traffic. Furthermore, our approach can fully exploit brokers placed in the core of the network, achieving a total reduction of traffic of over 50%. The evaluations also show the positive effects on user perceived delay. In the future, we aim to combine the relay strategy with a clustering algorithm to better control the distribution structure.

Acknowledgments. The authors A.B. and K.R. would like to thank the German Research Foundation (DFG) for financial support of the project within the Cluster of Excellence in Simulation Technology (EXC 310/1) at the University of Stuttgart.

References

1. Abadi, D., Ahmad, Y., Balazinska, M., Cetintemel, U., Cherniack, M., Hwang, J., Lindner, W., Maskey, A., Rasin, A., Ryvkina, E., et al.: The design of the borealis stream processing engine. In: CIDR 2005 (January 2005)
2. Ahmad, Y., Nath, S.: Colr-tree: Communication-efficient spatio-temporal indexing for a sensor data web portal. In: ICDE 2008, pp. 784–793 (April 2008)
3. Balazinska, M., Deshpande, A., Franklin, M., Gibbons, P., Gray, J., Nath, S., Hansen, M., Liebhold, M., Szalay, A., Tao, V.: Data management in the worldwide sensor web. IEEE Pervasive Computing 6(2), 30–40 (2007)
4. Benzing, A., Koldehofe, B., Rothermel, K.: Efficient support for multi-resolution queries in global sensor networks. In: Proc. of the 5th International Conference on Communication System Software and Middleware, COMSWARE 2011, pp. 11:1–11:12. ACM, New York (2011)
5. Beynon, M.D., Kurc, T., Catalyurek, U., Chang, C., Sussman, A., Saltz, J.: Distributed processing of very large datasets with datacutter. Parallel Computing 27(11), 1457–1478 (2001)
6. Bianchi, S., Felber, P., Gradinariu, M.: Content-Based Publish/Subscribe Using Distributed R-Trees. In: Kermarrec, A.-M., Bougé, L., Priol, T. (eds.) Euro-Par 2007. LNCS, vol. 4641, pp. 537–548. Springer, Heidelberg (2007)
7. Boukerche, A., Roy, A., Thomas, N.: Dynamic grid-based multicast group assignment in data distribution management. In: DS-RT 2000: Proceedings of the Fourth IEEE International Workshop on Distributed Simulation and Real-Time Applications, pp. 47–54 (2000)

8. Dreyfus, S.E., Wagner, R.A.: The steiner problem in graphs. Networks 1(3), 195–207 (1971)
9. Eugster, P.T., Felber, P.A., Guerraoui, R., Kermarrec, A.M.: The many faces of publish/subscribe. ACM Computing Surveys 35(2), 114–131 (2003)
10. Gamer, T., Scharf, M.: Realistic simulation environments for IP-based networks. In: Simutools 2008, pp. 83:1–83:7. ICST (2008)
11. Gibbons, P., Karp, B., Ke, Y., Nath, S., Seshan, S.: Irisnet: An architecture for a worldwide sensor web. IEEE Pervasive Computing 2(4), 22–33 (2003)
12. Hartwell, P.: Cense: A central nervous system for the earth. In: 2011 IEEE Technology Time Machine Symposium on Technologies Beyond 2020, p. 1 (2011)
13. Iwanicki, K., van Steen, M.: Using area hierarchy for multi-resolution storage and search in large wireless sensor networks. In: ICC 2009, June 14-18, pp. 1–6 (2009)
14. Jayaram, K.R., Jayalath, C., Eugster, P.: Parametric subscriptions for content-based publish/subscribe networks. In: Gupta, I., Mascolo, C. (eds.) Middleware 2010. LNCS, vol. 6452, pp. 128–147. Springer, Heidelberg (2010)
15. Kurian, J., Sarac, K.: A survey on the design, applications, and enhancements of application-layer overlay networks. ACM Comput. Surv. 43(1), 5:1–5:34 (2010)
16. Ohsawa, Y., Sakauchi, M.: A new tree type data structure with homogeneous nodes suitable for a very large spatial database. In: ICDE 1990, February 5-9, pp. 296–303 (1990)
17. Pietzuch, P., Ledlie, J., Shneidman, J., Roussopoulos, M., Welsh, M., Seltzer, M.: Network-aware operator placement for stream-processing systems. In: ICDE 2006, p. 49. IEEE (2006)
18. Reed, C., Botts, M., Davidson, J., Percivall, G.: OGC ® sensor web enablement: Overview and high level achhitecture. In: 2007 IEEE Autotestcon, pp. 372–380 (2007)
19. Rizou, S., Dürr, F., Rothermel, K.: Fulfilling end-to-end latency constraints in large-scale streaming environments. In: IPCCC 2011, pp. 1–8 (November 2011)
20. Srivastava, U., Munagala, K., Widom, J.: Operator placement for in-network stream query processing. In: PODS 2005, pp. 250–258. ACM (2005)
21. Tariq, M.A., Koldehofe, B., Koch, G.G., Rothermel, K.: Distributed spectral cluster management: A method for building dynamic publish/subscribe systems. In: DEBS 2012: Proceedings of the 6th ACM International Conference on Distributed Event-Based Systems, pp. 213–224. ACM (2012)
22. Tariq, M.A., Koldehofe, B., Rothermel, K.: Efficient content-based routing with network topology inference. In: DEBS 2013: Proceedings of the 7th ACM International Conference on Distributed Event-based Systems, DEBS 2013, pp. 51–62. ACM, New York (2013)
23. Varga, A.: Omnet++. In: Wehrle, K., Güneş, M., Gross, J. (eds.) Modeling and Tools for Network Simulation, pp. 35–59. Springer (2010)
24. Yeo, C., Lee, B., Er, M.: A survey of application level multicast techniques. Comp. Comm. 27(15), 1547–1568 (2004)

A Fuzzy-Logic Based Coordinated Scheduling Technique for Inter-grid Architectures

Abdulrahman Azab[1,2], Hein Meling[1], and Reggie Davidrajuh[1]

[1] Dept. of Electrical Engineering and Computer Science, Faculty of Science and Technology, University of Stavanger, Norway
abdulrahman.azab@ux.uis.no, {hein.meling,reggie.davidrajuh}@uis.no
[2] Dept. of Computer and Systems Engineering, Faculty of Engineering, Mansoura University, Egypt
abdulrahman.azab@mans.edu.eg

Abstract. Inter-grid is a composition of small interconnected grid domains; each has its own local broker. The main challenge is to devise appropriate job scheduling policies that can satisfy goals such as global load balancing together with maintaining the local policies of the different domains. Existing inter-grid methodologies are based on either centralised meta-scheduling or decentralised scheduling which carried is out by local brokers, but without proper coordination. Both are suitable interconnecting grid domains, but breaks down when the number of domains become large. Earlier we proposed SLICK, a scalable resource discovery and job scheduling technique for broker based interconnected grid domains, where inter-grid scheduling decisions are handled by gateway schedulers installed on the local brokers. This paper presents a decentralised scheduling technique for the SLICK architecture, where cross-grid scheduling decisions are made using a fuzzy-logic based algorithm. The proposed technique is tested through simulating its implementation on 512 interconnected Condor pools. Compared to existing techniques, our results show that the proposed technique is better at maintaining the overall throughput and load balancing with increasing number of interconnected grids.

1 Introduction

Grid computing provides the infrastructure for aggregating different types of resources (e.g. desktops, mainframes, storage servers) for solving intensive problems in different scientific and industrial fields, e.g. DNA analysis, weather forecasting, modelling and simulation of geological phenomenon [1]. Based on the delivered service, grid computing can be classified into computational grids, and data grids [2]. The target of computational grid, which is our main focus, is to aggregate many grid compute resources as one powerful unit on which computational intensive applications can run and produce results with low latency. Computational grid model is mainly composed of three components: (i) clients that consume grid resources by submitting computational jobs, (ii) resource brokers who are responsible of allocating submitted jobs to matching workers, and

K. Magoutis and P. Pietzuch (Eds.): DAIS 2014, LNCS 8460, pp. 171–185, 2014.
© IFIP International Federation for Information Processing 2014

(iii) workers that execute submitted jobs. Due to the rapid growth in the demand for compute resources, as more and more compute intensive applications are being built, there is a need to scale up the grid infrastructure with more workers to fulfil those demands. To scale up, without negatively impacting overall performance and throughput is challenging, as increasing the number of nodes in a single grid could lead to a performance bottleneck since the broker may become overloaded.

Introducing multiple load balanced brokers for the same resource set requires some form of coordination between the brokers [3]. One possible solution is to establish an interconnection between existing grid domains. This would enable migration of grid jobs between domains to avoid job starvation. The concept of interconnecting grid domains was first introduced by the Condor project in 1992, by means of a technique called *flocking* [4]. The initial idea was to use *gateway* machine in each Condor pool, i.e. a grid domain, to manage the interconnection between domains. Due to the lack of coordination between the broker and the gateway inside domains, this has now been replaced by a client initiated approach [5], which enables client nodes to submit jobs to external brokers when no matches are found by their local brokers. This however, is not practical when a large number of interconnected domains must be configured, each with hundreds of clients that communicate with many external brokers. Other grid systems (e.g. gLite [6], Condor-G [7], UNICORE [8], Nimrod-G [9]) used the concept of meta-scheduling [10], known also as super-scheduling. Meta-schedulers work in a layer above traditional brokers so that instead of submitting to their local brokers, users submit their demands to a meta-scheduler which transfers the submissions to a broker on a grid domain which can fulfil the demand. The problem with this approach is the lack of coordination between meta-schedulers. Another approach, *broker overlay*, is to establish the interconnection through an overlay network between brokers [11,12,13,14,15,3]. This approach has proven to be scalable [11] but it doesn't achieve load balancing. The reason is that for each external job submission, the local broker sends a query to its neighbouring brokers looking for a match. Any matching outside its neighbourhood will not be detected. Avoiding this problem by constructing a fully-connected logical topology between brokers is not practical, since that will result in increased scheduling overhead as the number of links between brokers increase.

This paper presents a coordinated scheduling technique for interconnected grids, which is an addition to our SLICK broker overlay architecture [16]. In SLICK, brokers maintains resource information about workers in its domain in a reduced information set (RIS) data structure. The RIS of each domain is disseminated to other brokers through a simple gossip based protocol [17]. Thus, each broker obtains a RIS from all the other domains in the system, and maintains this information in a data structure that we call global information set (GIS). Jobs with no matching workers in their local domains are exported to external domains with matching workers. Selecting the domain to export a job to is performed through a matchmaking process between the job requirements and the resource attributes of each RIS in the local GIS. Previously in SLICK [16], we proposed a simple

matchmaking technique which finds any match. This paper proposes a fuzzy scheduler that finds the best matching domain for jobs.

The proposed technique is modelled using the PeerSim P2P network simulator [18]. Using the simulation model we have tested the proposed technique
by interconnecting simulated Condor pools [19] using SLICK. Job allocation
throughput and load balancing of the proposed technique is tested against existing scheduling techniques. The results show that for a system capacity of 50,000
nodes divided into 512 domains, the proposed technique achieves load balancing
and reasonable throughput. In the broker overlay, we used a broker-to-broker
neighbourhood degree of $k = \frac{\ln N}{\ln 2}$, where N is the total number of brokers.

The paper is organised as follows: Section 2 gives the background for the
problem, and surveys related work. Section 3 describes the design of the SLICK
gateway and the Fuzzy scheduling technique. Section 5 presents the simulation
model and our evaluation. Section 6 concludes the paper.

2 Scheduling in Inter-grid Architectures

The interconnection of grid domains may be implemented in one of three levels: (1) *Client level* where the client machine can have access to multiple domains using associated access rights [4,20], (2) *Worker level* where worker nodes
can install the task executors of multiple domains and thus becomes available
for task submissions from either of those domains [21,6], and (3) *Broker level*
where the interconnection is carried out through local resource brokers. Two
different methodologies follow the latter approach: (a) *Central meta-scheduler*,
and (b) *broker overlay*. The role of a central meta-scheduler [10] is to manage
the inter-grid submission requests, allocating each to a broker with matching
resource requirements in its domain [7,9]. Scheduling in broker overlay architectures can be further classified into: (i) *non-coordinated*, and (ii) *coordinated* [3].
For non-coordinated scheduling, there is no cooperation between brokers making
scheduling decisions for tasks assigned to external domains. One methodology
is to have a shared directory service, as in UNICORE [8], where brokers can retrieve information about workers in external domains for making cross-domain
scheduling. Another methodology is implemented in Tycoon [15], where each
broker declares a public independent auction for its available resources and external brokers can compete to gain access to them. For coordinated scheduling,
a broker communicates with other brokers for negotiation about their available
resources before taking the inter-grid scheduling decision. This communication
is implemented through two main methodologies: (A) *Broadcasting*, e.g. one-to-
all, where cross-domain job requests are sent to all external brokers and take
decisions based on positive responses [13,12,14]. This methodology is applicable
only for small number of domains, as otherwise the negotiation process would
negatively influence the overall throughput. (B) *Multi-casting*, where instead of
negotiating with all external brokers, each broker only negotiate with a select set
of neighbouring brokers based on a broker overlay structure [3,11,12,14]. This
methodology is both scalable and fault-tolerant, but due to the need to disseminate of resource information, its ability to identify available resources depends

on the neighbourhood degree [22]. This means that for a broker to search for
some specific resource information, multi-hop communication may be necessary,
since a broker overlay network can offer reliable dissemination among available
brokers. However, there can be a significant latency involved in such multi-hop
communication [23,22]. Due to this obstacle, coordinated-scheduling based inter-
grid systems only rely on a small set of resource specification parameters, e.g.
three parameters [3], for coordination.

In SLICK we implement multi-casting based coordinated scheduling, where
each broker keeps a replica of the resource information of each external domain,
and periodically synchronises local replicas with its neighbours.

3   Design

SLICK performs inter-grid job scheduling over a broker overlay of interconnected
grid domains. Each broker in the overlay has a fixed number of neighbours
$k < N$, where N is the total number of brokers. The k value is determined by
the overlay topology, that is, $k = 2$ for the Ring topology, and $k = \frac{\ln N}{\ln 2}$ for
the Hypercube topology. The system architecture is shown in Figure 1.

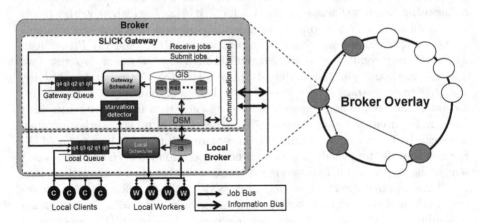

Fig. 1. System Architecture

The SLICK *gateway* is designed to be installed on broker nodes as an additional
layer on the top of the broker to manage the interaction with external domains. In
this paper, we present our implementation of the SLICK gateway for Condor[1] [19]
interconnected domains.

3.1   Condor

Condor provides a way to harness idle computational cycles for use by computational intensive distributed applications. A Condor pool is composed of: (i) *users*

---

[1] The new name of the Condor project is 'HTCondor'.

(clients), which submit jobs for execution, (ii) *executors* (workers), which runs compute jobs, and (iii) a *central manager* (broker), which is responsible for collecting job submission requests and allocate jobs to workers. One machine can operate as both client and worker. Condor uses an extensive machine and job description language called ClassAds [24]. The ClassAd describing a machine's computational power is simply number of *slots* that it can support, which is equal to the number of CPU cores on the machine. A Condor ClassAd job description can represent: (i) a *Simple job*, which has one process and needs one slot to run or (ii) a *Job cluster*, which is a collection of simple jobs and needs n slots to run, where n is the number of jobs in the job cluster. Upon a job submission to the broker, it is placed in a queue. The job waits until the broker finds a worker with resources matching the job requirements. Matchmaking is carried out between the job's ClassAd and each worker's machine ClassAd. The job is allocated to the first matching worker with idle slots. Jobs of one job cluster can be allocated to multiple worker machines based on which matching workers have idle slots.

3.2   Domain Resource Description

Condor worker software automatically detects the number of CPU cores and the size of the virtual memory of the local machine, in addition to other machine specifications (e.g. operating system), and builds the machine ClassAd. Each machine ClassAd contains more than 100 attribute-value pairs, which would result in a large amounts of network traffic in the broker overlay, if we want to disseminate the machine ClassAds of the entire domain to other domains. To overcome this problem, we divide machine ClassAds into groups based on similarities in the hardware and software specifications, e.g. all Linux machines with x86_64 architecture, physical memory > 2 GB, supports Java, ..., are in group 1. The number of machine group is the number of all available machine specifications which is supported by Condor [25], and exist in ≥ 1 worker machines in the system. The domain resource description is stored in the SLICK gateway as a RIS, which is composed of: (i) a collection of key-value pairs, where the key is a machine group id and the value is the total number of slots which machines belong to the associated group. (ii) a time-stamp, ts, representing the read time of the RIS. The structure of the RIS is described in [16].

3.3   Resource Information Sharing

As described above, in addition to its local RIS, each domain keeps a replica of the RIS of the other domains in the system in the GIS, as shown in Figure 1. The RIS replication between brokers in the overlay is carried out by a data synchronisation manager, DSM. The DSM in each broker implements a simple anti-entropy gossip protocol [17], to synchronise the local GIS with its neighbours. The gossip protocol is described in [16].

4 Inter-grid Scheduling

The roles of the SLICK gateway are: (i) Receive jobs submitted by external brokers throughout the overlay and schedule them to the local job queue[2]. (ii) Schedule starving local jobs to external brokers. A job j is declared as *starving* by the *starvation detector* (see Figure 1), if (CurrentTime - SubmissionTime(j)) $> \beta$, where β is a timeout value. Whenever a job is detected to be starving, it is moved to the gateway queue (GQ). The gateway scheduler performs matchmaking between jobs in GQ and each RIS stored in the GIS, and submits each job to a matching broker.

In our previous paper introducing the SLICK [16] architecture, we implemented a simple matchmaking technique, *any-match*. Matchmaking was performed between the job description ClassAd and the RIS replicas of only neighbour domains in the overlay. Upon finding any match D_x for job j, implied that domain D_x contained one or more workers who's machine group matches the requirements of job j. This would result in job j being allocated to domain D_x. This technique works well for scheduling simple jobs. In this section we introduce a new matchmaking technique, *best-match*, where either a simple job or a job cluster is allocated to the domain with the highest match. The new technique is illustrated with an example of a job cluster in Figure 2.

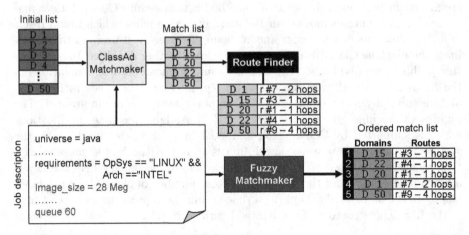

Fig. 2. Matchmaking of a Condor job cluster using the SLICK gateway scheduler

1. An initial matchmaking is performed between the description of the job cluster j and each $RIS_x \in GIS$ of a domain D_x. The ClassAd matchmaker works similar to the Condor matchmaker, called *condor_negotiator*, where the result is a true/false value for each RIS. The result is true for D_x if there exists a set of workers $\{W : |W| > 1 \land W \in D_x\}$, and the machine group of each worker $w \in W$ matches the job requirements of j. In the example

---

[2] This may result in contention between local jobs and external jobs. We are planning to add a contention manager to avoid this problem in the future.

above, Arch is Intel, OpSys is Linux, and Java is installed. The output is a
list of matching domains, *match list*.

2. The match list is passed to the *router*, which finds the route from the local
   domain D to each domain D_x in the list. If the brokers of D and D_x are
   neighbours in the overlay, then the route is a direct path with zero hops.
   Otherwise, the route with the smallest number of hops between D and D_x,
   $r(D_x)$ selected. The route description is added to each domain in the list.
3. The new match list together with the job description are passed to the fuzzy
   matchmaker, where an *ordered match list* is generated based on best-match-
   first. The role of the fuzzy matchmaker is described in Section 4.1.
4. The local gateway scheduler allocates j to the first domain in the list. The
   other domains in the list are substitutes in case of failure or rejection.

4.1   Fuzzy Matchmaker

The fuzzy matchmaking is implemented based on Takagi-Sugeno fuzzy model [26],
in which output membership functions are either linear or constant. In this implementation, constant output membership functions are used. Here we continue
using the example in Figure 2, but with only three domains in the match list for
simplicity. The following steps are carried out by the fuzzy matchmaker:

Generation of Input Membership Functions. Each domain in the match list
is viewed as a fuzzy set. Each fuzzy set has two *dynamic* input membership functions, related to two crisp inputs: (i) The number of CPU slots required by the job
(60 slots in Figure 2), and (ii) Image_size which is the maximum amount of memory consumed by the job while running on the worker node (28 MB in Figure 2).
The input membership functions for each domain are generated as follows:

1. The fuzzy matchmaker contacts the broker of each domain D_x in the list
   to obtain two values: (i) the current number of idle slots v_{D_x}, and (ii) the
   current queue size q_{D_x}.
2. The $\sharp$ CPU slots membership function is generated by (1), where S_{D_x} is the
   set of all CPU slots in D_x, read from RIS_x, and v_{D_x}. Three examples of $\sharp$
   CPU slots membership functions are shown in Figure 3a, where $|S_{D_1}| = 100$,
   and $v_{D_1} = 35$

$$Y_{D_x}(x) = \begin{cases} 1 & x \in [0, v_{D_x}] \\ \frac{x - |S_{D_x}|}{v_{D_x} - |S_{D_x}|} & x \in [v_{D_x}, |S_{D_x}|] \end{cases} \qquad (1)$$

3. The Image_size membership function is generated by (2) based on the fact
   that a job with an image size I must be allocated to a worker with virtual
   memory capacity $\geq I$. The x-axis is divided into intervals $(x_{i-1}, x_i]$, where
   $i \in \{1, 2, \ldots, 6\}$, assuming that the image size of any job won't exceed 60 MB.
   The Image_size membership function of domain D_x is generated as follows:
   For each interval $(x_{i-1}, x_i]$, we generate a set of CPU slots S_{x_i} as a subset

of the total CPU slots in the domain, and the virtual memory size of each slot's machine $\in S_{x_i} \geq x_i$. The result will be a histogram. The membership function is generated using (2c) by connecting the second edge of each bar in the histogram to the next bar's using a straight line, and divide the result by the total number of slots in the domain, $|S|$ in order to keep $Y(x) < 1$. Three examples of the Image_size membership function are shown in Figure 3b.

$$S_{D_x}(x_i) = \{s|\ s \in S_{D_x} \wedge vm(s) \geq x_i\} \tag{2a}$$

$$y_{D_x}(x) = |S_{D_x}(x_i)|\quad \forall x \in (x_{i-1}, x_i] \tag{2b}$$

$$Y_{D_x}(x) = \frac{1}{|S_{D_x}|}\left[\frac{(y_{D_x}(x_{i-1}) - y_{D_x}(x_i))(x - x_i)}{x_{i-1} - x_i} + y_{D_x}(x_i)\right]\quad \forall x \in (x_{i-1}, x_i] \tag{2c}$$

Fuzzification of Inputs. The fuzzification process is to take the inputs, determine the degree to which they belong to each of the appropriate fuzzy sets via input membership functions. Using the two inputs of Figure 2, 60 slots and 28 MB image size, the degree of membership in the three domains, D_{15}, D_{22}, and D_{20} is determined by the intersection as shown in Figure 3a.

Applying Fuzzy Operator. Once the inputs have been fuzzified, we know the degree to which each part of the antecedent has been satisfied for each rule. A separate rule must be created for each domain, D_x in the match list of the matchmaking process for job j. The rule for N domains can be formulated as follows:

if $CPUSlotsOf(j)$ **is** $AllocatableInCPUSlots(D_i)$
and $MemoryImageOf(j)$ **is** $AllocatableInVirtualMemory(D_i)$
then j **is** $AllocatableIn(D_i)$

where $i = 1, 2, \ldots, N$ and D_i is the domain identifier. The **and** operator used in the rule above is implemented as a minimum function: V_1 **and** $V_2 = \min(V_1, V_2)$. Using the example of Figure 3, $membership_{D_{15}} = \min(1, 0.63) = 0.63$.

Applying the Implication Method. Before applying the implication method, we set each rule's weight. The rule weight of the fuzzy set associated with each domain D_x is calculated as:

$$RW(D_x) = \frac{1}{|r_{D_x}| \times (1 + \frac{q_{D_x}}{|S_{D_x}|})}$$

where $|r_{D_x}|$ is the number of hops in the shortest route from the local domain to D_x, q_{D_x} is the queue size of D_x, and $|S_{D_x}|$ is the total number of slots in D_x. Once

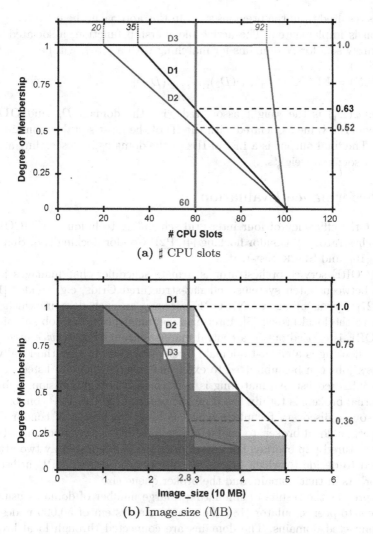

Fig. 3. Fuzzy input membership functions

proper weighting has been assigned to a rule, each of the resulted values from implementing the fuzzy operator in each rule is multiplied with its associated rule weight. The output membership function associated with each fuzzy set will be a single number representing the unique identifier of the associated domain $(ID(D_x)\ i = 1, \ldots, N)$. The outputs of all rules are aggregated into a single fuzzy set whose membership function assigns a weighting for every output value, so that the domain with the highest match will have the highest resulted weight.

Defuzzification. The input to the defuzzification process is the aggregate output fuzzy set and the output is a single number. The fuzzy set is the collection of weights resulted from the previous step. In this approach, the maxima aggregate function is implemented. The active membership function, associated with N input fuzzy sets for N domains for matching with a job j, will be:

$$\mathbf{OUT}(j,N) = \mathbf{MAX}[w(D_1),\ w(D_2),\ \ldots,\ w(D_N)]$$

Where: $w(D_i)$ is the weight associated with the domain D_i, and $\mathbf{OUT}(j,N)$ represents the value associated with the ID of the most suitable domain to allocate j. The final output is a List of IDs of the domains in descending according to the associated weights.

5   Performance Evaluation

We test the efficiency of four inter-grid scheduling techniques: UNICORE service orchestrator [8], Condor flocking [4], P2P Condor flocking [11], SLICK first-match [16], and SLICK best-match.

UNICORE service orchestrator is a meta-scheduler that manages job allocation between batch systems and flat-structured Grids, e.g. condor [19] and PBS [27], by installing a UNICORE *gateway* on each domain which is connected to the local broker [8]. Inter-grid communication and job submission in UNICORE is carried out in a central manner through the *service orchestrator*. Condor flocking is a client-to-domain interconnection. In case the local workers are busy, jobs can be submitted to external brokers which are listed in a manually configured list. No matching is performed before submission. Submission to external brokers is totally based on the order of the list. P2P condor flocking is a resource discovery technique which is built on the top of condor Central-Manager, i.e. local broker, to enable interconnecting condor pools, i.e. domains, in a structured p2p overlay. For cross-domain submissions, Only two attributes are used to decide to which broker to submit two: average CPU utilisation of the workers in that domain, and the broker queue size.

We present the results of simulating a large number of domains using Peer-Sim peer-to-peer simulator [18]. We simulate a system of 50,000 nodes in 512 interconnected domains. The domains are connected through local brokers in a HyperCube logical topology, i.e. in case of N interconnected domains, each broker will have k neighbours in its routing table where $k = \frac{\ln N}{\ln 2}$. In case of 512 brokers, each broker will have 9 neighbours. We implement a HyperCube instead of a full Mesh since it uses a smaller neighbourhood degree k and at the same time achieves efficient data synchronisation, described in [28]. In case of UNICORE service orchestrator, a logical star topology is used since UNICORE implements central meta-scheduling. Worker machine specifications are of two machine configuration groups:

- group1: 2 CPU slots, 4GB Memory, Windows OS, No java support.
- group2: 4 CPU slots, 8GB Memory, Linux OS, Java support

Workers are divided equally between the two groups, 25,000 each, but scattered among the domains. We create a load of total 80,000 synthetic jobs. Job resource requirements are randomly set to be matching either group1 or group2. The execution time of each job is uniformly distributed $t \in [100, 300]$ time units. Jobs are divided into 100 sequences. Each sequence is assigned to one broker. Using a uniformly distributed frequency $f \in [50, 100]$ time units, a uniformly distributed number of jobs $j \in [50, 100]$ is submitted periodically by each sequence. The process continues until all the 80,000 jobs are submitted. The total simulation time of the experiment is set to 2000 time units. The simulation is configured such that each of the following takes places in a one simulation time unit:

- The local scheduler processes one job from the local queue, i.e. either allocating the job in the local domain in case of local matching.
- The gateway scheduler processes one job from the gateway queue, in case of SLICK, i.e. allocating the job to the matching domain. The job transmission time is proportional to the route length from the local domain to the matching domain, e.g. if the route length is 3 hops then the job transmission time is 3 time units.
- Each SLICK broker synchronises GIS with one neighbour broker in the overlay. The GIS synchronisation algorithm is described in [16]. Due to the size reduction of the resource information, each GIS synchronisation takes only one time unit.

We use two benchmarks: *Job allocation throughput*, and *Load balancing*.

Job Allocation Throughput. is measured by reading the total number of waiting jobs in the system/time, Figure 4a, and number of job allocation trials Figure 4b. In terms of decreasing the number of waiting jobs, it is clear that both SLICK any-match and best-match techniques manage to reach a steady state. The any-match manages to allocate all jobs within 1800 time units, while best-mach does in 1345 time units. This shows the positive influence of applying the new technique on the performance. With other systems, a bottleneck case happens. This can be described that: For the UNICORE case, this is due to the fact that there is only one central meta-scheduler to carryout interconnections, which for cross-domain submissions allocates only one job per time unit. In case of flocking and p2p flocking, the reason of the bottleneck is the difference in worker specifications. for flocking, the brokers in the flocking list may be already saturated and/or don't have matching workers. In p2p flocking, the best broker is chosen based on its queue size and average CPU utilisation of its domain. However, the domain with the least loaded queue and lowest CPU utilisation may not have matching workers in other terms, e.g. operating system. The breakdown in curves after ≈ 800 time units is because we configured all job sequences to complete their submissions by that time. This was done in order to validate the system performance when job allocation is carried out only inter-domain and not intra-domain. The job allocation trials benchmark, Figure 4b, tells how many jobs needed to be reallocated to another domain how many times in order to start running. The value of $y(x_i)$ is the number of jobs which needed to be reallocated x_i times. $y(0)$ is the number of jobs which have not been reallocated, i.e. were successfully allocated in their local domains. In case of SLICK best-match, the number of re-allocations doesn't exceed 4. +50% of jobs are reallocated once. This is a positive indication that almost all scheduling decisions are accurate. In case of SLICK any-match, the number of re-allocations exceeds 300 sometime. This is mainly because a matching domain doesn't necessarily has a number of idle slots matching a particular job in the time of this job's submission. All jobs are managed to find a suitable domains though. Other systems show different behaviours, but not much can be concluded since none of them manage to allocate all jobs. So, the displayed behaviour is not for a small portion of jobs.

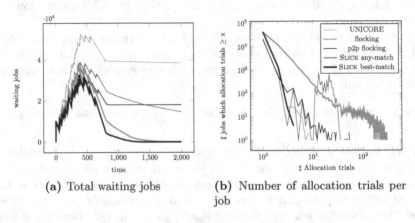

(a) Total waiting jobs

(b) Number of allocation trials per job

Fig. 4. system throughput: Overall Job Allocation Performance

Load Balancing. is measured by calculating for brokers, throughout the simulation: How long did it take to allocate all jobs owned by the domain of each broker, and what is the average waiting time. In Figure 5, it is clear that for SLICK any-match technique, the total allocation time never exceeded 1500 time units and the average waiting time is below 800. The output is even better in case of SLICK best-match, the total allocation time is below 1000, and the average waiting time is below 700. For UNICORE, none of the domains were able to finish the job allocation before the end of the simulation at 2000 time units. The same case occurs for more than half of the brokers in case of flocking and p2p flocking. The value of 2000 for both total allocation time and average waiting time indicates that this broker's jobs were not totally allocated.

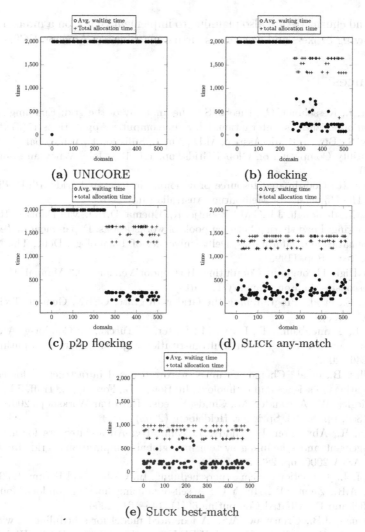

Fig. 5. Load balancing: Average waiting time and total allocation time of jobs submitted to each of 512 domains

6   Conclusions

This paper presented a coordinated scheduling technique for interconnected Grid domains. The key feature of the proposed technique is to allocate starving local jobs to the best-match domain, which is carried out by a fuzzy matchmaking. The proposed technique is tested through simulating its implementation on 512 interconnected Condor pools. It was proven that the proposed technique provides accurate cross-scheduling decisions compared to other techniques. Results also show that the proposed technique achieves load-balancing, high throughput, and is stable under high loads. We are planning to develop a failure control model for broker failures and churn. We are also planning to implement SLICK on a inter-grid prototype having brokers and workers as virtual machines on Amazon EC2.

References

1. Foster, I., Kesselman, C., Tuecke, S.: The anatomy of the grid: Enabling scalable virtual organizations. International J. Supercomputer Applications 15(3) (2001)
2. Yeo, C.S., Buyya, R., de Assuno, M.D., Yu, J., Sulistio, A., Venugopal, S., Placek, M.: Utility Computing on Global Grids, pp. 110–130. John Wiley and Sons, Inc. (2007)
3. Ranjan, R.: Coordinated resource provisioning in federated grids. Ph.D. dissertation, The University of Melbourne, Australia (July 2007)
4. Evers, X., de Jongh, J.F.C.M., Boontje, R., Epema, D.H.J., van Dantzig, R.: Condor flocking: Load sharing between pools of workstations. Department of Technical Mathematics and Informatics, Delft University of Technology, Delft, The Netherlands, Tech. Rep. (1993)
5. C. for High Throughput Computing, HTCondor Version 7.9.3 Manual, University of Wisconsin-Madison (January 16, 2013)
6. Laure, E., et al.: Programming the Grid with gLite. CERN, Geneva, Tech. Rep. (March 2006)
7. Frey, J., Tannenbaum, T., Livny, M., Foster, I., Tuecke, S.: Condor-g: A computation management agent for multi-institutional grids. Cluster Computing 5(3), 237–246 (2002)
8. Schuller, B., et al.: Chemomentum - unicore 6 based infrastructure for complex applications in science and technology. In: Bougé, L., Forsell, M., Träff, J.L., Streit, A., Ziegler, W., Alexander, M., Childs, S. (eds.) Euro-Par Workshops 2007. LNCS, vol. 4854, pp. 82–93. Springer, Heidelberg (2008)
9. Buyya, R., Abramson, D., Giddy, J.: Nimrod/g: An architecture for a resource management and scheduling system in a global computational grid. In: Procee. HPC ASIA 2000, pp. 283–289 (2000)
10. Schopf, J.: Ten actions when superscheduling. In: Global Grid Forum. (2001)
11. Butt, A.R., Zhang, R., Hu, Y.C.: A self-organizing flock of condors. Journal of Parallel and Distributed Computing 66(1), 145–161 (2006)
12. Weissman, J.B., Grimshaw, A.S.: A federated model for scheduling in wide-area systems. In: Proceedings of the 5th IEEE International Symposium on High Performance Distributed Computing, HPDC 1996, pp. 542–550. IEEE Computer Society, Washington, DC (1996)
13. Shan, H., Oliker, L., Biswas, R.: Job superscheduler architecture and performance in computational grid environments. In: Proc. of the 2003 ACM/IEEE Conference on Supercomputing (SC), pp. 44–58 (2003)
14. Daval-Frerot, C., Lacroix, M., Guyennet, H.: Federation of resource traders in objects-oriented distributed systems. In: Proceedings of the International Conference on Parallel Computing in Electrical Engineering, PARELEC 2000, pp. 84–88. IEEE Computer Society, Washington, DC (2000)
15. Lai, K., Rasmusson, L., Adar, E., Zhang, L., Huberman, B.A.: Tycoon: An implementation of a distributed, market-based resource allocation system. Multiagent Grid Syst. 1(3), 169–182 (2005)
16. Azab, A., Meling, H.: Slick: A coordinated job allocation technique for inter-grid architectures. In: 7th European Modelling Symposium, EMS (November 2013)

17. Vahdat, A., Becker, D.: Epidemic routing for partially connected ad hoc networks. Duke University, Tech. Rep. (July 2000)
18. Montresor, A., Jelasity, M.: PeerSim: A scalable P2P simulator. In: Proc. of the 9th Int. Conference on Peer-to-Peer (P2P 2009), Seattle, WA, pp. 99–100 (September 2009)
19. Litzkow, M., Livny, M., Mutka, M.: Condor - A hunter of idle workstations. In: Proceedings of the 8th International Conference of Distributed Computing Systems (June 1988)
20. Aiftimiei, C., Andreetto, P., Bertocco, S., Dalla Fina, S., Dorigo, A., Frizziero, E., Gianelle, A., Marzolla, M., Mazzucato, M., Sgaravatto, M., Traldi, S., Zangrando, L.: Design and implementation of the glite cream job management service. Future Gener. Comput. Syst. 26(4), 654–667 (2010)
21. NorduGrid: Nordic Testbed for Wide Area Computing and Data Handling, http://www.nordugrid.org/
22. Rowstron, A., Druschel, P.: Pastry: Scalable, decentralized object location, and routing for large-scale peer-to-peer systems. In: Guerraoui, R. (ed.) Middleware 2001. LNCS, vol. 2218, pp. 329–350. Springer, Heidelberg (2001)
23. Stoica, I., Morris, R., Liben-nowell, D., Karger, D.R., Kaashoek, M.F., Dabek, F., Balakrishnan, H.: Chord: A scalable peer-to-peer lookup protocol for internet applications. IEEE/ACM Transactions on Networking 11, 17–32 (2003)
24. Raman, R., Livny, M., Solomon, M.: Matchmaking: Distributed resource management for high throughput computing. In: Proceedings of the Seventh IEEE International Symposium on High Performance Distributed Computing (HPDC7), Chicago, IL (July 1998)
25. 2.5 Submitting a Job, http://research.cs.wisc.edu/htcondor/manual/v7.8/
26. Takagi, T., Sugeno, M.: Fuzzy identification of systems and its applications to modeling and control. IEEE Transactions on Systems, Man and Cybernetics 15, 116–132 (1985)
27. Bode, B., Halstead, D.M., Kendall, R., Lei, Z., Jackson, D.: The portable batch scheduler and the maui scheduler on linux clusters. In: Proceedings of the 4th Annual Linux Showcase & Conference, ALS 2000, vol. 4, p. 27. USENIX Association, Berkeley (2000)
28. Azab, A., Meling, H.: Decentralized service allocation in a broker overlay based grid. In: Jaatun, M.G., Zhao, G., Rong, C. (eds.) Cloud Computing. LNCS, vol. 5931, pp. 200–211. Springer, Heidelberg (2009)

Distributed Vertex-Cut Partitioning

Fatemeh Rahimian[1,2], Amir H. Payberah[1]
Sarunas Girdzijauskas[2], and Seif Haridi[1]

[1] Swedish Institute of Computer Science, Stockholm, Sweden
{fatemeh,amir,seif}@sics.se
[2] KTH - Royal Institute of Technology, Stockholm, Sweden
sarunasg@kth.se

Abstract. Graph processing has become an integral part of big data analytics. With the ever increasing size of the graphs, one needs to partition them into smaller clusters, which can be managed and processed more easily on multiple machines in a distributed fashion. While there exist numerous solutions for edge-cut partitioning of graphs, very little effort has been made for vertex-cut partitioning. This is in spite of the fact that vertex-cuts are proved significantly more effective than edge-cuts for processing most real world graphs. In this paper we present JA-BE-JA-VC, a parallel and distributed algorithm for vertex-cut partitioning of large graphs. In a nutshell, JA-BE-JA-VC is a local search algorithm that iteratively improves upon an initial random assignment of edges to partitions. We propose several heuristics for this optimization and study their impact on the final partitioning. Moreover, we employ simulated annealing technique to escape local optima. We evaluate our solution on various graphs and with variety of settings, and compare it against two state-of-the-art solutions. We show that JA-BE-JA-VC outperforms the existing solutions in that it not only creates partitions of any requested size, but also requires a vertex-cut that is better than its counterparts and more than 70% better than random partitioning.

1 Introduction

A wide variety of real-world data can be naturally described as graphs. Take for instance communication networks, social networks, biological networks, etc. With the ever increasing size of such networks, it is crucial to exploit the natural connectedness of their data in order to store and process them efficiently. Hence, we are now observing an upsurge in the development of distributed and parallel graph processing tools and techniques. Since the size of the graphs can grow very large, sometimes we have to partition them into multiple smaller clusters that can be processed efficiently in parallel. Unlike the conventional parallel data processing, parallel graph processing requires each vertex or edge to be processed in the context of its neighborhood. Therefore, it is important to maintain the locality of information while partitioning the graph across multiple (virtual) machines. It is also important to produce equal size partitions that distribute the computational load evenly between clusters.

K. Magoutis and P. Pietzuch (Eds.): DAIS 2014, LNCS 8460, pp. 186–200, 2014.

Fig. 1. Partitioning a graph into three clusters, using (a) edge-cut partitioning and (b) vertex-cut partitioning

Graph partitioning is a well known NP-Complete problem in graph theory. In its classical form, graph partitioning usually refers to *edge-cut* partitioning, that is, to divide vertices of a graph into disjoint clusters of nearly equal size, while the number of edges that span separated clusters is minimum. However, tools that utilize edge-cut partitioning do not achieve good performance on real-world graphs (which are mostly power-law graphs) [1,2,3], mainly due to unbalanced number of edges in each cluster. In contrast, both theory [4] and practice [5,6] prove that power-law graphs can be efficiently processed in parallel if *vertex-cuts* are used.

A *vertex-cut* partitioning divides edges of a graph into equal size clusters. The vertices that hold the endpoints of an edge are also placed in the same cluster as the edge itself. However, the vertices are not unique across clusters and might have to be *replicated* (cut), due to the distribution of their edges across different clusters. A good vertex-cut is one that requires minimum number of replicas. Figure 1 illustrate the difference between these two types of partitioning.

While there exist numerous approximate solutions for edge-cut partitioning, very little work has investigated vertex-cut partitioning. Figure 2 shows a graph with three different vertex-cut partitionings. The graph edges are partitioned into two clusters. Two colors, yellow and blue, are representing these two partitions. Vertices that have edges of one color only, are also colored accordingly, and the vertices that have to be replicated are colored white. A very naïve solution is to randomly assign edges to partitions. As shown in Figure 2(a), nearly all the vertices have edges of different colors, thus, they have to be replicated in both partitions. Figure 2(b) illustrates what happens if we use an edge-cut partitioner, and then assign the cut edges to one of the partitions randomly. As shown, the vertex-cut improves significantly. However, the number of edges in the partitions is very unbalanced. What we desire is depicted in Figure 2(c), where the vertex-cut is kept as low as possible, while the size of the partitions, with respect to the number of edges, is balanced.

An alternative solution for vertex-cut partitioning of a graph G is to transform it to its corresponding line graph $L(G)$ (where $L(G)$ represents the adjacencies between edges of G) and then use an edge-cut partitioning algorithm. However, in most real-world graphs the number of edges are orders of magnitude higher than the number of vertices, thus, the line graph often has a significantly higher number of vertices. Consequently, the complexity of the partitioning could grow drastically. It is, therefore, necessary to devise algorithms that performs the vertex-cut partitioning on the original graph.

In this paper, we present a distributed vertex-cut partitioning algorithm, called JA-BE-JA-VC, based on local search optimization, which is mainly inspired by our

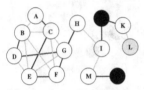 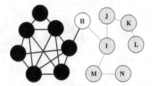 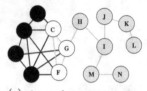

(a) A random vertex-cut. Edges are evenly distributed, but nearly all the vertices have to be replicated.

(b) Partitioning based on edge-cut and then assigning the cut edges randomly to one partition. Only one vertex is replicated, but edges are not evenly distributed.

(c) A good vertex-cut partitioning. Three vertices are replicated and the number of edges in the two partitions are balanced.

Fig. 2. Vertex-cut partitioning into two clusters. The color of each edge/vertex represents the partition it belongs to. The white vertices belong to both partitions.

previous work for edge-cut partitioning [7]. The algorithm starts with a random assignment of edges to partitions. For simplicity we represent each partition with a distinct *color*. Over time, vertices exchange information (about the color of their edges) with each other and try to locally reduce the vertex-cut, by negotiating over the assignment of their edges to partitions. Every vertex attempts to assign all its edges to the same partition (same color), because this means the vertex does not have to be cut. If this case is not possible due to the contention between neighboring vertices, then the vertex tries to have the minimum number of distinct assignments. Two vertices will decide to exchange the colors of their candidate edges, if the vertex-cut can be reduced. Otherwise, the edge colors are preserved.

The aforementioned heuristic is likely to get stuck in local optima due to initial random partitioning and the nature of the problem, which is NP-Complete. Thus, we employ the well-known simulated annealing technique [8] to escape local optima and find a better vertex-cut. Note, JA-BE-JA-VC will always maintain the initial distribution of partition sizes. That is, if the initialization is uniformly random, the partition sizes are expected to be balanced. If we require to have partitions of a different distribution, e.g., one partition twice as big as the others, then we only need to change the initialization step to produce the required distribution.

We observe through experiments, that JA-BE-JA-VC produces quality partitions on several large graphs and scales well with varying number of partitions. We also study the trade-off between the vertex-cut and the computation cost, in terms of the number of iterations to compute the partitioning. Finally, we compare JA-BE-JA-VC to the state-of-the-art vertex-cut partitioner [9], as well as the state-of-the-art edge-cut partitioner [7], and study their existing the trade-offs. We show that JA-BE-JA-VC consistently outperforms [7] and [9] on producing requested size partitions, while not sacrificing the vertex-cut. Even for varying number of partitions, JA-BE-JA-VC always reduces the vertex-cut to lower than 30% and down to 10% for some graphs.

2   Problem Statement

We are given an undirected graph $G = (V, E)$, where V is the set of vertices and E is the set of edges. A k-way balanced *vertex-cut* partitioning divides the set of edges E into k subsets of equal size, where k is an input parameter. Each partition also has a subset of vertices that hold at least one of the edges in that partition. However, vertices are not unique across partitions, that is, some vertices may appear in more than one partition, due to the distribution of their edges across several partitions. A good edge partitioning strives to minimize the number of vertices that belong to more than one partition.

A k-way balanced vertex-cut partitioning can be given with the help of a partition function $\pi : E \to \{1, \ldots, k\}$ that assigns a *color* to each edge. Hence, $\pi(e)$, or π_e for short, refers to the color of edge e. Edges with the same color form a partition. We denote the set of edges that are connected to vertex p by E_p. Accordingly, $E_p(c)$ indicates the subset of edges of p that have color c:

$$E_p(c) = \{e \in E_p : \pi_e = c\} \tag{1}$$

We refer to $|E_p(c)|$ as the *cardinality* of color c at vertex p. Then, the *energy* of a vertex p is shown with $\gamma(p, \pi)$ and it is defined as the number of different colors that has a cardinality greater than zero.

$$\gamma(p, \pi) = \sum_{|E_p(c)|>0} 1, \forall\, c \in \{1, \ldots, k\} \tag{2}$$

In other words, the energy of a vertex p for a partition function π is the number of different colors that are assigned to the edges of p, which is equivalent to the number of required replicas (vertex-cut) for p. The energy of the graph is sum of the energy of all its vertices:

$$\Gamma(G, \pi) = \sum_{p \in V} \gamma(p, \pi) \tag{3}$$

Now we can formulate an optimization problem as follows: find the optimal partitioning π^* such that:

$$\pi^* = \arg \min_{\pi} \Gamma(G, \pi) \tag{4}$$

$$s.t.\ |E(c_1)| = |E(c_2)|, \forall\, c_1, c_2 \in \{1, \ldots, k\} \tag{5}$$

where $|E(c)|$ is the number of edges with color c. Note, in all practical cases the second condition is relaxed, such that it requires partitions of **approximately** equal size. This is important, because the number of edges of the graph is not necessarily a multiple of k. Therefore, throughout this paper, we address the relaxed version of the problem.

3   Solution

In order to partition the edges of a given graph, we use an approach inspired by Ja-be-Ja [7], our previous work on edge-cut partitioning. Our algorithm, called JA-BE-JA-VC, is vertex-centric and fully distributed, and no central point with a global

Algorithm 1. Optimization sketch

```
 1: procedure RUN()
 2:     if self.isInternal() is not TRUE then
 3:         selfEdge ← self.selectEdge()                          ▷ Select an edge (Algorithm 2)
 4:         candidates ← self.selectCandidates()   ▷ Select a list of candidate vertices (Algorithm 3)
 5:         for all partner in candidates do        ▷ Look for a swap partner among the candidates
 6:             if partner is not internal then
 7:                 if policy is DominantColor then
 8:                     selfColor ← self.getDominantColor()
 9:                     partnerColor ← partner.getDominantColor()
10:                     if selfColor ≠ partnerColor and partner.hasEdge(selfColor) then
11:                         partnerEdge ← partner.selectEdge(selfColor)
12:                         swapColor(selfEdge, partnerEdge)
13:                         break
14:                     end if
15:                 else                                        ▷ If the policy is based on Edge Utility
16:                     partnerEdge ← partner.selectEdge()
17:                     if swapUtility(selfEdge, partnerEedge) > 0 then
18:                         swapColor(selfEdge, partnerEedge)
19:                         break
20:                     end if
21:                 end if
22:             end if
23:         end for
24:     end if
25: end procedure
```

knowledge is required. Vertices of the graph execute the algorithm independently and iteratively. In this algorithm, initially a random color is assigned to each edge of the graph. This is equivalent to a random assignment of edges to partitions. Then we allow vertices to exchange the color of their edges, provided that the exchange leads to a better cut of the graph. In the initialization step we can control the required partition size distribution. If edges are initially assigned to partitions uniformly at random, then size of the partitions is expected to be equal. We could also use any other distribution for initial edge assignment, and JA-BE-JA-VC guarantees to preserve this distribution during the course of optimization.

The optimization step is illustrated in Algorithm 1. In each iteration, first a vertex checks whether or not it is *internal*. An internal vertex is a vertex that is surrounded with the edges of the same color (i.e., $\gamma(p, \pi) = 1$). If the vertex is internal, it does not need to perform any optimization and waits for its turn in the next round. Otherwise, the vertex proceeds with the following three steps: (i) *edge selection*, (ii) *partner selection*, and (iii) *swap*. Each of these steps could be realized by means of various policies. Here we explain a few possible policies for these steps separately.

3.1   Edge Selection

In this step a vertex selects one of its edges for color exchange. We consider two policies for edge selection: (i) *random* and (ii) *greedy*. In the random policy, a vertex chooses one edge of its edges randomly. Although random selection is very straight forward, it will not lead our local search in the right direction. Consider, for example, a vertex with a majority of edges with blue color and just very few

Algorithm 2. Edge Selection

```
1: procedure SELECTEDGE(COLOR)
2:     if color is null then
3:         color ← self.getColorWithMinCardinality()
4:     end if
5:     edges ← self.getEdges(color)
6:     return edges.getRandomElement()
7: end procedure
```

Algorithm 3. Partner Selection

```
1: procedure SELECTCANDIDATES()
2:     candidates ← self.getNeighbours().getSubset()        ▷ a subset of direct neighbors
3:     candidates.add(getRandomVertices())        ▷ a subset of random vertices from the graph
4:     return candidates
5: end procedure
```

Algorithm 4. Calculate Swap Utility

```
1: procedure SWAPUTILITY(edge1, edge2)
2:     c1 ← edge1.getColor()
3:     c2 ← edge2.getColor()
4:     u1c1 ← getEdgeValue(edge1.src, edge1.dest, c1);        ▷ utility of edge1 before swap
5:     u2c2 ← getEdgeValue(edge2.src, edge2.dest, c2);        ▷ utility of edge2 before swap
6:     u1c2 ← getEdgeValue(edge1.src, edge1.dest, c2);        ▷ utility of edge1 after swap
7:     u2c1 ← getEdgeValue(edge2.src, edge2.dest, c1);        ▷ utility of edge2 after swap
8:     return ((u1c2 + u2c1) × T_r) − (u1c1 + u2c2)
9: end procedure
```

red edges. If this vertex selects a random edge for a color exchange, it is more likely that the vertex selects a blue edge (because it has a majority of blue edges), and such selection is not in the interest of the vertex. Whereas, if the vertex selects an edge with red color, it will have a higher chance of unifying the color of its edges. With a greedy policy, a vertex selects one of its edges, e.g., e, which has a color with minimum cardinality:

$$e \in E_p(c^*), \quad c^* = arg\min_c |E_p(c)|$$

Since random policy is ineffective in our optimization process, we only consider the greedy edge selection in our experiments. Algorithm 2 describes how an edge is selected with this policy.

3.2 Partner Selection

In this step a vertex selects a subset of other vertices from the graph as candidates for a color exchange. A vertex considers two sets of vertices for partner selection: (i) *direct neighbors*, and (ii) *random* vertices. Direct neighbors of a vertex p are a set of vertices that are directly connected to p. Every vertex has knowledge about its directly connected neighbors. Since some vertices may have a very large degree, this local search could become exhaustive for such vertices if they have to check each and every of their neighbors. Hence, vertices only consider a fixed-size random subset of their direct neighbors.

Vertices choose their partners for color exchange first from their direct neighboring. To increase the chance of finding a swap partner, vertices also consider a few random vertices from the graph. This random subset of vertices could be acquired through a peer sampling service [10,11,12,13] or random walk [14] that is continuously running on all the graph vertices. In our previous work [7] we have extensively discussed these two vertex selection policies (i.e., direct and random) and how they can be realized. Moreover, we showed that the best outcome is achieved while the *hybrid* of direct and random neighbors are taken into account. We, therefore, use the hybrid policy, where as shown in Algorithm 1 (Line 5) and Algorithm 3 vertices first check a subset of their direct neighbours, and then if they do not succeed, they check some random vertices.

3.3   Swap Heuristics

To make a decision for color exchange we consider two heuristics: (i) *dominant color* and (ii) *edge utility*.

Dominant Color (DC). We define the *dominant color* of a vertex p as the color with the maximum cardinality at p. That is:

$$c_p^* = arg \max_c |E_p(c)|$$

With this heuristic, a vertex p looks for a partner which (i) is not internal, and (ii) has an edge with vertex p's dominant color. If vertex p finds such a vertex, it exchanges with that vertex one of its non-dominant colors for the dominant color. In other words, every vertex tries to unify the color of its edges, in order to reduce its energy. Since the global energy of the graph is sum of all vertices' energy, this optimization has the potential to lead us toward a globally optimal state. Although condition (i) prevents disturbing those vertices that are already stabilized, vertices are still acting very greedily and do not consider the benefits of the other endpoint of the edge that they are negotiating over. Consequently, this policy could end up in contention between neighboring vertices, and the color of some edges might fluctuate. In Section 4, we will study the evolution of the partitioning under such policy.

Edge Utility (EU). An alternative policy is to assign a *utility* value to every edge based on the cardinality of the colors at its endpoints. The main idea of this heuristic is to check that whether exchanging the color of two edges decreses the energy of the their connected vertices or not. If it does, two edges swap their colors, otherwise they keep them. To every edge e_{pq} (with two endpoints p and q) we assign a value v, with respect to color c, that indicates the relative number of neighboring edges of e with color c. That is:

$$v(e, c) = \begin{cases} \frac{|E_p(c)|-1}{|E_p|} + \frac{|E_q(c)|-1}{|E_q|} & if \ c = \pi_e \\ \frac{|E_p(c)|}{|E_p|} + \frac{|E_q(c)|}{|E_q|} & otherwise \end{cases}$$

Table 1. Datasets used in the experiments

Graph Name	$|V|$	$|E|$	power-law	Avg. Clustering Coeff.	Diameter	Source
Data	2851	15093	no	0.486	79	Walshaw Archive [15]
4elt	15606	45878	no	0.408	102	Walshaw Archive [15]
Astroph	17903	196972	yes	0.6306	14	Stanford Snap Datasets [16]
Email-Enron	36692	367662	yes	0.4970	11	Stanford Snap Datasets [16]

Note, in the first case, $E_p(c)$ and $E_q(c)$ include edge e, and that is why we need to decrement them by one. Next, the objective is to maximize the overall value of edges during the color exchange process. More precisely, vertex p exchanges the color of its edge e_{pq} with the color of another edge $e'_{p'q'}$, if and only if:

$$v(e, c') + v(e', c) > v(e, c) + v(e', c')$$

where $c = \pi_e$ and $c' = \pi'_e$. Hence, the swap utility is calculated as follows:

$$utility = (v(e, c') + v(e', c)) - (v(e, c) + v(e', c'))$$

Simulated Annealing. Since our swap policy is based on local optimization with limited information at each vertex and no central coordinator, it is prone to getting stuck in local optima. Therefore, we need to employ some techniques to help it get out of local optima and move towards better configurations over time. To achieve this goal, we use simulated annealing [8] with constant cool down rate. Two parameters of the simulated annealing are the *initial temperature* T_0 and the *cool down rate* δ. The *temperature* at round r is then calculated as follows:

$$T_r = max(1,\ T_0 - r \cdot \delta)$$

Finally, as shown in Algorithm 4 we bias the utility computation with the value of temperature at each round, as follows:

$$utility = ((v(e, c') + v(e', c)) \times T_r) - (v(e, c) + v(e', c'))$$

4   Experiments

In this section, we first introduce the datasets and metrics that we used for evaluating our solution. Then, we study the impact of our simulated annealing parameters on the partitioning quality. Next, we show how different policies, introduced in Section 3.3, perform. We also measure the performance of these policies in scale, and compare them to two state of the art solutions.

To evaluate JA-BE-JA-VC we used four graphs of different nature and size for evaluating our ideas. These graphs and some of their properties are listed in Table 1. Note, graphs Astroph and Email-Enron have power-law degree distribution. We measure the following metrics to evaluate the quality of the partitioning:

- *Vertex-cut*: this metric counts the number of times that graph vertices has to be cut. That is, a vertex with one cut has replicas in two partitions, and a vertex with two cuts is replicated over three partitions. This is an important metric, because when a graph vertices are scattered over several partitions, every computation that involves a modification to a vertex, should be propagated to all the other replicas of that vertex, for the sake of consistency. Therefore, vertex-cut directly affects the required communication cost of the partitioned graph.

- *Normalized vertex-cut*: this metric calculates the vertex-cut of the final partitioning relative to the random partitioning, thus, it shows to what extent the algorithm can reduce the vertex-cut.
- *Standard deviation of partition sizes*: this metric measures the Standard Deviation (STD) of normalized size of the partitions. First, we measure the size of the partitions (in terms of the number of edges) relative to the average (expected) size. Then, we calculate how much the normalized size deviates from the perfect normalized size, i.e., 1.

4.1   Experimental Setting

We conducted several experiments to tune the two parameters of the simulated annealing, namely T_0 and δ. For these experiments we selected the Data graph (Table 1) and $k = 2$. As shown in Figure 3(a), the vertex-cut decreases when T_0 increases. However, Figure 3(b) illustrates that this improvement is achieved in a higher number of rounds, that is, a bigger T_0 delays the convergence time. Similarly, a smaller δ results in a better vertex-cut, at the cost of more rounds. In other words, T_0 and δ are parameters of a trade-off between vertex-cut and the convergence time and can be tuned based on the priorities of the applications. Moreover, we found out that for a larger k, it is better to choose a smaller δ, because when the number of partitions increases, the solution space expands and it is more likely for the algorithm to get stuck in local optima. Unless otherwise mentioned, in the rest of our experiments $T_0 = 2$ and we use *delta* $= 0.0005$ for $k = 32$ and $k = 64$, and $\delta = 0.001$ for other values of k. Moreover, each node selects 4 candidates in a round, including three random nodes among its neighbors (line 3 in Algorithm 3) and one random node from the whole graph, provided by the peer sampling service (line 4 in Algorithm 3).

4.2   Performance

We observe the evolution of vertex-cut over time on different graphs, with two different swap policies: (i) *DC*, i.e., dominant color, and (ii) *EU*, i.e., edge utility. For this experiment $k = 4$, and the results are depicted in Figure 4. As shown, the main gain with the DC policy is acquired in the very beginning, when the vertex-cut drops sharply. After the first few iterations, the vertex-cut does not change considerably. In contrast, the EU policy results in a lower vertex-cut, but in a larger number of iterations. It is important to note, the convergence time is independent of the graph size and is mainly determined by the parameters of the simulated annealing. The algorithm converges soon after the temperature reaches value 1.

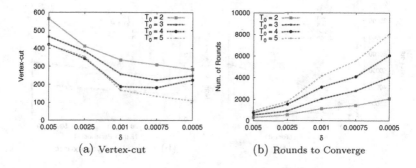

(a) Vertex-cut

(b) Rounds to Converge

Fig. 3. Tuning SA parameters on Data graph (K=2)

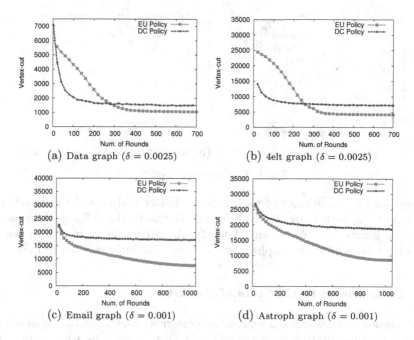

(a) Data graph ($\delta = 0.0025$)

(b) 4elt graph ($\delta = 0.0025$)

(c) Email graph ($\delta = 0.001$)

(d) Astroph graph ($\delta = 0.001$)

Fig. 4. Evolution of vertex-cut with different swap policies (K=4)

It is interesting to note, for the first two graphs, the DC policy can produce a better vertex-cut in a short time, but in the long run, the EU policy outperforms it. For the other graphs in Figures 4(d) and 4(c), the EU policy is always performing better. This is due to the different structural properties of these graphs. More precisely, Astroph and Email-Enron are power-law graphs (Figures 4(d) and 4(c)), that is the the degree distribution of graph vertices resembles a power-law distribution. More structural properties of these graphs are listed in Table 1.

We also measure the vertex-cut for various number of partitions. For this experiment, we only use the EU policy. Figure 5(a) depicts how the vertex-cut

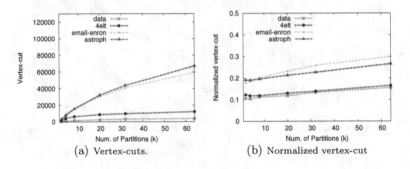

(a) Vertex-cuts.   (b) Normalized vertex-cut

Fig. 5. The improvements for different number of partitions

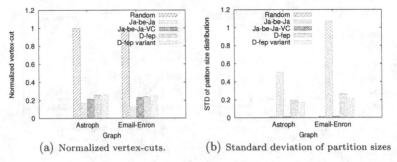

(a) Normalized vertex-cuts.   (b) Standard deviation of partition sizes

Fig. 6. Comparisons (k=20)

changes for various number of partitions. To better understand this result, we
also report the vertex-cut of JA-BE-JA-VC relative to that of a random partitioning in Figure 5(b). As shown, JA-BE-JA-VC reduces the vertex-cut to nearly
10-15% for Data and 4elt graphs, and to 20-30% for our power-law graphs.

4.3   Comparisons to the State of the Art

In this section we show that our solution outperforms two state-of-the-art solutions
in that it produces partitions with equal size, while requiring a very low vertex-cut.
First, we use an edge-cut partitioner, Ja-be-Ja [7] to partition the graph. Then, the
cut edges are randomly assigned to one of the partitions, where their endpoints belong to. This is similar to the example in Figure 2(b). We also compare JA-BE-JA-
VC to the state-of-the-art vertex-cut partitioner by Alessio et al. [9], which includes
two policies of its own, namely D-fep, and D-fep Variant. This experiment is performed on Astroph and Email-Enron graphs with $k = 20$. To make the comparisons
more meaningful, we report the normalized vertex-cut, that is the vertex-cut relative to that of a random partitioning. As shown in Figure 6(a), Ja-be-Ja produces
the minimum vertex-cut. However, Figure 6(b) shows that the partition sizes are
very unbalanced. The number of cut vertices in D- fep and its variant is more than
that of Ja-be-Ja, but their partition sizes are much more balanced. JA-BE-JA-VC
has a better vertex cut than D-fep, while the partition sizes are nearly equal.

As explained in Section 4.1, the convergence time of JA-BE-JA-VC is independent of the graph size and is mainly affected by the parameters of the simulated annealing process. While this is true for Ja-be-Ja, [9] shows that both D-fep and its variant converge in only very few rounds and produce very good vertex-cuts for graphs Astroph and Email-Enron. However, as depicted in Figure 6(b) these algorithms do not maintain the balance of the partition sizes. In fact, without proper coordination, the standard deviation of the partition size distribution could grow to prohibitively large levels. JA-BE-JA-VC, however, maintains the initial distribution of edge colors, and can even be used to produce partitions of any desired size distribution, with a better vertex-cut. This comes, however, at the cost of longer running time.

5 Related Work

In this section we study some of the existing work on both edge-cut and vertex-cut partitioning.

5.1 Edge-Cut Partitioning

A significant number of algorithms exist for edge-cut partitioning [17,18,19,20,21,22,23]. These algorithms can be classified into two main categories: (i) centralized algorithms, which assume cheap random access to the entire graph, and (ii) distributed algorithms.

A common approach in the centralized edge-cut partitioning is to use Multilevel Graph Partitioning (MGP) [19]. METIS [20] is a well-known algorithm based on MGP that combines several heuristics during its coarsening, partitioning, and un-coarsening phases to improve the cut size. KAFFPA [23] is another MGP algorithm that uses local improvement algorithms based on flows and localized searches. There exist also other works that combined different metaheuristics with MPG, e.g., Soper et al. [24] and Chardaire et al. [25] used Genetic Algorithm (GA) with MPG, and Benlic et al. [26] utilized Tabu search.

Parallelization is a technique that is used by some systems to speedup the partitioning process. For example, PARMETIS [21] is the parallel version of METIS, KAFFPAE [27] is a parallelized version of its ancestor KAFFPA [23], and [28] is a parallel graph partitioning technique based on parallel GA [29].

Although the above algorithms are fast and produce good min-cuts, they require access to the entire graph at all times, which is not feasible for large graphs. Ja-be-Ja [7] is a recent algorithm, which is fully distributed and uses local search and simulated annealing techniques [8] for graph partitioning. In this algorithm each vertex is processed independently, and only the direct neighbors of the vertex, and a small subset of random vertices in the graph need to be known locally. DIDIC [30] and CDC [31] are two other distributed algorithms for graph partitioning, which eliminate global operations for assigning vertices to partitions. However, they may produce partitions of drastically different sizes.

5.2 Vertex-Cut Partitioning

While there exist numerous solutions for edge-cut partitioning, very little effort has been made for vertex-cut partitioning. SBV-Cut [32] is one of the recent work for vertex-cut partitioning. The authors proposed a solution to identify a set of balanced vertices that can be used to bisect a directed graph. The graph can then be further partitioned by a recursive application of structurally-balanced cuts to obtain a hierarchical partitioning of the graph.

PowerGraph [5] is a distributed graph processing framework that uses vertex-cuts to evenly assign edges of a graph to multiple machines, such that the number of machines spanned by each vertex is small. PowerGraph reduces the communication overhead and imposes a balanced computation load on the machines. GraphX [6] is another graph processing system on Spark [33,34] that uses a vertex-cut partitioning to improve its performance.

ETSCH [9] is also a graph processing framework that uses a distributed vertex-cut partitioning algorithm, called DFEP [9]. DFEP works based on a market model, where the partitions are buyers of vertices with their funding. Initially, all partitions are given the same amount of funding. The algorithm, then, proceeds in rounds, such that in each round, a partition p tries to buy edges that are neighbors of the already taken edges by p, and an edge will be sold to the highest offer. There exists a coordinator in the system that monitors the size of each partition and sends additional units of funding to the partitions, inversely proportional to the size of each partition.

6 Conclusions

We presented JA-BE-JA-VC, a distributed and parallel algorithm for vertex-cut partitioning. JA-BE-JA-VC partitions edges of a graph into a given number of clusters with any desired size distribution, while the number of vertices that have to be replicated across clusters is low. In particular, it can create balanced partitions while reducing the vertex-cut. JA-BE-JA-VC is a local search algorithm that iteratively improves upon an initial random assignment of edges to partitions. It also utilizes simulated annealing to prevent getting stuck in local optima. We compared JA-BE-JA-VC with two state-of-the-art systems, and showed that JA-BE-JA-VC not only guarantees to keep the size of the partitions balanced, but also outperforms its counterparts with respect to vertex-cut.

References

1. Abou-Rjeili, A., Karypis, G.: Multilevel algorithms for partitioning power-law graphs. In: Proc. of IPDPS 2006, p. 10. IEEE (2006)
2. Lang, K.: Finding good nearly balanced cuts in power law graphs (2004) (preprint)
3. Leskovec, J., Lang, K., Dasgupta, A., Mahoney, M.: Community structure in large networks: Natural cluster sizes and the absence of large well-defined clusters. Internet Mathematics 6(1), 29–123 (2009)

4. Albert, R., Jeong, H., Barabási, A.: Error and attack tolerance of complex networks. Nature 406(6794), 378–382 (2000)
5. Gonzalez, J., Low, Y., Gu, H., Bickson, D., Guestrin, C.: Powergraph: Distributed graph-parallel computation on natural graphs. In: Proc. of OSDI 2012, pp. 17–30 (2012)
6. Xin, R., Gonzalez, J., Franklin, M., Stoica, I.: Graphx: A resilient distributed graph system on spark. In: Proc. of GRADES 2013, pp. 1–6. ACM (2013)
7. Rahimian, F., Payberah, A., Girdzijauskas, S., Jelasity, M., Haridi, S.: Ja-Be-Ja: A distributed algorithm for balanced graph partitioning. In: Proc. of SASO 2013. IEEE (2013)
8. Talbi, E.: Metaheuristics: From design to implementation, vol. 74. John Wiley & Sons (2009)
9. Guerrieri, A., Montresor, A.: Distributed Edge Partitioning for Graph Processing. CoRR abs/1403.6270 (2014)
10. Voulgaris, S., Gavidia, D., Van Steen, M.: Cyclon: Inexpensive membership management for unstructured p2p overlays. Journal of Network and Systems Management 13(2), 197–217 (2005)
11. Jelasity, M., Montresor, A.: Epidemic-style proactive aggregation in large overlay networks. In: Proc. of ICDCS 2004, pp. 102–109. IEEE (2004)
12. Payberah, A.H., Dowling, J., Haridi, S.: Gozar: Nat-friendly peer sampling with one-hop distributed nat traversal. In: Felber, P., Rouvoy, R. (eds.) DAIS 2011. LNCS, vol. 6723, pp. 1–14. Springer, Heidelberg (2011)
13. Dowling, J., Payberah, A.: Shuffling with a croupier: Nat-aware peer-sampling. In: Proc. of ICDCS 2012, pp. 102–111. IEEE (2012)
14. Massoulié, L., Le Merrer, E., Kermarrec, A., Ganesh, A.: Peer counting and sampling in overlay networks: Random walk methods. In: Proc. of PODC 2006, pp. 123–132. ACM (2006)
15. Leskovec, J.: The graph partitioning archive (2012), http://staffweb.cms.gre.ac.uk/~wc06/partition
16. Leskovec, J.: Stanford large network dataset collection (2011), http://snap.stanford.edu/data/index.html
17. Baños, R., Gil, C., Ortega, J., Montoya, F.G.: Multilevel heuristic algorithm for graph partitioning. In: Cagnoni, S., et al. (eds.) EvoWorkshops 2003. LNCS, vol. 2611, pp. 143–153. Springer, Heidelberg (2003)
18. Bui, T., Moon, B.: Genetic algorithm and graph partitioning. Transactions on Computers 45(7), 841–855 (1996)
19. Hendrickson, B., Leland, R.: A multi-level algorithm for partitioning graphs. SC 95, 28 (1995)
20. Karypis, G., Kumar, V.: A fast and high quality multilevel scheme for partitioning irregular graphs. Journal on Scientific Computing 20(1), 359–392 (1998)
21. Karypis, G., Kumar, V.: Parallel multilevel series k-way partitioning scheme for irregular graphs. Siam Review 41(2), 278–300 (1999)
22. Walshaw, C., Cross, M.: Mesh partitioning: A multilevel balancing and refinement algorithm. Journal on Scientific Computing 22(1), 63–80 (2000)
23. Sanders, P., Schulz, C.: Engineering multilevel graph partitioning algorithms. In: Demetrescu, C., Halldórsson, M.M. (eds.) ESA 2011. LNCS, vol. 6942, pp. 469–480. Springer, Heidelberg (2011)
24. Soper, A., Walshaw, C., Cross, M.: A combined evolutionary search and multilevel optimisation approach to graph-partitioning. Journal of Global Optimization 29(2), 225–241 (2004)

25. Chardaire, P., Barake, M., McKeown, G.: A probe-based heuristic for graph partitioning. Transactions on Computers 56(12), 1707–1720 (2007)
26. Benlic, U., Hao, J.: An effective multilevel tabu search approach for balanced graph partitioning. Computers & Operations Research 38(7), 1066–1075 (2011)
27. Sanders, P., Schulz, C.: Distributed evolutionary graph partitioning. arXiv preprint arXiv:1110.0477 (2011)
28. Talbi, E., Bessiere, P.: A parallel genetic algorithm for the graph partitioning problem. In: Proceedings of the 5th International Conference on Supercomputing, pp. 312–320. ACM (1991)
29. Luque, G., Alba, E.: Parallel Genetic Algorithms: Theory and Real World Applications. SCI, vol. 367. Springer (2011)
30. Gehweiler, J., Meyerhenke, H.: A distributed diffusive heuristic for clustering a virtual p2p supercomputer. In: Proc. of IPDPSW 2010, pp. 1–8. IEEE (2010)
31. Ramaswamy, L., Gedik, B., Liu, L.: A distributed approach to node clustering in decentralized peer-to-peer networks. Transactions on Parallel and Distributed Systems 16(9), 814–829 (2005)
32. Kim, M., Candan, K.: SBV-Cut: Vertex-cut based graph partitioning using structural balance vertices. Data & Knowledge Engineering 72, 285–303 (2012)
33. Zaharia, M., Chowdhury, M., Franklin, M., Shenker, S., Stoica, I.: Spark: Cluster computing with working sets. In: Proc. of HotCloud 2010, p. 10. USENIX (2010)
34. Zaharia, M., Chowdhury, M., Das, T., Dave, A., Ma, J., McCauley, M., Franklin, M., Shenker, S., Stoica, I.: Resilient distributed datasets: A fault-tolerant abstraction for in-memory cluster computing. In: Proc. of NSDI 2012, p. 2. USENIX (2012)

Multi-agent Systems Design and Prototyping with Bigraphical Reactive Systems[*]

Alessio Mansutti, Marino Miculan, and Marco Peressotti

Laboratory of Models and Applications of Distributed Systems,
Department of Mathematics and Computer Science, University of Udine, Italy
alessio.mansutti@gmail.com, {marino.miculan,marco.peressotti}@uniud.it

Abstract. Several frameworks and methodologies have been proposed
to ease the design of Multi Agent Systems (MAS), but the vast majority of them is tightly tied to specific implementation platforms. In this
paper, we outline a methodology for MAS design and prototyping in the
more abstract framework of *Bigraphical Reactive Systems* (BRS). In our
approach, components and elements of the application domain are modelled as *bigraphs*, and their dynamics as graph rewriting rules. Desiderata
can be encoded by means of type systems or logical formulae. Then, the
BDI agents (i.e., their beliefs, desires and intentions) are identified and
extracted from the BRS. This yield a prototype which can be run as
distributed bigraphical system, evolving by means of distributed transactional rewritings triggered by cooperating agents depending on their
internal intentions and beliefs.

This methodology allows the designer to benefit from the results and
tools from the theory of BRS, especially in the requirement analysis and
validation phases. Among other results, we mention behavioural equivalences, temporal/spatial logics, visual tools for editing, for simulation and
for model checking, etc. Moreover, bigraphs can be naturally composed,
thus allowing for *modular design* of MAS.

1 Bigraphical Reactive Systems

Bigraphical Reactive Systems (BRSs) [12] are a flexible and expressive meta-
model for ubiquitous computation. System states are represented by *bigraphs*,
which are compositional data structures describing at once both the locations
and the logical connections of (possibly nested) components of a system (see
Figure 1). Like graph rewriting, the dynamic behaviour of a system is defined
by a set of *(parametric) reaction rules*, which can modify a bigraph by replacing
a *redex* with a *reactum*, possibly changing agents' positions and connections.

BRSs have been successfully applied to the formalization of a broad variety of
domain-specific calculi and models, from traditional programming languages to
process calculi for concurrency and mobility, from context-aware systems to web-
service orchestration languages; a non exhaustive list is [2,4,9,17]. Very recently
bigraphs have been used in structure-aware agent-based computing for modelling

---

[*] Work partially supported by MIUR PRIN project 2010LHT4KM, *CINA*.

K. Magoutis and P. Pietzuch (Eds.): DAIS 2014, LNCS 8460, pp. 201–208, 2014.

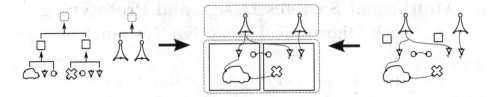

Fig. 1. Forming a bigraph from a place graph and a link graph

the structure of the (physical) world where the agents operates (e.g., drones, robots, etc.) [13]. Another inspiring recent development is a formal connection between ontologies and a particular class of BRS recovering inference and (non-monotone) reasoning as graphs rewrites and reachability tests.

Beside their normative and expressive power, BRSs are appealing because they provide a range of interesting general results and tools, which can be readily instantiated with the specific model under scrutiny: simulation tools, systematic construction of compositional bisimulations [12], graphical editors [8], general model checkers [15], modular composition [14], stochastic extensions [10], etc.

The key point of BRSs is that "the model should consist in some sort of reconfigurable space". Agents may interact in this space, even if they are spatially separated. This means that two agents may be adjacent in two ways: they may be at the same (abstract) *place*, or they may be connected by a *link*. This leads to the definition of *bigraphs* as an enriched hyper-graph combining two independent graphical structures over the same set of *nodes*: a hierarchy of places called *place graph* , and a hyper-graph of connections called *link graph* [12, Def. 2.3]. Each node in a bigraph is decorated with a type called *control* specifying additional properties such as the number of available link endpoints (*ports*). The set of available controls is called *signature* and is often denoted as Σ. We refer the reader to [12] for a precise and extensive presentation of BRS.

Figure 1 shows how a place graph and a link graph are merged yielding a bigraph. In particular, it portrays the state of a system composed by interconnected cars. These cars can move across an abstract topology described by a graph of locations; each location is presented as a (rectangle-shaped) node whose sub-nodes represent the cars at each location (car-shaped), the antenna coverage (triangle-shaped), and location interconnections (circle-shaped). Finally, a cross-shaped node is used to mark the destination of cars linked to it.

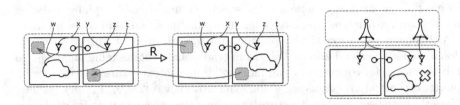

Fig. 2. Applying a parametric rewriting rule

The dynamic behaviour of a system is described in terms of *reactions* of the form $a \rightarrow a'$ where a, a' are bigraphs of the given BRS. Reactions are defined by parametric rewriting rules i.e. pairs of bigraphs (R_L, R_R) equipped with a function from the sites (parameters) of R_R to those of R_L called *instantiation rule*. An example is provided in Figure 2 where the rewriting rule R (on the left) is applied to the bigraph in Figure 1 (yielding the bigraph on the right); the instantiation map is denoted by red arrows, keeping track of which nodes are created or deleted in the process (this extra information is functional to the results presented in this paper and is not required by the bigraphical framework).

BRS usually include a *sorting discipline* for ruling out spurious (i.e. non well-formed) states. In their general form, sortings are judgements over bigraph and reactions and can be used to model additional properties such as desiderata for the systems e.g. "a car reaches its destination" as will be discussed later.

2   From BRS to MAS

The first step for translating a specification given as a BRS (optionally enriched with properties and desiderata) to a MAS is to distinguish between *subjects* and *objects* in the domain model, i.e. which entities can perform actions and which cannot. This distinction is not necessarily unique and is intrinsically part of the specification; in fact, many approaches found in literature assume similar distinctions, although usually tailored to specific implementations (e.g. by means of specific classes in the ontology modelling the problem domain [3, 16]).

Subjects and objects may be defined as specific configurations of portions of the bigraph, but a simpler characterization can be done in the signatures, i.e. by partitioning Σ into the set of subject (Σ_s) and the set of object (Σ_o) controls. This solution prevents ambiguities (e.g. arising from overlapping configurations) and simplifies the mapping between agents and their BRS specification. Controls can be either *active* or *passive*: reactions can take place only within an active context (i.e. a context obtained by nesting only active controls). A subject can be temporary inhibited by a passive context, like, for instance, a virtualized machine that is halted by its supervisor in response to some suspicious behaviour.

A bigraph in the BRS is a model of the global state of the system and hence it is natural to read nodes decorated with subject controls as BDI agents in the prototype MAS. Then, bigraphical reactions model agent reconfigurations where node creation/destruction translates in agent creation/termination accordingly to the instantiation map. An example of reconfiguration induced by a bigraphical rewrite is illustrated in Figure 3 where the signature Σ is defined as the union of $\Sigma_s = \{\Box{:}0, \triangle{:}2\}$ and $\Sigma_o = \{\bigcirc{:}1\}$. Each bigraph is mapped into a family of agents hierarchically organised mirroring the place graph structure (which represents strong relations e.g. spatial or administrative ones); hence agents are aware of their parent and children along this hierarchy. Object nodes are collapsed in the internal state of the agent associated to their nearest ancestor. This mapping is consistent with the forest structure of place graphs, the idea that ancestors represent the environment and object the passive entities carrying data. From

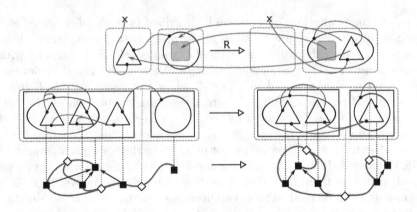

Fig. 3. The MAS induced by a BRS over $\Sigma_s = \{\square{:}0, \triangle{:}2\}$ and $\Sigma_o = \{\bigcirc{:}1\}$

this perspective, circular nodes in Figure 3 can be read as sandboxes used by square agents to wrap and host foreign (triangular) ones.

The mapping induced by Σ_s and Σ_o defines a partition of the place graph assigning to each agent a portion of the global state. This portion corresponds to the public image of the agent's internal state (*public state*) and strong consistency is assumed only for this information (whereas other approaches assume a shared consistent state [13], as in the case of blackboard systems). A similar approach is adopted for the link graph however, hyper-edges are intrinsically "less-local" than place dependencies and it is very common for an hyper-edge to span over several nodes, e.g. in the case of a shared communication medium like a network. Therefore, assuming that agents sharing a hyper-edge are consistently aware of each other may be very demanding. To mitigate this shortcoming, consistency (and hence agent public states) is limited to the hyper-edge handles (i.e. the name associated to a hyper-edge). This solution can be read as if agents were linked only through some mediating proxy (middleware). However, the use of handles does not preclude the presence of (full) hyper-edges in agent beliefs since these are not required to be consistent (differently from public states). Links and handles are pictured in Figure 3 as green thick lines and diamonds.

Agent beliefs are the view that an agent has of the system i.e. a bigraph which is not guaranteed to be consistent with the global state. The only part of it that can be safely assumed to be consistent is the agent *public state*, i.e., the portion of the global bigraph mapped into the agent and its neighbouring agents. Note that a system-wide snapshot of public states always yields a consistent view of the global state represented by means of a bigraph (from the specification BRS). Inconsistencies may appear only between agents beliefs but are readily addressed by means of logical timestamps thanks to the mapping between BRS and MAS states. In practice, each agent will maintain an internal counter that is incremented at every update of its public state and attaches this value to its public state, hence effectively implementing logical timestamps – since bigraphs are uniquely partitioned and assigned to agents by the aforementioned mapping. This simple mechanism offers a way to locally resolve conflicts between cooperating agents and their beliefs. (Terminated agents are handled by death certificates as usual.)

A cornerstone in the theory of bigraphs is the concept of *idempotent pushouts*[1] (IPO) [12, Def. 4.4]. IPOs characterize the *minimal contexts* enabling a given reaction. The advantages of IPOs for our purposes are twofold: first, these minimal contexts can be used as minimal hypothesis during *planning* tasks; secondly the bound on the context simplifies distributed rewritings. In fact, an agent interested in performing some action can check its beliefs or actual context against those obtained from the IPO construction and negotiate the rewrite with the agents involved. The operation can be refined by locks or push/pull notification with the agent neighbourhood. Moreover, IPOs guarantee that reconfiguration operations will involve only the minimal number of agents.

In general, reactions of BRS are non-deterministic, but can be easily restricted by suitable sortings (over states and executions), e.g. by requiring or forbidding specific occurrences [1], type systems [7] and modal logics [5]. The same tools and techniques are used to decorate a BRS MAS specification with (global) properties and desiderata. The presence of deadlocks highlights conflicts between desires/goals and (non-confluent) non-determinism may be the symptom of an incomplete specification. However, in some cases, non-determinism may be desirable (e.g. to express events from outside the system) and therefore has to be supported by the model.

3   Structural Properties and Desiderata

In this Section we describe how properties and desiderata for a given BRS specification can be expressed by means of spatial and temporal logics. In particular, "spatiality" and "temporality" are used to characterize the states and transitions of the given BRS respectively. This is achieved by combining a temporal logic such as CTL (computational tree logic) on top of BiLog, a spatial logic for bigraphs [5]: BiLog formulae are seen as the atomic predicates of CTL. Although more complex combinations are possible (even spatial-temporal logics precisely designed for BRS), this rather simple stratification already yields a great expressive power. Moreover, this stratification allows us to readily adapt model checking algorithms for CTL by extending them with BiLog ones. In the following, we elaborate the BRS of "interconnected cars" introduced in the previous Sections and present how structural properties and desiderata are modelled in this spatial-temporal logic for bigraphs.

The first structural property we discuss requires that "cars always reach their destination". This requirement is captured by the formula:

$$\mathbf{AF}[\mathsf{Car}_{c,x} \mid \mathsf{Target}_x] \tag{1}$$

---

[1] IPO are connected to the concept of borrowed context extensively used in the theory of graph rewriting systems; actually both are instance of GRPO.

where BiLog sub-formula enclosed by the square brackets is satisfied only by those states where the car node is next to the target it is connected with. The **AF** operator is the CTL "all-future" temporal operator and states that, for every path starting from the current state, the BiLog predicate eventually holds. For instance, (1) holds for the bigraph in Figure 1 but not for any state where the car is spatially disconnected from its target (hence (1) effectively rules out "bad initial states"). Likewise, we can model the requirement "cars are always connected to some antenna wherever there is one" as follows:

$$\mathbf{AG}([(id_{\langle 1,x \rangle} \mid /_y) \otimes \mathsf{Zone}(\mathsf{Car}_{y,x})] \vee [\mathsf{Car}_{a,x} \mid \mathsf{Connection}_{a,c}]) \qquad (2)$$

In other words, a car is disconnected only if it is in a zone covered by no antenna.

Predicates (1) and (2) can be thought as temporal-structural requirements about the system; on the other hand, we can use the same logic to express *desires*, e.g., the desire "there exists a route such that the car is never disconnected" (at least until the target is reached) is expressed by:

$$\mathbf{E}([\mathsf{Car}_{c,x} \mid \mathsf{Connection}_{a,c}] \ \mathbf{U} \ [\mathsf{Car}_{c,x} \mid \mathsf{Target}_x]) \qquad (3)$$

which combines (1) with a stronger version of (2). A predicate expressing a desire, like (3), may not be valid for a whole BRS, but this does not means that unsafe states are reached. In fact, agents will try to find suitable paths (i.e., by careful planning) accordingly to their desires and chosen goals.

4   Discussions and Future Work

In this paper we have outlined a methodology for modelling and simulating MAS as distributed BRS. The idea follows the direction of recent and interesting results where information is presented as suitable BRSs or used as a shared topological abstraction for agents [13]. Building upon the solid theory of bigraphs, this methodology offers a rapid prototyping tool aiding the designer in the requirement analysis and validation phases. Among the several theoretical results and practical tools offered by the BRS framework, we mention behavioural equivalences, temporal/spatial logics, visual tools for editing, for simulation and for model checking, etc. Moreover, bigraphs can be naturally composed, thus allowing for modular design of MAS. Overall, this methodology paves the way for cross-fertilizing transfer of results between MAS and BRS.

The use of bigraphs is eased by the support to *attached properties* offered by recent tools like BigRED and LibBig[2]. This feature allows bigraph components to be decorated with additional informations in the form of (typed) properties. In particular, LibBig supports property-aware matchings/rewritings, whose solutions are optimal w.r.t. property-based costs; this allows the designer to easily model and test in a declarative style cost-based policies (e.g. picking up the antennas with the strongest signal, or finding a shortest path).

---

[2] A Java library for extensible BRSs is available at `http://mads.dimi.uniud.it/`.

The development of a distributed runtime for BRS is in its early stages and would surely benefit from tools and results developed for MAS. For instance, protocols and techniques like *speculative reasoning* [11] could be applied to compute distributed bigraphical reactions more efficiently and possibly ported to other bigraphical tools (in particular, model checkers).

We plan to investigate the connection between distributed matchings and the attribute-based agent-communication at the core of the language for autonomic systems SCEL [6]. In both cases interactions are based on the public state (the *interface* in SCEL lingo). Another topic to be investigated is the extraction of a MAS from an (enriched) BRS; this construction resembles bigraphical refinements [14], suggesting the possibility to apply results from the field of (bigraphical) language engineering to the approach presented in this paper.

References

1. Bacci, G., Grohmann, D.: On the decidability of bigraphical sorting. In: Haveraaen, M., Lenisa, M., Power, J., Seisenberger, M. (eds.) Proc. CALCO Young Researchers Workshop, number 05/2010 in Technical Report, pp. 1–14 (2009)
2. Bacci, G., Grohmann, D., Miculan, M.: Bigraphical models for protein and membrane interactions. In: Ciobanu, G. (ed.) Proc. MeCBIC. Electronic Proceedings in Theoretical Computer Science, vol. 11, pp. 3–18 (2009)
3. Bernon, C., Cossentino, M., Gleizes, M.P., Turci, P., Zambonelli, F.: A study of some multi-agent meta-models. In: Odell, J., Giorgini, P., Müller, J.P. (eds.) AOSE 2004. LNCS, vol. 3382, pp. 62–77. Springer, Heidelberg (2005)
4. Birkedal, L., Debois, S., Elsborg, E., Hildebrandt, T., Niss, H.: Bigraphical models of context-aware systems. In: Aceto, L., Ingólfsdóttir, A. (eds.) FOSSACS 2006. LNCS, vol. 3921, pp. 187–201. Springer, Heidelberg (2006)
5. Conforti, G., Macedonio, D., Sassone, V.: Spatial logics for bigraphs. In: Caires, L., Italiano, G.F., Monteiro, L., Palamidessi, C., Yung, M. (eds.) ICALP 2005. LNCS, vol. 3580, pp. 766–778. Springer, Heidelberg (2005)
6. De Nicola, R., Loreti, M., Pugliese, R., Tiezzi, F.: A formal approach to autonomic systems programming: the SCEL language. ACM Transactions on Autonomic and Adaptive Systems, 1–29 (2014)
7. Elsborg, E., Hildebrandt, T.T., Sangiorgi, D.: Type systems for bigraphs. In: Kaklamanis, C., Nielson, F. (eds.) TGC 2008. LNCS, vol. 5474, pp. 126–140. Springer, Heidelberg (2009)
8. Faithfull, A.J., Perrone, G., Hildebrandt, T.T.: BigRed: A development environment for bigraphs. In: ECEASST, vol. 61 (2013)
9. Hildebrandt, T., Niss, H., Olsen, M.: Formalising business process execution with bigraphs and reactive XML. In: Ciancarini, P., Wiklicky, H. (eds.) COORDINATION 2006. LNCS, vol. 4038, pp. 113–129. Springer, Heidelberg (2006)
10. Krivine, J., Milner, R., Troina, A.: Stochastic bigraphs. In: Proc. 24th MFPS. Electronic Notes in Theoretical Computer Science, vol. 218, pp. 73–96 (2008)
11. Ma, J., Broda, K., Goebel, R., Hosobe, H., Russo, A., Satoh, K.: Speculative abductive reasoning for hierarchical agent systems. In: Dix, J., Leite, J., Governatori, G., Jamroga, W. (eds.) CLIMA XI. LNCS, vol. 6245, pp. 49–64. Springer, Heidelberg (2010)
12. Milner, R.: The Space and Motion of Communicating Agents. Cambridge University Press (2009)

13. Pereira, E., Kirsch, C.M., de Sousa, J.B., Sengupta, R.: BigActors: a model for structure-aware computation. In: Lu, C., Kumar, P.R., Stoleru, R. (eds.) ICCPS, pp. 199–208. ACM (2013)
14. Perrone, G., Debois, S., Hildebrandt, T.T.: Bigraphical refinement. In: Derrick, J., Boiten, E.A., Reeves, S. (eds.) Proc. REFINE. Electronic Proceedings in Theoretical Computer Science, vol. 55, pp. 20–36 (2011)
15. Perrone, G., Debois, S., Hildebrandt, T.T.: A model checker for bigraphs. In: Ossowski, S., Lecca, P. (eds.) Proc. SAC, pp. 1320–1325. ACM (2012)
16. Ribino, P., Cossentino, M., Lodato, C., Lopes, S., Sabatucci, L., Seidita, V.: Ontology and goal model in designing BDI multi-agent systems. In: *WOA@AI*IA*. CEUR Workshop Proceedings, vol. 1099, pp. 66–72. CEUR-WS.org (2013)
17. Zhang, M., Shi, L., Zhu, L., Wang, Y., Feng, L., Pu, G.: A bigraphical model of WSBPEL. In: Proc. TASE, pp. 117–120. IEEE Computer Society (2008)

Author Index

Printed in the United States
By Bookmasters